THE
TUDORS
IN 100 OBJECTS

THE
TUDORS
IN 100 OBJECTS

JOHN MATUSIAK

The
History
Press

To my daughter, Beth.

First published 2016

The History Press
The Mill, Brimscombe Port
Stroud, Gloucestershire, GL5 2QG
www.thehistorypress.co.uk

British Library Cataloguing in Publication Data.
A catalogue record for this book is available from the British Library.

ISBN 978 0 7509 6180 6

Typesetting and origination by The History Press
Printed in Turkey by Imak

Contents

Dynasty, Politics, Nation

1   Silver-gilt boar badge from
     Bosworth Field   11
2   The first state bed of Henry VII   13
3   The Winchester round table   17
4   Letter to Pope Clement VII
     requesting the annulment
     of Henry VIII's marriage to
     Catherine of Aragon   21
5   Edward VI, base silver shilling   23
6   Kett's oak   26
7   Lady Jane Grey's prayer book   29
8   Mary Tudor's wedding chair   33
9   Jewelled salamander pendant
     recovered from the Spanish
     galleas Girona, 1588   35
10   Lock of Elizabeth I's hair   39

Birth, Childhood, Marriage and Death

11   Birthing chair   45
12   Baby rattle   47
13   Wooden doll   50
14   Hornbook   53
15   Betrothal ring   57
16   *Memento mori*   61
17   Sir Henry Sidney's heart coffin   63

Women, Work, Craftsmen and Paupers

18   Linen sampler   69
19   Ducking stool   71
20   Agrarian almanac   75
21   Cloth seal   77
22   Miner's jacket   81

23   Apprenticeship register   83
24   Leather bombard   87
25   Glass goblet   89
26   Nonsuch chest   93
27   Alms box   97

Food, Drink and Fashion

28   Pewter plate and spoon   101
29   Chafing dish   105
30   Colander shard   109
31   Apple baker   111
32   Christmas pie   115
33   Ye Olde Mitre pub   117
34   Child's knitted mitten   121
35   Shoe   123
36   Jerkin   127
37   Codpiece   129
38   Effigy corset of Elizabeth I   133
39   Sun mask   137
40   Tablets of Venetian ceruse   139

Home, Hearth and Travel

41   Fuming pot   145
42   Prince Arthur's hutch   147
43   Leaded window   151
44   Oak chest   153
45   Floor watering pot   156
46   Garderobe   159
47   Hot water cistern   163
48   Bee skep   165
49   Chimney   169
50   The bridge at Great Mitton   171

Culture and Pastimes

51	Shakespeare's signet ring	177
52	Thomas Tallis keyboard	179
53	Misericord depicting a chained bear	182
54	Hawking vervel	185
55	Dice and shaker	189
56	Playing cards	191
57	World's oldest football	195

Health and Healing

58	Medicine chest	199
59	Urethral syringe	201
60	Condom	205
61	Apothecary jar	207
62	Arrow remover	211
63	Lithotomy dilator	213
64	Seal matrix from the leper hospital of St Mary Magadalene, Mile End	217

Religion

65	Portable communion set	211
66	Pilgrim's badge	225
67	Reliquary	227
68	Tyndale's New Testament	230
69	Statue of the dead Christ	233
70	The Glastonbury Grace Cup	237
71	Pilgrimage of Grace banner	241
72	Thomas Cranmer's cell door	245
73	Priest hole, Oxburgh Hall	247

Superstition

74	Caul locket	253
75	John Dee's *sigillum dei aemaeth*	257
76	Elizabethan 'angel'	261
77	The Danny jewel	265
78	Interrogation stool for witches	267
79	Witch bottle	271

Warfare, Weapons and Defence

80	The Flodden helm	275
81	Chanfron	277
82	Rapier	281
83	Bollock dagger	285
84	Elizabeth I's 'pocket pistol'	287
85	Signal station at Culmstock beacon, Devon	290

Crime and Punishment

86	Executioner's axe	295
87	'Scavenger's daughter'	299
88	Rack	301
89	Execution cauldron	305
90	The Halifax gibbet	309

Novelties and New Horizons

91	Printing press	313
92	Spectacles	315
93	Pocket watch	317
94	Prosthetic arm	321
95	Flushing toilet	325
96	Matchlock revolver	327
97	Microscope	331
98	Sebastian Cabot's 'planisphere'	333
99	William Lee's knitting frame	227
100	Gresham's grasshopper	339

Introduction

All books, arguably, are journeys of discovery for their authors, but none more so, perhaps, than this one. The task of recreating Tudor England through the medium of 100 objects was, to say the least, daunting. Merely selecting and locating the objects concerned, let alone researching and interpreting them, and synthesising them thereafter into a coherent and representative whole, involved not only time but the acquisition of a whole new level of expertise in a range of unfamiliar and frequently abstruse – even arcane – areas. Neither knitting, beekeeping, plumbing nor furniture-making, nor a whole host of other areas from midwifery to magic, were areas in which I could lay any claim to expertise before my writing began. But what appeared initially to be a task fraught with challenges and pitfalls would ultimately prove to be as fascinating as it was fulfilling, and the basis for what became the most consistently enthralling project I have undertaken.

As the book unfolded, a whole material world gradually emerged from the shadows, which has all too often been ignored by more formal social histories of the period. In unravelling the story of individual artefacts, countless other threads, linking these items to the broader contemporary world, emerged at every turn. The result, I hope, is a surprisingly comprehensive and rich panorama, which captures both the allure and anomalies of the age whose spirit it attempts, however humbly, to evoke.

My immeasurable thanks are due to all those individuals who assisted so readily and generously in offering suggestions and advice, and particularly those who supplied the images that help bring each chapter to life so vividly. As always, the team at The History Press – and particularly Mark Beynon and Lauren Newby – have been a model of helpfulness, matched only by the efforts of my wife, whose patience was frequently tested, but never more than when I became lodged, seemingly interminably, in a cramped priest hole, with daylight waning, tension mounting and a long drive home ahead.

To all concerned, I raise my glass at journey's end.

Dynasty, Politics and Nation

I

Silver-gilt boar badge from Bosworth Field

In the high summer of 1485, the entire political future of a troubled and comparatively insignificant kingdom on the damp and misty fringe of Europe hung in the balance. By that time, those old enough to have witnessed the winding course of the thirty-year contest between the two rival branches of the Plantagenet line that we now call the Wars of the Roses had grown wearily accustomed to its interminable twists and turns. Though the fighting was sporadic, the armies small and the material losses inconsiderable, the crown had nevertheless become little more than a political football as Henry VI lost his throne to Edward IV at Towton in 1461, only to retrieve it in 1470 with the help of Edward's former henchman, Warwick 'the Kingmaker', before losing it once more to his vanquished enemy eight years later. With Edward's eventual death in 1483, moreover, and the subsequent succession of his brother, Richard III, the dynastic merry-go-round began yet another giddy circuit when Henry Tudor, great-grandson of a fugitive Welsh brewer wanted for murder, made his way to Market Bosworth in England's midland heart to stake his own flimsy claim to primacy. At the head of some 8,000 men and outnumbered by two to one, he would nevertheless triumph in a particularly foul and inglorious fray fought on blood-soaked fen and moorland, which left the crown of his enemy's butchered corpse to be rudely plucked from a thicket.

Yet despite the crucial importance of the battle which marked the dawn of Tudor England, the precise location of 'Bosworth Field' had remained a matter of debate for centuries until the chance discovery of

11

the object pictured here. It was not until the late 1990s, in fact, that a team of archaeologists and historians began to look afresh at local place names and conduct soil tests for historical wetlands that revealed crucial new evidence locating the battle at Sutton Cheney in Leicestershire, some 2 miles away from where it was traditionally considered to have taken place. Employing original accounts that described the battlefield as marshy, local farmland was systematically scoured with metal detectors, though it was not until the final week of a six-month extension to the 1999 survey that a single 30mm lead ball was located and a series of groundbreaking discoveries began to unfold. Indeed, after a full season of further work, thirty lead munitions – far more than from all the other fifteenth- and sixteenth-century battlefields in Europe put together – were uncovered, along with the remains of swords and buckles, silver coins from Burgundy, and a variety of shot fired from handguns.

As if to quell the misgivings of any remaining doubters once and for all, however, there finally emerged the most iconic and conclusive object of all those discovered on Bosworth Field: a silver-gilt boar, the location and nature of which, beside the site of Fen Hole, not only confirmed the battle site but evoked the most poignant of images. For the boar was Richard III's own emblem, given in large numbers to his supporters, and while most of these badges were of base metal, this one is silver-gilt, and could only have been given to a knight or someone of even higher status. The recipient was therefore in all likelihood a knight in the king's own retinue and someone who may well have ridden with him in his final desperate cavalry charge, launched as victory was slipping from his grasp in a vain bid to kill his protagonist and win the day. In the process, we are told, the king not only killed the Lancastrian standard bearer and threw down another man but personally attacked Henry Tudor, who kept him at bay until help came. Thereafter, however, the king's small body of knights was driven back remorselessly until he himself was cut down when his horse became stuck in a mire – not far at all, it seems, from the small medieval marsh where this object was retrieved – and the succession of England's first Tudor king was finally assured.

2

The first state bed of Henry VII

In the twenty-four years that followed his crushing victory at the Battle of Bosworth Field, Henry VII both confirmed and consolidated the Tudor dynasty's grasp on power by a canny combination of sound finance, tough justice and peace abroad. Above all, however, he married wisely and procreated vigorously. Elizabeth of York, his swiftly acquired bride, was the eldest daughter of Edward IV, and the resulting union of the red and white roses was the surest possible safeguard against any further scheming by his enemies. For the new queen was not only sprung from the requisite royal stock but fertile. Within a year of her marriage she had borne a son, Arthur, and five years later a second boy, the future Henry VIII, would follow. Prince Arthur, the so-called 'rosebush of England', was in effect the living embodiment of lasting union between the once contending houses of Lancaster and York, leaving the queen's other surviving offspring, including two daughters, both as handy insurance policies against the vagaries of sixteenth-century medicine and as priceless bargaining chips in the game of European diplomacy. Indeed, it is no exaggeration to say that if Tudor England was founded on the field of battle, it would thrive or falter on the fortunes of the royal marriage bed.

The uncanny identification of Henry VII's 'first state bed' in 2010 therefore ranks as arguably one of the most evocative and significant early Tudor discoveries of all time. Found by chance in the car park of a Chester hotel after being dismantled and discarded, it was sold at auction for £2,200, as a Victorian bed, to an antique furniture restorer. When the restoration had been completed, however, the eagle-eyed craftsman duly contacted the chief executive of the World Monuments Fund Britain, suspecting that the object actually belonged to the Tudor period. And though the bed's origins remain a matter of some academic debate, dendrochro-

nology confirms that the wood was indeed cut in Germany in the 1480s, while written records trace the bed back to at least 1495, when the king went to Lathom to visit the Stanley family, who had been instrumental in securing his victory at Bosworth. Even more intriguingly, however, the headboard depicts Henry VII and his queen as Adam and Eve transmuted into Christ and surrounded by the fruits of paradise, which would appear to symbolise the couple's imminent hopes for an heir. Notwithstanding the later addition of an inscription from the Matthew Bible of 1537, there is compelling evidence to suggest, therefore, that the bed was actually created at the time of the first Tudor's marriage on 18 January 1486. If so, it is wholly plausible that not only Prince Arthur but Henry VIII, too, was subsequently conceived thereon, raising the bed's value, according to experts, to some £20 million.

3

The Winchester round table

In light of his slender claim to the throne, it was small wonder that the first Tudor should have taken such pains to emphasise his legitimacy. For, quite apart from the lowly fugitive past of his great-grandfather, Henry VII had other embarrassments to contend with. His paternal grandfather Owen, for instance, had found fortune and influence only by seducing Henry V's French widow after some years' service as an official in her household. And while Margaret Beaufort, the mother of the victor of Bosworth, was descended from John of Gaunt, it was only from what contemporaries discreetly termed the 'wrong side of the blanket'. Equally significantly, the same Parliament that eventually legitimised her and her children had done so only on the express grounds that they should be barred from the throne. Besides which, if Henry VII's claim to the throne came in any case through his mother, it was strictly speaking she rather than he who should have been crowned in 1485. With such a tangle of impediments, it was therefore only the general squandering and sullying of royal blood in the fourteenth century, coupled with the desperation of the hour, that had eventually thrust Henry Tudor to the pinnacle of the Lancastrian cause, and this was something that neither he nor his successor would lightly forget.

In consequence, the Tudor court was awash from the outset with a relentless torrent of high- and low-level propaganda. It was no coincidence, of course, that Henry VII was responsible for introducing the term 'majesty' into the English language or that, in so doing, he consciously developed the practices of pageantry and invested the notion of Tudor kingship with a mystique all of its own. Processions, the shouting of loyal salutations, the doffing of caps and reverent genuflexions in the

John Cook

royal presence all formed part of the same tireless theme that such spectacle was designed to drive home. Meanwhile, grooms, pages, servers and sundry menials were all attired in the Tudor livery of white and green embossed with the Tudor rose. Indeed, lest any should doubt or forget the might and splendour of England's new dynasty, there were also roses in the chains and necklaces worn by the king and queen, on the wooden ceilings and tiled floors of all royal dwellings and even on the gilded harnesses of royal horses. For the same reason,

Arthur, the first Tudor prince, was named specifically after the legendary king, with his Welsh connections, and the choice of Winchester as the boy's christening place was deliberately intended to reinforce the new dynasty's ancient connections.

But it was Henry VIII's decision in 1522 to emblazon the round table at Winchester with his own image that symbolised more than any other act the new dynasty's determination to stake its claims to primacy. By that time, the king had already liquidated the two main surviving claimants to his throne from the House of York, clinically dispatching Edmund de la Pole in 1513 after he had spent seven helpless years imprisoned in the Tower, and treating Edward Stafford, Duke of Buckingham, to the fleeting hospitality of the gallows eight years later. In these circumstances, then, with a visit from Emperor Charles V pending, the second Tudor duly took the ultimate step of symbolically linking his kingship with the legendary Arthur himself and the illustrious knights of ancient Britain's dim and distant past.

The table concerned, which hangs today in the Great Hall at Winchester, is in fact nothing more than a forgery created around the year 1290 to celebrate the marriage of one of Edward I's daughters. It has a diameter of 5.5m, is built from English oak and weighs 1,200kg; it originally had twelve legs and seating, ostensibly, for the twenty-four knights of the round table as well as the king himself. But at the time of its construction, it was common throughout Europe for festive events known as 'round tables' to be staged where royal courts engaged in feasting, dancing, and jousting, and attending knights assumed the identities of Arthur and his followers. Indeed, the earliest event of this kind appears to have been held in Cyprus in 1223, while René of Anjou even erected an Arthurian castle for a similar extravaganza of 1446.

Even so, the Winchester round table appears to have been both widely renowned and respected. 'At Venta Symeno alias Winchester in ye castle most famously knowne, standeth fixed ye table at the walle side of ye kinges Hal, which (for ye majesty of Arthure) they cal ye round table', wrote John Leland in *The Assertion of King Arthur* (1544). Caxton, too, mentioned the Winchester table in his preface to Malory's *Morte D'Arthur* and seemed to regard it as authentic, though fame and fashion are fickle, and later generations would prove altogether less reverential. Indeed, no doubt because of its resemblance to a dartboard, the table was ultimately used for target practice by Roundhead troops in 1645, and only in 1789, when the entire object was repainted, were the bullet holes finally filled.

Henricus Dei gra Rex Angliæ et franciæ, defensor fidei ac Dñs Hiberniæ Rmo in chro pri Dño B: S. R. E. Car li de Rauenna &c. Amico nro Carmo Sal. Sepe antea, non obscurè experti sumus, q̃ multa de beneuolo Rmæ D. vræ erga nos ãio, et affectu, nobis polliceri queamus, hunc etiam oratores nri, qui nuper ex italia redierūt, ita abunde testantur, ut non antea satisfactum nobis esse putemus, q̃ grati aĩmi testimonio, tam egregia vræ Rmæ D. de nobis bene merendi uoluntatem, aliqua in parte compensauerimus. Literas vero, quas omni humanitate refertas ad nos dedit, locupletes sui in nos pectoris indices, gratissimas, charissimasq̃ habemus, veluti ab illo datas, quem inter precipuos nros amicos iampridem adnumerauimus, et cuius amplitudinis, et ornamenti summa q̃ maxime studiosi, vram igr Rmã D. impensè rogamus, tũ ut in pulcherrimo isto suo nobis gratificandi instituto, perstare velit, tum etiã, ut quæcunq̃ nra opera, audacter utatur, quotiens sibi usui, ornamento ue esse posse putauerit. Mittimus demum ob nõnulla nra negocia ad Cesaream Mtem oratorem, Ill. D. Tho: comitem Wolcorie, et Wormondie, Consanguineū, et consiliariū nrūm dilectissimū, priuatiq̃ nri Sigilli custodem, quã ob rem, vram Rmã D. oramus, ut nõ alio officio illum prosequi, nec aliã fidem in omnibus habere, q̃ si nos coram loquentes audiret. Et feliciter valeat. Londini, ex Regia nra, Die xvij januarij M.D.XXIX.

4

Letter to Pope Clement VII

requesting the annulment of Henry VIII's marriage to Catherine of Aragon

Ultimately, it would take much more than propaganda to remedy Henry VIII's dynastic insecurity. It would require a male child that could not be had, and a divorce that could only be obtained by a breach with Rome. When, on 18 February 1516, Catherine of Aragon's procreative exertions had borne their first lasting fruit with the arrival of Princess Mary, there had been renewed hope. Clutching the girdle of her patron saint and namesake, and kept ignorant of her father's recent demise for fear that grief might affect the final passage of her pregnancy, she had finally emerged from a difficult labour with at least the partial satisfaction of a daughter. But the queen's harrowing catalogue of previous failures remained a cause of considerable disquiet for her impatient husband. A stillborn daughter had already fallen from her womb in 1510 and at the end of November 1514 she had also given birth to a premature child, 'a prince who lived not long after'. Indeed, before the Princess Mary's birth, Catherine had brought forth four sons in all, none of whom survived longer than a few weeks. And only a year or so later, the king's infidelities had begun to make their mark.

In the years that followed, Anne Boleyn tightened her grip upon Henry's affections; Thomas Wolsey's best efforts to bring about an equitable solution short of an outright break with the Holy See would result in his disgrace and downfall in 1529. But on 18 January of that same year the King of England was still sufficiently optimistic to write to his 'most dear friend' the Cardinal of Ravenna, in a spirit of co-operation and goodwill, announcing the imminent arrival in Rome of his mistress's father, Thomas Boleyn, Earl of Wiltshire. The earl, whom the king saw fit to describe as 'Our most beloved kinsman', was to serve as ambassador in the Holy City to Emperor Charles V in yet another effort to break the deadlock that had dogged all previous divorce negotiations, and the cardinal was 'vehemently' begged 'to attend to him with the same courtesy and grant him in all things the same trust as if Your Most Reverend Lordship heard Us speaking in person'. At the same time, the recipient was entreated to continue in his 'most fair determination to please Us' and also 'to make bold use of anything in Our power whenever it seems useful or honourable to Your Most Reverend Lordship'.

Ultimately, however, both the cardinal's good offices and Boleyn's diplomacy would prove no more fruitful than Thomas Wolsey's own, and nineteen months later a group of eighty-one English noblemen and clergy, including the Archbishop of Canterbury, were prepared to attach their seals to another letter, composed in an altogether less amiable tone. Sent from London on 13 July 1530, it would take two months to arrive in the Pope's hands, and warned, with what would prove to be prophetic candour, that 'a refusal of annulment would require recourse to extreme measures for the good of the kingdom which we would not hesitate to take'.

5

Edward VI, base silver shilling

Anne Boleyn was quickly come and gone, and on 12 October 1537, that 'most precious jewel' of a healthy son was born at last to Henry VIII's third wife, Jane Seymour. The mother, however, would soon be cold in the grave from a grievous post-natal infection, and only nine years later, this self-same 'boy of wondrous hope' was left a vulnerable orphan cast adrift amid the surging sectarian and faction-ridden currents of mid-Tudor politics. First, under the partly right-minded but wholly wrong-headed stewardship of his uncle and Lord Protector, Edward Seymour, England would continue its agonising descent into the foreign wars and economic upheaval begun by his father. Then, after Seymour's ousting in 1549, the desperate quest for stability under John Dudley, Duke of Northumberland, became all too often the pretext for injustice and repression. As England finally succumbed to France in March 1550 with the Treaty of Boulogne, its new Church veered leftwards to an ever more radical brand of Protestantism, and the corridors of power continued to heave with faction and ambition, while in the wider world the unfamiliar scourge of inflation racked the common people and strained social bonds to the limit. To cap all, even nature herself seemed to assume an unforgiving aspect towards Edward VI's embattled kingdom, as 'sweating sickness' cut two consecutive swathes through high and low alike in 1551 and 1552.

Yet it was probably the 'hideous monster of base moneys' and inflation that most affected common people in their everyday struggle for survival. The practice of debasing the coinage by reducing its precious metal content had in fact been instituted by Cardinal Wolsey in 1526, but escalated drastically with the so-called 'Great Debasement' of 1542. Suspected by

many economists to be the master plan of Thomas Wriothesley, Earl of Southampton and the king's principal secretary, the aim was to increase the supply of money available to the Crown for war with Scotland and France without recourse to Parliament. To begin with, Henry VIII kept secret what he was doing, collecting all the silver and gold that was paid in to him as loans and benevolences, and issuing it out again from the Mint, mixed with alloy, so that he was able to pay out about a quarter as much again as he received. In consequence, however, the silver coins struck from 1542 to 1551 steadily sank in value. In March 1542, for example, the silver content of English coins averaged 75 per cent of each coin's face value. But by March 1545 the value of the silver content had fallen to 50 per cent, and by March 1546 to 33.33 per cent. Indeed, even before the end of Henry VIII's reign the surface layer of silver had become so thin that it would invariably wear off revealing the copper below, especially in the area of the king's nose, giving rise to his nickname 'Old Coppernose'.

Even so, during the course of the next reign the practice escalated still further, leading to soaring food prices and incalculable disruption to trade as English coins became increasingly unacceptable abroad. In contrast with Henry VIII's expansion of the money supply to £126,000, Edward's Lord Protector, the Duke of Somerset, managed to increase it by £1,000,000 and, as a result, prices rose from the 1547 index point of 116.4 to a figure of 202.3 in 1551. 'The evilness of money,' declared the radical preacher Hugh Latimer in 1548, 'hath made all things dearer,' and the silver coin pictured here could not capture more aptly the economic, social and indeed political malaise of mid-Tudor England. Struck at the Tower Mint only one year after Latimer's lament, it was worth no more than a quarter of what a similar coin had been before the repeated debasements of the previous reign. And at the coin's centre, appropriately enough, resides a lone boy, encumbered by a heavy crown. Only from 1551 onwards under the leadership of John Dudley did currency reforms begin, but they would not be completed until 1560 during the reign of Elizabeth I, and not before two rebellions had torn young Edward's realm asunder.

www.hammeredcoinage.com

6

Kett's oak

On an otherwise inconsequential stretch of dual carriageway between Hethersett and Wymondham in Norfolk stands a bent and blasted oak tree. Weary from its centuries-long duel with prevailing headwinds and propped up against collapse by functionally minded municipal workmen, it nevertheless continues to defy the noxious fumes and jarrings of passing rush-hour traffic and remains a gnarled yet poignant block of living Tudor history, as the steadily corroding plaque at its base makes clear. For this is 'Kett's oak', so named after the heroic local farmer who, in the summer of 1549, is said to have set out from this spot at the head of a rebel host en route to Norwich in a tragic quest for social justice.

The previous decade had seen a crisis in English agriculture as the rising population increased the impact of landlords' determination to fence off their lands and thereby deprive the less wealthy of their traditional grazing rights on open pasture. Some landowners, too, were not only 'enclosing' their land in this way, but forcing tenants off their farms so that they could 'engross' their holdings and convert arable land into pasture for sheep, which had become more profitable as demand for wool increased. With the majority of people depending on agriculture for their livelihood, and the added burdens of inflation, unemployment, rising rents and declining wages to contend with, outbreaks of unrest were inevitable, and Norfolk was to be stricken by the most serious of all.

Robert Kett himself, ironically, had at first been intended as a target of the rebels, but when they duly descended upon his land, the 57-year-old yeoman farmer, far from resisting, joined their cause and swiftly emerged as leader of the budding insurrection. Indeed, the following day, Tuesday 9 July, Kett and his fellow protestors set off for Norwich, gathering support from nearby towns and villages along the way before setting up camp at Mousehold Heath and drawing up a list of twenty-nine demands, which the government rejected so resolutely that violence became inevitable. In the late evening of 21 July, therefore, realising that without access to

Martinburo

the supplies of Norwich his followers would starve, Kett duly decided to attack, and by the next day England's second city was in his hands after thousands of rebels charged down from their camp at Mousehold at first light and began swimming the River Wensum between the Cow Tower and Bishops Gate. Though the city's defenders loosed volleys of arrows into the rebels as they crossed, the attack could not be thwarted, and as a running battle ensued, the same government messenger who had been sent to declare Kett an outlaw was forced to flee for his life after attempting to address the insurgents in the Market Square.

Yet the rebel victory could not be consolidated indefinitely; after the defeat of a force led by the Earl of Northampton, the government subsequently dispatched the Earl of Warwick at the head of 14,000 men, including German, Spanish and Welsh mercenaries, to wreak an awful revenge. By 24 August, indeed, the earl had forced an entry into Norwich, and was soon reinforced with a further 1,500 German *Landsknechte* – a ruthless and hard-bitten mix of mercenary hand-gunners and pikemen. Faced by such a formidable army, even Kett's redoubtable fighters, who had already burned large sections of the city and recaptured parts of it initially taken by Warwick, had no choice but to abandon their camp at Mousehold and head for open country and a final stand against what would prove impossible odds.

So it was that on the morning of 27 August 1549, 3,000 peasant rebels were basely slaughtered by well-armed, well-trained professional soldiers at a place called Dussindale, which has never been successfully identified. The morning after the battle, moreover, a number of Kett's followers were hanged outside Norwich's Magdalen Gate and at the so-called 'Oak of Reformation', which had served as their camp headquarters. Kett himself, meanwhile, was captured at the village of Swannington the night after the battle and taken, together with his brother William, to the Tower of London to await trial for treason. Found guilty, the brothers were returned to Norwich at the beginning of December, whereupon Robert was hanged from the castle walls on 7 December 1549 and William from the west tower of Wymondham Abbey on the same day. Estimates of deaths among Warwick's mercenary army, by contrast, vary from 300 to as few as thirty.

Can we be sure, however, that Kett's oak really is what long tradition claims? To complicate matters, there are some suggestions that the tree may not have been the initial meeting place of the Norfolk rebels but rather the site where a number of them were eventually hanged. Confusingly, too, another 'Kett's oak', now over 800 years old, stands near Ryston Hall, not far from Downham Market, apparently marking the point where, according to Francis Blomefield's eighteenth-century *History of Norfolk*, Matthew Parker, the future Archbishop of Canterbury, preached to the rebels and exhorted them to lay down their arms, 'which nearly cost him his life'. But if written sources are ambivalent on the matter, oral tradition, for better or worse, has stood firm over four and a half centuries and continues to endow the solitary ancient tree just outside Wymondham with a special significance and poignancy all of its own.

Lady Jane Grey's prayer book

According to the anonymous *Chronicle of Queen Jane*, Lady Jane Grey made her way to trial at the Guildhall in the City of London on 13 November 1553 bearing two books – 'a black velvet boke hanging before hir, and another boke in hir hande open'. But neither the first nor the second, which is likely to have been her favourite prayer book pictured here, would have the slightest influence in protecting her from subsequent events. Found guilty of falsely signing a number of documents as 'Jane the Queen', she was sentenced to be 'burned alive on Tower Hill or beheaded' as Mary Tudor, the rightful queen with whom she had contested the throne for a mere nine days, saw fit. Just under two months later, on the morning of 12 February 1554, Jane Grey was certainly carrying this very same dark blue leather prayer book as she mounted the scaffold for her appointment with the executioner's axe – an appointment that had been postponed for three days in the vain hope that she might submit to the efforts of the queen's chaplain, John Feckenham, and save her soul by renouncing Protestantism. 'Being nothing at all abashed', we are told, 'neither with feare of her owne deathe, which then approached', or 'the sight of the ded carcase of hir husbande', which had been carried by horse and cart past the rooms where she had been awaiting her own ordeal, Jane bore herself at the end with exemplary courage. Only the two gentlewomen accompanying her, we are told, 'wonderfully wept'.

But perhaps the most poignant moment of all came in the final moments before the execution when the 16-year-old victim passed her prayer book to Sir Thomas Brydges in the expectation that he would give it to his 61-year-old brother, Sir John, the Lieutenant of the Tower of London, who had supervised Jane's incarceration and, 'though much addicted to

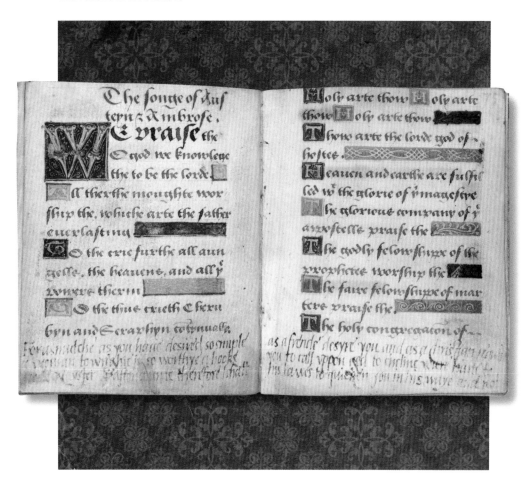

the old religion', had grown deeply fond of her. Within were messages of farewell both to Sir John and to Jane's father, who would himself be feeling the ample weight of the axe upon his neck only eleven days hence. The book, it seems, had not only been given to her in early September 1548 by the former queen, Katherine Parr, as she lay dying of puerperal fever after the birth of her only child, but had actually been written by that same lady while still in good health. The handwriting upon its 143 vellum leaves is conclusively hers, just as the slightly faded message beginning at the bottom of the page reproduced here is undoubtedly Jane's:

> Forasmuche as you haue desired so simple a woman to wrighte in so worthy a booke, gode mayster Lieufenante therefore I shalle as a frende desyre you, and as a christian require you, to call vpyon God, to encline youre harte to his laws, to quicken you in his waye, and not to take the worde of trewethe vtterlye oute of youre mouthe.

Lyue styll to dye, that by deathe you may purchase eternall life; and remember howe the ende of Mathusael, whoe as we reade in the scriptures, was the longest liuer that was of a manne, died at the laste. For, as the Precher sayethe, there is a tyme to be borne, and a tyme to dye; and the daye of deathe is better than the daye of our birthe. Youres, as the Lorde knowethe, as a frende, Jane Duddeley.

Though she had been spared at first after the failed attempt to bar Mary Tudor from the throne, the subsequent Protestant rebellion of Thomas Wyatt the Younger in January 1554 had finally sealed Jane's fate – though unlike her father, the Duke of Suffolk, who had played a prominent role in events, she bore no responsibility. Instead, the rising had been precipitated by Queen Mary's planned marriage to the future Philip II of Spain, which had sparked a half-cocked outburst of opposition centred upon Kent, resulting in a march on London and leaving the government with little choice other than to carry out the verdict against both Jane and her husband, the Duke of Northumberland's son Guildford Dudley. Yet Jane's message to her father remains a moving expression of resignation and devotion, notwithstanding his bullying role in forcing her to comply in the first place with Northumberland's scheme to install her as queen after the death of Edward VI. 'Although it hath pleased God to hasten my death by you, by whom my life should rather have been lengthened', she told her father forgivingly, 'yet can I patiently take it, that I yield God more hearty thanks for shortening my woeful days, than if all the world had been given unto my possession, with life lengthened at my own will'.

Ultimately, when her final minutes arrived, Jane would grant her executioner forgiveness and plead to be dispatched quickly. Referring to her head, she asked whether it would be taken off 'before I lay me down', to which the axeman answered no. Then, after blindfolding herself and failing to find the block with her hands, she cried for assistance before eventually repeating Christ's last words, as recounted by the evangelist Luke, and commending her spirit into God's hands. The message to her father, meanwhile, was duly passed on by Sir John Brydges as promised, though only on condition that the lieutenant might afterwards retain the prayer book itself as a memento. Today it resides in the British Museum.

8

Mary Tudor's wedding chair

Stand with your back to Winchester Cathedral's west wall today, and you will find yourself at the very spot where Mary Tudor, daughter of Catherine of Aragon, waited in the last nervous moments before she began her procession to marry Philip of Spain on 25 July 1554. The soaring magnificence of the nave would surely have given the queen renewed confidence in her own power and that of her realm, though even by this time the political and emotional imbalance between herself and her spouse-to-be was apparent. At 37, Mary was eleven years older than the groom, and Philip considered her little more than 'our dear and well beloved aunt', even revealing to one of his Spanish confidants, almost casually, that the marriage itself had been 'made for no fleshly consideration'. The queen too, for that matter, had initially harboured reservations about the match on the grounds that the groom was 'likely to be supposed amorous, and such is not my desire, not at my time of life, and never having harboured thoughts of love'. But she had come in due course to hanker for him, and while Mary pined and doted, her bridegroom maintained the icy objectivity of the calculating Habsburg power-broker that he undoubtedly was, viewing the queen and her realm as little more than handy political counters in his ongoing struggle with France and tireless crusade for the embattled Catholic faith.

Even so, Mary's long walk to the wedding stool pictured was certain to have been a journey of especial joy and satisfaction. She had witnessed, after all, the disgrace of her mother and experienced bitter rejection of her own at the hands of her father, Henry VIII. She had also seen the old religion, which had become her only consolation during her darkest years, dismissed, discarded and derided over almost two decades. Finally, after the death of her Protestant brother Edward, she had been made to endure

John Cook

an anxious struggle for the throne that was rightfully hers. Now, however, she was to wed at last a prince of her mother's homeland in a realm that was already restored to its ancient faith by her succession. Fittingly, therefore, the cathedral's nave and quire were magnificently adorned with cloth of gold and gaudy banners hanging high above from brackets that remain in place to this day. For further effect a raised walkway and dais had been constructed so that the couple could be seen by the thousands of onlookers who packed the building. Clad in white, gold and purple cloth, they were intended to look as though they were floating along their elevated walkway, with the arching backdrop of the nave above them.

The chair at which Mary was given away, meanwhile, had been specially constructed for the occasion and was matched by an identical one for Philip, which has since disappeared. Of comparatively simple construction and never intended to survive for posterity, it had nevertheless been suitably upholstered in leather and fine fabric, and as she took her place upon it there were royal fanfares and other music specially composed for the occasion. It was the first time, indeed, that horns, wind and other instruments were used in an English religious service. And the fact that there were two identical chairs of state with matching canopies was a subtle indication of a crucial political fact that none were meant as yet to know – that Philip was to be made King of England in his own right rather than as consort by marriage.

The same historic chair, which can be found today in Winchester Cathedral's Triforium Gallery, had therefore symbolised a fact of extraordinary political significance. As a result, England would soon follow Spain into war with France, and in losing Calais sacrifice her last remaining Continental foothold. Mary, too, would pursue her Protestant enemies with a determination that mirrored Spain's notorious Inquisition and in doing so extinguish the dominance of the 'old religion' on these shores once and for all. Ultimately, some 284 Protestant martyrs would lose their lives in Mary's fires, while a further 800 or so sought shelter in exile abroad, only to return in the next reign as Protestantism emerged once more, phoenix-like, to stage its final triumph under Elizabeth I.

9

Jewelled salamander pendant

recovered from the Spanish galleas Girona, 1588

By the close of the sixteenth century the Tudor dynasty had not only established a lasting national religion but also secured the kingdom's independence from foreign domination. Victory over the Spanish Armada and the vanquished fleet's subsequent destruction by powerful westerly winds in September 1588 marked the beginning of the end of Philip II's threat, as up to 5,000 men perished by drowning, starvation and slaughter at the hands of English troops after their shipwreck on the Irish coast. Some survivors were concealed by the local population, but few were taken into Irish service and fewer still returned home. In the end, indeed, only sixty-seven ships and fewer than one in three men survived, many of whom were near death from disease by the time of their return, as food and water ran low and the cramped, insanitary conditions took their inevitable toll. Thereafter, many more died in Spain, or on hospital ships in Spanish harbours, from diseases contracted during the voyage. When Philip II learned of the result of the expedition, he was reported to have declared that he had 'sent the Armada against men, not God's winds and waves'. Nor was his opinion likely to have been denied by any English man or woman. 'God's Protestant wind' had, it seems, blown decisively, and the exquisite salamander pendant pictured remains a powerful reminder of its potency.

Recovered from the wreck of the Spanish galleas *Girona*, which sank on 26 October off Lacada Point near the Giant's Causeway on the north Antrim coast, the gold pendant set with rubies reflects the full glory of an imperial Spain bloated with bullion from the New World, and bears striking testament, too, to the skill and influence of native American craftsmen. For while large numbers of native gold ornaments were melted down, the ideas of those craftsmen were retained, which explains the residing appeal of jewels in the form of animals throughout the sixteenth century. In 1526 Hernán Cortés, conqueror of the Aztec empire in Mexico, had recorded that among the ornaments shipped to his homeland was a 'winged lizard'. In legend, moreover, the salamander was believed to possess the magical property of being able to survive and extinguish fire – something which made it an exceptionally appropriate good luck charm for any voyage on a wooden fighting vessel and may well explain its appearance on the *Girona*, since the ill-fated galleas was no ordinary treasure ship. On the contrary, by the time of her destruction she was carrying not only the officers of two other craft but the surviving leaders of the Armada itself, who had been chosen from the noblest and wealthiest families in Spain.

In consequence, the ship foundered with an extraordinary store of precious objects on board, many of which provide a fascinating testament to the nature of contemporary Spanish culture. Alongside items of purely ornamental personal decoration, such as gold chains and buttons, for example, a good deal of the sumptuous gold jewellery recovered bore emblems of the religious orders of chivalry. A gold cross, inlaid with red enamel, of a Knight of the Order of Santiago de Compostella belonged to the ship's ill-fated captain Don Alonzo Martinez de Leiva, one of the youngest and most admired of the fleet's commanders, who had been named its Commander Designate in the event of Medina Sidonia's death. A gold ring with the initials 'IHS' on the bevel, the symbol of the Jesuit Order, was also among the hoard, as was a splendid *Agnus Dei* reliquary containing wax pellets blessed by the pope at the start of the 'grand enterprise' and believed to command miraculous powers of protection. Madame de Champagney's so-called *no tengo* ring, meanwhile, was being worn by her 21-year-old grandson, Don Tomas Perrenoto, at the time of his drowning, and hundreds of gold and silver coins were likewise discovered, along with silver candlesticks and silver-gilt tableware designed to grace the table of those very ship's officers, priests and grandees who had so confidently set sail in August from A Coruña with the express intention of putting paid to Tudor England once and for all. *No tengo mas que dar te* – 'I have nothing more to give you' – runs the full inscription on Perrenoto's ring, which would prove, of course, all too tragically prophetic.

Ulster Museum

37

10

Lock of Elizabeth I's hair

This lock of hair, preserved at Wilton House, near Salisbury in Wiltshire, is said to have been given to Philip Sidney by Queen Elizabeth I in 1572. One of the most prominent figures of the Elizabethan age, Sidney was not only brother to the Countess of Pembroke but a renowned poet, courtier and soldier who in the same year travelled to France as part of the embassy to negotiate a marriage between the queen and the Duc D'Alençon. Aged just 18 at the time, the young courtier was one of a select band who captured the queen's affection and good offices, though only eight years later he would incur her displeasure by urging his 'most feared and beloved, most sweet and gracious sovereign' that a French marriage 'will be unprofitable to you'. Forced to retire from court after subsequently challenging the Earl of Oxford to a duel, which the queen personally forbade, Sidney eventually succumbed to a bullet wound in the thigh at the Battle of Zutphen in 1586, offering his water bottle to a wounded comrade as he lay dying, since 'thy necessity is greater than mine'.

The treasured lock, meanwhile, would eventually find its way to the country seat of the Earls of Pembroke, where it resides today. At the age of only 39, Elizabeth was clearly greying rapidly, though the characteristic red tinge, which is always associated not only with the queen herself but with the Tudor dynasty in general, is plainly visible. Whether her troubled earlier years and the rigours of rule had already taken a heavy toll is uncertain, but religious dissent, plots and threats from abroad were already ongoing sources of pressure, which would escalate as her reign progressed. And by the end of her rule the queen's physical decline was much more apparent still, so that by December 1597, when she was described by the French ambassador André Hurault-Sieur de Maisse, the image of womanly perfection that her propagandists had

sought so assiduously to project was no longer remotely intact. 'On her head,' wrote de Maisse, 'she wore a garland and beneath it a great reddish-coloured wig, with a great number of spangles of gold and silver, and hanging down over her forehead some pearls, but of no great worth.' On either side of her ears, meanwhile, 'hung two great curls of hair, almost down to her shoulders and within the collars of her robe, spangled as the top of her head'. But it was her face, which the ambassador described as 'very aged', that reflected the impact of the years so forcefully. 'It is long and thin,' he recorded:

> And her teeth are very yellow and unequal, compared with what they were formerly, so they say, and on the left side less than on the right. Many of them are missing so that one cannot understand her easily when she speaks quickly.

What was already becoming evident in 1572, therefore, was by 1597 a plain, manifest and glaring fact of nature. Her teeth, moreover, had long been a problem, causing a German visitor to comment upon their blackness – 'a defect,' he added, 'that the English seem subject to, from their great use of sugar'. And in December 1578, predictably enough, she found herself 'so excruciatingly tormented' with toothache that she was forced 'to pass whole nights without rest'. Though urged by her physicians to have the painful teeth removed, it was not until the Bishop of London, John Aylmer – 'a man of high courage' – had one of his own extracted in her presence that the 'Fairie Queen' was 'thereby encouraged to submit to the operation herself', notwithstanding the fact that Aylmer himself 'had not many to spare'.

By the late 1590s, moreover, the queen's political mystique was fading in parallel with her physical appearance. The triumph over the Armada had given way to military disappointment and war-weariness, as a result of Drake's disastrous campaign against Spanish America in 1595 and his death from dysentery off the coast of Panama the following year. Troubled relations with Parliament, rebellion in Ireland, inflation, bad harvests and mounting challenges to the religious settlement also took their toll upon the so-called 'Cult of Gloriana' which has nevertheless moulded modern-day perceptions of Elizabeth so successfully. Indeed, by the time of her death in the bedraggled early hours of 24 March 1603, she had already been sunk in 'dullness and lethargy' and refusing all medicine since January.

The queen's hair, at least, remained intact; rumours that she had long since become bald are unfounded. Only a few years earlier, in fact, the impetuous Earl of Essex had burst into her bedchamber without permission to find the ageing Elizabeth with 'her hair all about her ears'. And Sidney's lock, fine and prematurely grey though it was, gives further lie to the residing myth, propagated by Hilaire Belloc among others, that 'at thirty she was bald as an egg'.

Birth, Childhood, Marriage and Death

II

Birthing chair

Long before male physicians came to dominate the delivery room, the use of birthing chairs or similar contraptions had been common around the world. On the walls of the Birth House at Luxor, for example, is a picture, dating to around 1450 BC, of an Egyptian queen giving birth on a stool. It was only in the seventeenth century, when Louis XIV of France required his wife to lie down while giving birth so that he could observe the event from behind a screen, that the prone position for delivery began its steady ascent to popularity – a process assisted, it has been suggested, by the fact that male doctors, who assumed increasing control of proceedings during the eighteenth century, considered it undignified for them to crouch at the mother's feet while she pushed her baby forth into the outside world. In Tudor England, however, where childbirth was the sole preserve of midwives, the birthing or 'groaning' chair continued to enjoy unrivalled popularity. Causing less constriction of the pelvis, chairs like the one here, made from elm and oak around 1600, allowed the squatting mother to push more effectively, and its removable keyhole seat provided both a clear route for the emerging baby and access for the women in attendance. Such chairs, or in some cases stools, were usually placed in front of the fireplace at the time of delivery and were used by all classes, although in this case the elaborate carved leaf motif clearly suggests a wealthier owner.

The danger entailed by pregnancy and childbirth, which was often an annual event for Tudor women, requires little elaboration. As well as preparing a layette and a nursery, an expectant mother would, as a matter of routine, make provision for someone to care for her child in the event of her dying at its birth, and even if she survived the ordeal there was also the prospect that she might experience permanent injury. Puerperal fever, for example, killed both Katherine Parr and Jane Seymour, who had been stricken by delirium before suffering 'an naturalle laxe', or catastrophic haemorrhage, less than a fortnight after the birth of Edward VI.

Caesarean section and forceps were also unknown, and many women might expect to see fewer than half their children grow to full maturity.

Certainly, the midwives or 'wise women' who assisted at births varied considerably in standard. Some, it seems, believed in over-hasty intervention and, according to some accounts, broke the birth membrane with coins, thimbles or even specially sharpened fingernails. If, on the other hand, the baby's journey along the birth canal were delayed for any reason, it might be assisted by the application of pig fat. Yet most Tudor midwives appear to have been comparatively skilled and successful practitioners of their art, so that no more than 1 per cent of women actually appear to have died in childbirth – a figure that would not be bested or even equalled by male doctors until the 1920s. Believing that dirt and foul odours brought sickness, they were often scrupulously clean in their habits, and displayed great proficiency in the management of difficult birthing presentations.

Not altogether surprisingly, then, midwives enjoyed a special status in Tudor society, crossing social boundaries and tending to noblewomen and beggars alike. Unlike other married women, they had the legal power to testify in court and were also authorised by the Church to perform emergency baptisms. Furthermore, since childbirth was not considered a medical issue per se, midwives and not physicians were the source of authoritative knowledge about any obstetric and postpartum matters. The royal doctors who attended Jane Seymour, for instance, were merely distinguished academics with limited practical experience, who had in all likelihood failed to check that her afterbirth had been properly expelled. Ironically, then, a woman of inferior station might well have received better treatment at the hands of her friends and relatives than that accorded to the most revered female in the land.

What, meanwhile, was the role of husbands in the hugger-mugger world of Tudor childbirth? It was not until the 1960s, of course, that their presence during labour became fashionable. In sixteenth-century England, by contrast, they were strictly prohibited from attendance of any kind. Instead, female family members and friends, known as 'gossips', were the only people on hand to assist the midwife in her life-or-death duties. Typically, gossips might tend to routine tasks, such as putting straw under the birthing chair – a practice which explains why the term 'a woman in the straw' became a popular euphemism for a birthing mother in the Tudor era. The main task of the waiting Tudor father, however, was to tend to the needs of his wife's entourage – a task which could only be neglected at some cost, since those who failed to provide adequate hospitality were apt to find themselves duly stigmatised by unfavorable 'gossip' about their lack of generosity.

12

Baby rattle

Rattles are among the oldest and most commonplace toys in the world. They appear in pre-Columbian America, in pharaonic Egypt and even as far back as the era of the ancient Hittites. Yet the one shown here is of particular interest. Measuring 9cm in length, it opens into a ball shape with four copper alloy bells attached that may have served as a locator for children who happened to venture out of sight of busy adults. Under this there is a long stem which ends in a whistle, and at the whistle's end are the initials of the pewterer who fashioned the handle, cast as part of the design – A.B. or A.I.B. The whole object is covered in cross-hatching except the ball, which has an Elizabethan-style design around it. Rattles of similar design were common until the end of the eighteenth century, but with one intriguing difference: in later examples the hard 'teething' piece on which the baby could cut its first teeth was usually a piece of coral, imported from Africa or the southern Mediterranean, while in this instance the teething piece is the canine tooth of a wolf, against which the baby could press its gums to relieve the pain. And it is here, perhaps, that the especial curiosity of this object resides, for beyond its more obvious practical purpose it also seems to have served as an amulet.

Wolves' teeth, in particular, symbolised supernatural power which could be transferred from the animal to the child in a way that would not only protect it against danger but also ensure its health and happiness. And at a time when infant mortality was so grievously high, their use in such a personal, everyday item might well have seemed especially appropriate. Overall, around a quarter of babies died before their first birthday, with some estimates suggesting that between a third and a half of children did not survive past the age of 5. Ben Jonson's well-known and touching lament – 'Farewell, thou child of my right hand, and joy' – on the death of his son Benjamin, who died in 1603, reminds us of the grief that was all too commonly experienced by Tudor parents. Shakespeare, too, lost his son Hamnet, who died at the age of 11 in 1596, while Catherine

of Aragon's seven pregnancies produced only one lasting survivor, her daughter Mary.

Clearly, then, Providence was no respecter of rank, and quite apart from the harrowing impact of disease and infection, the unsupervised toddler, ranging free about the humbler Tudor home with its uneven surfaces, open fires and boiling pans, faced a further host of potentially deadly dangers. Court records are full of ill-starred infants meeting with accidents when they ventured out of doors and windows, or toddled off down the street and fell in ditches. In one particularly heartbreaking instance a baby left swaddled in a cot in a not untypical Derbyshire village while its mother went out was fatally injured by a scavenging wild pig that entered the house in her absence.

So it was hardly surprising that our Tudor forebears also placed such a dividend upon early baptism, and not merely because those who died without christening might be condemned to eternal damnation. Children, it was believed, 'came on better' after baptism – a belief which certainly survived in some places into the twentieth century. Even children still alive in the womb, for that matter, might be christened before birth by a clergyman in those cases where there was imminent risk of a stillbirth. In such cases, the sacraments could be administered *in utero*, though a neutral rather than a 'Christian' name was usually applied to the stricken child. In most cases, the name 'Creature' sufficed or in a handful of cases where the female gender of the baby had been determined, 'Creatura'. Thankfully, however, at least a few of these children subsequently survived, for in the vestry-book of a Staplehurst church there is a reference on 19 July 1579 to the marriage of 'John Haffynden and Creature Cheseman, yong folke'.

13

Wooden doll

Wooden and lead alloy dolls entered England in large numbers during the Tudor period, and this particular specimen, manufactured in Thuringia in 1530, is an exceptionally fine example of the work of the German craftsmen who produced them. Such was their popularity, indeed, that some contemporaries expressed peevish disapproval. 'The rootes which are counterfited and made like litle puppettes and mammettes which come to be sold in England in boxes with heir and such forme as man hath, are nothyng elles but folishe fened trifles and not naturall', complained the staunch Calvinist William Turner in his *Herball* of 1562. Yet he could not stem the tide of German imports, as is demonstrated by the number of cruder lead alloy, hollow-cast figurines, dressed in the German and Swiss fashions found around the areas of Frankfurt, Cologne and Geneva during the mid- to late sixteenth century, now residing in various English museums. Nor, for that matter, could he stifle Teutonic ingenuity on a broader front, since the first doll's house was produced in the mercantile region of southern Germany in 1558. And in the meantime, the steady supply of more roughly crafted, natively manufactured dolls, dubbed 'Bartholomew babies' as a result of their sale in large numbers at St Bartholomew's fair in London, seems to have continued unabated.

Clearly, then, the modern stereotype of tyrannical Tudor parents not only ignoring their offspring's psychological needs but abusing them with gusto at every opportunity is at the very least partially wide of the mark. Where excessive mistreatment occurred it was more likely to be inflicted by employers, and in such instances it was not unheard of for parents to resort to legal action against offenders. Moreover, while Tudor children were seen in some respects as little more than small adults, their elders nevertheless recognised that they passed through different developmental stages. The age of 7, for example, seems to have been set as a key watershed in a child's existence, especially among more privileged families.

Until then, boys were very much 'brought up among the women', being dressed and treated the same as girls. From their 7th birthdays onwards, however, their masculinity was asserted, with changed clothing and more frequent entry into male company. Poorer children, by contrast, were typically expected to begin work at this age, albeit in limited roles as bird-scarers and the like, although we hear in one account of how a 5-year-old pig herder from Huggate in Yorkshire was killed in an accident with his animals.

Thereafter, depending largely upon the social class of child, the next stage was around 12 for girls and 14 for boys, at which time they were considered ready for betrothal, although marriage rarely occurred until at least the age of 15 for girls and 18 for boys. Once again, however, some aristocratic matches were arranged well before this, even in infancy, after which the child concerned might be raised in the household of their prospective spouse. Certainly, members of the royal family were married at a particularly young age and considered perfectly capable of consummating the union by their mid-teens, as was the intention with Prince Arthur and Catherine of Aragon in 1501. Henry VIII's grandmother, Margaret Beaufort, was married at 12 and gave birth at 13.

For the less privileged, meanwhile, the age of marriage was usually highest of all, not least because most wives needed to be old enough to manage their household duties and strong enough to carry a child while also conducting manual labour. Similarly, the prospective husband was often expected to earn enough money to pay for the bride's dowry or wait in many cases for his father to die to acquire the necessary funds, which could, of course, take years. Although early matches were encouraged, therefore, the actual age of marriage in Tudor England seems on average to have been around 24 for women and 27 for men.

And what, in the meantime, may be said of Tudor 'teenagers'? The concept, of course, is a modern one, but outbreaks of violence and mischief on the part of repressed adolescents were not altogether uncommon, especially on the streets of London at festival times. The May Day riots of 1517, for example, saw thousands of wild apprentices wreak havoc in the capital against merchants and craftsmen from Flanders, Florence, Genoa and the Baltic. And though, according to one eyewitness, 'the terror was greater than the harm done', this did not prevent the rioters from closing the city gates to prevent the king's soldiers from reinforcing the guard. Nor, after a token pardon, did it prevent the authorities from selecting forty or so unfortunates as an example to the rest. 'At the city gates', wrote a visitor to London soon afterwards, 'one sees nothing but gibbets and the quarters of these scelerats, so that it is horrible to pass near them.'

14

Hornbook

The so-called hornbook was not in fact a book at all, but a small wooden board with a handle like the one from the British Museum pictured here, which is embellished with the ubiquitous Tudor rose in the form of a brass diamond-shaped mount. On the front, a sheet of vellum inscribed with a lesson – typically the alphabet and the Lord's Prayer – was attached to one side and covered by a thin, transparent layer of horn to serve as protection. In spite of their simplicity, however, hornbooks played a fundamental role in the education of Tudor children, serving as a primer in basic literacy and addressing the simple practical problem that parchment, and later paper, was simply too costly to be placed in the hands of young learners. In its own humble way, then, the sturdy hornbook represented in principle a sixteenth-century hardware solution to illiteracy, one of the major social problems of the day. On some hornbooks, indeed, the vellum insert could slide out from beneath the translucent horn and be replaced by other lessons. In this way the hornbook became a kind of sixteenth-century iPad, being passed down in some cases from generation to generation. Usually made of wood, lead or pewter and employed in the instruction of children from various social backgrounds, hornbooks were used at all levels of society. The future Queen Elizabeth I herself possessed one with a silver filigree frame. Shakespeare also mentions a 'Hornebook' in *Love's Labour Lost*, and there is every possibility that he, too, first learned his letters with the aid of such an item.

Most youngsters, of course, were taught only those practical skills that their parents considered useful for adult life, and only a small percentage of Tudor children went to school. By the mid-sixteenth century, therefore, it seems likely that no more than 20 per cent of men and 5 per cent of women were literate, at a time when literacy was in any case measured by little more than the ability to fashion a signature. Girls in most cases were either kept at home by their parents to help

with housework or sent out to work to earn money for the family, while boys from a slightly more elevated social background might begin rudimentary schooling at a 'petty' school at the age of 4 before moving on at the age of 7 to a grammar school where discipline was invariably rigorous and the school day long, starting at about 6 a.m. in the summer or 7 a.m. in winter and ending at about 5 p.m. Attendance, moreover, often ran to six days per week, and holidays were few – between eight and twelve weeks annually – with the result that Tudor pupils spent some 2,000 hours per year in school, or around double the time experienced by their twenty-first-century counterparts.

The gentry, meanwhile, usually preferred to employ private tutors, though by the end of the sixteenth century this trend was altering as the reputation of grammar schools continued to flourish. For those of slightly humbler social circumstances, there was also the option of parish schools, which, though less prestigious, were more numerous, with over half the parishes in England boasting one by the end of the Tudor period. Here children were taught not only singing, so that boys could become choristers, but also reading, writing and simple arithmetic, though schoolmasters of all types received no formal training and the quality of teaching varied enormously. Many, for instance, were clergymen trying to enhance their meagre wages, and it was not until 1559 that teachers became licensed.

Yet respect for learning increased steadily among most social groups in Tudor England. Since Protestantism was the religion of the 'word', a higher degree of literacy was needed to read the Scriptures, and although the dissolution of the monasteries and chantries resulted in the closure of some schools, a number were re-founded by both Henry VIII and Edward VI. Prompted by the influence of individuals like Baldassare Castiglione on the continent and Sir Thomas Elyot in England, education became not only a prerequisite for advancement but the hallmark of gentility itself. Nor, for that matter, was this new emphasis upon education confined entirely to males. Even comparatively early in the century Thomas More was unable to see 'why learning may not equally agree with both sexes', though, like other humanist authors, More's real ideal was the educated wife who was able to provide intellectual companionship for her husband and educated moral training for her children. Furthermore, while Lady Jane Grey and others stand out as notable exceptions, there may well have been, according to some estimates, no more than sixty or so aristocratic women in the entire course of Tudor history who benefited from anything like the full flush of a Renaissance education. At the time of Queen Elizabeth's death in 1603, therefore, traditional attitudes seem to have been as entrenched as ever, prompted in no small measure by the pronouncements of men like her successor, James I, who, when told of the accomplishments of a learned woman, was heard to remark sarcastically, 'but can shee spin?'

15

Betrothal ring

Even though his ideas were never formally embraced by the Anglican Church, few foreigners, arguably, had a more far-reaching impact upon Tudor England than the German religious reformer Martin Luther. Furthermore, the betrothal ring that the former monk presented to Katharina von Bora – the wife with whom he had six children – remains an object of exceptional cultural resonance in its own right. In the centre is the crucified Saviour surrounded by a series of finely wrought gold devices representing all the symbols of the Passion. On one side a leaf of hyssop is depicted and on the other the spear with which Christ's body was pierced. Elsewhere a ladder may also be distinguished, along with other symbols connected with Christ's last act of atonement, such as the three nails, the rod of reeds used for his flagellation and the dice with which the soldiers cast lots for his robes – the whole surmounted by a central ruby. On the inside of the ring, meanwhile, the inscriptions are still perfect. They contain the names of the betrothed pair, and the date of their wedding day in German, *der 13 Junij 1525*.

As depicted in Lucas Cranach's portrait of the following year, the ring was worn by Katharina on the index finger of her left hand, though English tradition had always stipulated the right hand until Edward VI's first Book of Common Prayer officially reversed the convention in 1549. This, moreover, was only one of many changes to time-honoured wedding customs ushered in by the Reformation. Traditionally, for instance, the vows and exchange of rings had been performed outside the church, after which the congregation moved inside to celebrate Mass. But in 1559, England became the first place where the marriage ceremony was officially ordered to take place indoors. An early Tudor etiquette book had mentioned that members of the nobility and gentry could be married inside the church, while an earl's son or daughter might be married by the choir door, and a knight 'within the church or chapel door'. Those of

Stadtgeshichteliches Museum, Leipzig

lower station, however, still had to be content 'to be married without the church door' until the first Elizabethan Book of Common Prayer stipulated once and for all that 'the persons to be married shal come into the body of the Churche, wyth theyr friends and neighbours'.

The practice of sprinkling confetti, in its turn, can also be traced to this period, though it did not occur at the church but at the family home where the wedding reception occurred. 'As the bride enters the house', wrote Polydore Vergil, 'wheat is thrown upon her head', and another custom clearly related to fertility and procreation involved the presentation and scattering of flowers. In some cases, the bride presented her groom with a wreath, while her unmarried peers presented other wreaths to guests. In a double wedding of two English sisters in 1560 we hear of 'fine flowers and rosemary strewed for their homecoming, and so to their father's house, where a great dinner was prepared', though for most families, of course, the cost involved prohibited such extravagance. Indeed, for poorer folk the cost of nuptial festivities might have to be defrayed by the holding of a so-called 'bride ale', at which the bride sold cups of ale – usually in the churchyard – for as much as the guests might pay.

Certainly, even the weddings of the less fortunate were likely to be well attended, and processions preceding the marriage were normally noisy affairs, with loud music, bawdy jokes and laughter, which not infrequently led town councils to complain about the resulting disorder. Pregnant brides, meanwhile, had the consolation of knowing that marriage would render their child legitimate, so long as the birth did not occur before

Herzog August Bibliothek Wolfenbüttel

the actual vows had been taken. And any stigma attached to such women seems in any case to have been minimal, since sexual relations appear to have been generally considered a normal aspect of courtship. Nor do such liberal attitudes seem to have resulted in unrestricted promiscuity. Figures available for the later Tudor period suggest that only 3 per cent of children were actually illegitimate.

And what more may be said at this stage of the fate awaiting sixteenth-century brides after their wedding day? Here, perhaps, the example of Katharina von Bora herself may be of some relevance. The daughter of an impoverished nobleman, she had been sent to a convent at the age of 5, taking her nun's vows at 16 before finally growing dissatisfied with the cloistered life after hearing of the reformation movement led by her future husband. Along with eleven other nuns she escaped from the convent by hiding in the wagon of a fish merchant, before eventually marrying the 42-year-old Luther when she herself was 26. Thereafter, while her husband lived the life of a scholar, Katharina, like most sixteenth-century women, became a whirlwind of industry, not only managing family and household affairs but also running both a farm and a brewery, and, at times of sickness, a hospital. She was, said Luther, 'the morning star of Wittenberg', referring to her habit of rising at 4 a.m. in order to begin her daily tasks.

16

Memento mori

Death figured prominently in the Tudor psyche, as it did throughout contemporary European, and this outstanding example of a *memento mori*, or 'reminder of death', could not embody more aptly both the transience and potentially agonising end of any sixteenth-century life. A gruesome skeleton clothed in tattered flesh holds a scroll bearing the Latin inscription 'I am what you will be. I was what you are. For every man is this so'. That the artist, probably Hans Leinberger, has depicted the cadaver in a graceful pose that mimics that of Adam in Albrecht Dürer's famous engraving of Adam and Eve is probably intentional, for it was supposedly due to Adam's sin that humans were subject to death. Archduke Ferdinand of Austria possessed a similar item also attributed to Leinberger that is not quite so well-proportioned, and though the original owner of this particular object is unknown, the person concerned is certain to have been a sophisticated collector, for most *memento mori* in Tudor England usually consisted of finger rings of varying degrees of sophistication. In England, too, *memento mori* seals depicting skulls were common, along with mourning rings sometimes containing a snip of hair. Here, however, we have a consummate work of art in its own right – the complexity of the carving demonstrating all the finer qualities of boxwood, allowing the gut to be hollowed out with immense precision and the skin to be peeled away without the whole form collapsing.

Nor was the dedication of such painstaking artistry to so morbid a subject anything but appropriate, for 'making a good death' remained especially important to Tudor men and women constantly endangered by epidemic diseases such as typhoid, dysentery and smallpox – not to mention occasional visitations of bubonic plague and the mysterious, deadly ailment known as the 'sweating sickness', which had reputedly been brought to England by Henry VII's mercenaries in 1485. The threat from accidental death also remained ever present, as the 9,000 or so reports from Tudor coroners stored at the National Archives at Kew conclusively demonstrate.

Housewives and servants fetching water for domestic use from open pits, streams and wells, were, for example, involved in about 4 per cent of all accidental deaths, and the fact that women also picked riverside plants, cleaned linen and washed sheep before shearing in fast-flowing mountain streams lent added risk to their everyday lives. We hear, too, of the unfortunate John Broke, a Yorkshire cloth-maker, who was only one among countless others struck down by his Maker without warning when an oak tree 'suddenly rolled downhill and hit him' while he was building a fence.

Most poignantly of all, perhaps, there is the case of little Jane Shaxspere, a 2-year-old girl who fell into a mill pond and drowned while picking flowers, called 'yelowe boddles' or corn marigolds, in Upton Warren in Worcestershire, 20 miles from Stratford-upon-Avon, in 1569. William Shakespeare would have been around 5 years old at the time and, if Jane was indeed his younger cousin, as has been suggested, the parallels to Ophelia in *Hamlet* – who picked flowers and drowned when she fell into a river – are intriguing. Certainly the coroner, Henry Feeld, was scrupulous regarding the details:

> The same Jane Shaxspere the said sixteenth day of June about the eighth hour after noon of the same day suddenly and by misfortune fell into the same small channel and was drowned in the aforesaid small channel, and then and there she instantly died. And thus the aforesaid flowers were the cause of the death of the aforesaid Jane; and they are worth nothing.

The Tudor path to death was paved with an infinitely varied mosaic of ever-present hazards. The threat of destruction grew even more terrifying as the century progressed, for during the course of Henry VIII's reign the consolations of priestly absolution were finally undermined by the abandonment of Roman Catholicism. Yet, if fear of death may well have increased in post-Reformation England, fear of the dead, at least, may just have diminished marginally. For while the Tudors continued to believe in ghosts, the more enlightened of their rationally minded Protestant preachers made increasing efforts to eradicate such superstitions. Since purgatory was officially dismissed in the 1540s as an unbiblical superstition concocted in Rome, the implications were plain. Not only was there now no need for priests to deliver the last rites or for prayers for the dead to be said in chantry chapels, a further conclusion was equally obvious. For how could the dead return from a mythical staging-post between heaven and hell to plague their living counterparts? 'Souls departed,' wrote the reformer Robert Wisdom in 1543, 'do not come again and play boo-peep with us.'

17

Sir Henry Sidney's heart coffin

By the early twelfth century, it was already common practice to eviscerate and bury the body apart from the heart, brain, tongue etc. as part of the embalming process, and this procedure seems to have retained its popularity among certain members the Tudor aristocracy. In the case of Sir Henry Sidney, who died in 1586 and whose heart coffin is pictured here, his body was buried in Kent, while the heart was removed to Shropshire. The inscription reads, 'herlith the harte of syr henrye sydny l.p. anno.' Surviving coffins of this type are rare, however, and the motives for such dismemberment remain unclear, although another lead urn with the name of John Peck and dated 1562 was acquired in 2009 by Ryedale Folk Museum in North Yorkshire.

Sidney himself seems to have died a disappointed man, since he had gained neither the grant of lands nor the peerage which were reasonable hopes for a royal servant who had served both in Wales as President of the Council of the Marches and as Lord Deputy of Ireland. In 1582 he wrote a long letter to Sir Francis Walsingham, whose daughter was about to marry his son Philip. In it he recounted in detail how in each of his three terms in Ireland he had suppressed rebellion, and in each expended some £5,000 of his own money. Yet for all this he had nothing to show in terms of material reward and had been forced to sell off considerable parts of his lands in the Midlands to pay off his debts. Perhaps in Sidney's case, therefore, it was only natural that his heart should return to the place where it had once been happiest and was, arguably, finally broken.

There is, however, no such element of mystery concerning the choice of material for Sidney's heart coffin, since lead-lined caskets were standard for the wealthy, and had been for centuries. Lead could easily be sealed to provide a fluid- and gas-tight envelope, although in Henry VIII's case

it seems that his 140kg bulk may well have contributed to a fracture that resulted in leakage of 'body liquor' prior to burial. And if Sidney himself died heartbroken, he was at least spared the carelessness in death that seems to have been the fate of various other monarchs. When young Edward VI died on 6 July 1553, for instance, he was all but forgotten as John Dudley and his co-conspirators struggled unsuccessfully to establish the primacy of Lady Jane Grey over Mary Tudor. Even upon Mary's accession on 19 July no one was willing to take the funeral in hand until given specific orders from the new queen, who did not enter London until the first week of August. And at that point, too, there was further debate between Mary and her advisers over whether the funeral rites should be conducted according to the new Protestant Book of Common Prayer or the traditional Roman Catholic liturgy before the Protestant faction finally won the skirmish. The result was a four-week delay before the king's eventual burial on 8 August.

There is the harrowing case, too, of Henry VIII's brother-in-law, James IV of Scotland, who was killed at Flodden in 1513 and whose corpse was apparently abandoned in a lumber room of Richmond Palace. 'My Lord of Surrey, my Henry, wolde fayne know your pleasur in the buryeng of the King of Scotts body', wrote Catherine of Aragon to her husband in the wake of the battle, after suggesting that James's blood-soaked tunic might be dispatched to him as a fitting trophy. But while Henry spurned the garment, he continued to feel no need for a fitting funeral for his fallen enemy. Nor, for that matter, was he even inclined to hand back the corpse to the Scots. In John Stow's account a local workman actually cut off the Scottish king's head and took it home as a ghoulish keepsake.

Plainly, respect for the dead was sometimes at a premium in Tudor England. After her death at 2.00 p.m. on 7 January 1536 Catherine of Aragon herself became the victim of a hasty autopsy conducted by a candlemaker who seems to have found her heart 'quite black and hideous to look at'. Her husband's beloved illegitimate son, meanwhile, seems to have been another victim of a botched funeral procedure. For in spite of the king's orders that he be interred in lead, the young man's father-in-law, the Duke of Norfolk, failed to oversee the task personally. Eight days after he died, therefore, the corpse of Henry Fitzroy, Duke of Richmond, was loaded on to a cart and covered with straw, with only two servitors as escort, before being rudely hauled to Framlingham for entombment. And last but not least, of course, there was the even rougher treatment of poor Anne Boleyn, whose mortal remains were casually crammed into an old arrow chest, with her head tucked in for good measure.

British Museum

65

Women, Work, Craftsmen and Paupers

18

Linen sampler

'The good and virtuous woman,' wrote Sabba da Castiglione in his *Ricordi overo Ammaestramenti* ('Reminders or Teachings') of 1569, 'will teach her daughters to work with their hands and above all to sew.' 'Idleness,' he added with a characteristic dash of pomposity, 'is a great evil.' Yet the Italian's sentiments were heartily shared by his English counterparts, male and female alike, who viewed needlework as a seemly, safe and productive pastime for both young girls and grown women – morally apt in all its aspects and infinitely preferable, therefore, to less reputable activities like dancing and card-playing. High and low together, but especially ladies of refinement, were consequently encouraged to embroider items for their trousseau as well as chemises and handkerchiefs, or larger items such as tablecloths and wall hangings. And as the possibilities for permanent employment as a seamstress in a wealthy household became increasingly attractive, so samplers like the one above, produced by Jane Bostocke in 1598, became particularly significant. The earliest known example to include an embroidered date, its inscription commemorates the birth of a child, Alice Lee, two years earlier, though it is, in effect, a practice-piece for Jane Bostocke herself, who is likely to have been a member of the Lee family household, employed specifically for her needlework skills.

But may such an item be taken to confirm widespread stereotypes of female passivity and subjection in Tudor England? Certainly, Jane Bostocke's knowledge of the alphabet already placed her in a tiny minority among her contemporaries, and there were a host of other ways too in which women like Jane found themselves not only restricted by social conventions but sometimes nakedly exploited by the more ruthless elements of a Tudor patriarchy which shaped their destiny. 'The good nature of a woman', wrote Sir Thomas Elyot in 1531, 'is to be mild, timorous, tractable, benign, of sure remembrance, and shamefast', while the marriage service, in its turn, required brides to be 'bonaire and buxom in bed and at bord', or in other words cheerful and amenable both in bed and at table. Almost immediately after the Statute of Wills of 1540 had allowed men to bequeath the greater part of their land by will, moreover, another statute denied to married women – along with idiots, children and young men under the age of 21 – the right to bequeath any land at all.

Inferiority under the law and exploitation in marriage were accompanied by the harrowing physical effects of twenty years of continual childbirth, though the practice of abortion seems to have left little imprint upon the historical record. Contemporary books mention supposedly effective 'medicines' for terminating a pregnancy, but infanticide remained a criminal offence, and for this reason, perhaps, the total number of people indicted for killing unwanted children in the three counties of Essex, Hertfordshire and Sussex in the later sixteenth century was less than 1.5 per annum. Over the same period and areas, moreover, even fewer convictions occurred for rape, which was a reflection too, no doubt, on the fact that rape within marriage was considered an outright contradiction in terms. And if occasion demanded, of course, Tudor men of humbler stock had little to fear from the consequences of simply deserting their wives. A census of poor families conducted in Norwich in 1570, for instance, suggests that there were many, such as a certain Margery, aged 40, in the parish of St Martin at Bale, who was described as the wife, though never married, of one John Hill, lime-burner, who had 'departed from her a four year past and she know not where he is'.

For Jane Bostocke, secure in her seamstress role in the Lee family home and educated enough to form her letters, similar misfortunes were naturally a remoter prospect. Nor, it seems, did some of her gender accept their subservience quite as readily as others. When royal representatives came to Oxford in 1530 to advance the case for the annulment of the king's marriage, they were met by furious women armed with rocks, while a preacher in Salisbury who supported the king's actions had to be rescued before he 'suffered much at the hands of women'. At St Paul's in London, too, a woman responded to a sermon favouring the divorce by calling the preacher a liar and claiming that the king should be chastised for undermining the institution of marriage. And as if these more high-profile examples do not prove the point eloquently enough, there is the further case of Thomas Wylede, husbandman of Temple Normanton near Chesterfield, who in 1590 bequeathed 'one cow and a coverlet or some part towards a bed' to his daughter Ann, so long as she will 'be ruled by her mother'.

19

Ducking stool

The ducking stool or 'stool of repentance' has a long history, dating back to Anglo-Saxon and Norman England. In the Domesday Book, for example, there is mention of a *cathedra stercoris* – 'chair of filth' – at Chester, while from about 1215 onwards there are increasing references to 'cucking stools' deriving from the old verb *cukken*, and its Latin predecessor *cacare*, meaning to defecate. The suggestion, then, is that some form of immersion in human waste was the original punishment for offenders, though by Tudor times this particular option seems to have been discarded. Towards the end of this period the term 'ducking stool', which is first mentioned in written records in 1597, had begun to be used, and a record from 1769 confirms that 'ducking stool' is a corruption of the term 'cucking stool'. Cucking stools and ducking stools, however, were by no means necessarily one and the same thing, for whereas the former could be used for humiliation with or without ducking the person in water, the latter came to be applied more specifically to those stools on an oscillating plank which were used to plunge offenders into ponds and rivers.

It became mandatory for manors during the late medieval period to possess and maintain such ducking devices, though by the 1560s their use was already declining, and entries in the records of the court leet at Leominster, for example, indicate that the town was failing to maintain its own instrument properly and incurring several fines as a result. Primarily reserved for any 'troublesome and angry woman who, by her brawling and wrangling among her neighbours, doth break the public peace and beget, cherish and increase public discord', the ducking stool at Leominster, like other places, was also employed upon male traders who sold short measures or adulterated food, as well as men who brawled in public. Yet the general reputation of the ducking stool – like that of the scold's bridle, which was outlawed in Tudor England (but not Scotland) – eventually became so inextricably linked to the abuse of women that

Karen Roe

when the the contraption at Leominster was moved to its current position in the town's parish church, a short service of penance was deemed
appropriate, not merely for the excesses of former times, but for present-
day intolerance and prejudice, too.

Nor, it must be said, did the association of ducking with the maltreat-
ment of women arise without good reason. In 1378, Langland's *Piers
Plowman* referred to it as a form of *wyuen pine* or 'women's punishment',
and it had continued in use from time to time for sexual offences like
prostitution or the bearing of illegitimate children. For those convicted
of such misdemeanours, moreover, there was a further form of ritual
humiliation involving the so-called 'tumbrel' – a cart with wooden wheels
in which the transgressor was paraded through the streets. In 1571, for
example, the wife of the vicar of Epping was convicted in the court leet
of being 'garrulous to her neighbours' and humiliated in precisely this
fashion, while in December 1559 the wife of the goldsmith Henry Glyn
was wheeled in a cart through the City of London for selling the sexual
services of her own daughter – a not altogether uncommon offence, it
seems, for not long afterwards the widow of a certain Master Warner,

late sergeant of the Admiralty, was found guilty of being a bawd to her daughter and her maidservant, both of whom were unmarried and had subsequently become pregnant.

Yet in a society where rough justice born of tough conditions, a no-nonsense approach to morality and a boisterous sense of community 'fun' were commonplace, men and women frequently continued to be demeaned in equal measure. Unruly married couples, for example, were sometimes bound back-to-back and ducked. And while men were more usually treated to the stocks or pillory, they too were not above being paraded in tumbrels. Only one month after Henry Glyn's wife suffered disgrace, a London baker was similarly paraded for multiple instances of fornication, while in June 1560 a cart was drawn through the city exhibiting two men and three women – 'one man for he was the bawd, to bring women unto strangers' and the other man, along with his sister, since they 'were taken together naked'. Even men of some standing, for that matter, might be subjected to similar indignity, for on 16 June 1563 Dr Christopher Langton, an Eton- and Cambridge-educated Fellow of the College of Physicians, was paraded in a cage through baying Cheapside crowds in his best finery – a gown of damask lined with velvet, and a velvet coat and cape. Thus, wrote Henry Machyn, he was made to suffer 'on the market day ... for he was taken with two young wenches at once'.

Public humiliation was, it would seem, a common enough spectacle in Tudor England. Yet the cruder excesses rightly associated with it may well be assigned more properly to the following centuries, as the history of the notorious Leominster ducking stool once again confirms. There were numerous tranformations over time; records show that in 1566 a certain Walter Maddocke charged a little over 4s for installing wheels upon the gadget. But it was not until the eighteenth century that it was fitted with irons to restrain the miscreant and a new hoist which allowed the chair to be held higher in the air to increase the indignity and magnify the ordeal.

20
Agrarian almanac

For Tudor men and women in both town and village alike, the harvest remained a subject of perennial interest, for upon it rested the whole foundation of their material well-being and, in the final analysis, life or death itself. This, after all, was a time when at most two thirds of the population were wage-earners, and a considerable proportion of the rest subsistence farmers. It was a time, too, when some 80 to 90 per cent of wage-earners' incomes were spent on food, so that any increase in food prices meant hunger. When it is remembered, finally, that roughly one third of all people lived in any case below the poverty line, the disastrous consequences of harvest failure for sixteenth-century communities requires little further explanation. And such failures were all too frequent. In a normal decade, one harvest in four could be reckoned a failure, and while a little more than 40 per cent of harvests might be considered abundant, some twenty-four individual cases over the course of the Tudor period – a little more than one sixth of the total – could be considered 'bad', in which case, wrote Bishop John Ponet, the people might be 'driven of hunger to grind acorns for bread and drink water instead of ale'. Worse still, they might die in droves, as indeed happened when the heavy rains of 1555 and 1556 caused the worst harvest failures of the century, and the epidemics which then descended upon a malnourished and weakened population in 1556 and 1558 exacted a death toll of some 200,000 – around 6 per cent of the total population.

Under such circumstances, therefore, it was hardly surprising that agrarian almanacs of the kind featured here were produced. This one, dating from 1513 and now located in the library of Copenhagen University, not only records the cycle of the agricultural year, but also contains practical tips for landowners and farmers. The concentric circles, for example, note the varying hours of daylight during the year, while the image of Christ crucified, depicted elsewhere, demonstrates the strong relationship drawn in sixteenth-century society between work and prayer. Folded in order to be carried in a pocket or worn on a belt, the illustrations also demonstrate the various types of manual work predominating in each month and are accompanied by brief handwritten commentaries on each specific activity.

Around 90 per cent of Tudor men and women were engaged in agricultural employment of one kind or another and, as the almanac demonstrates, the labour involved was often strenuous. But it was also, if contemporary coroners' reports are any guide, surprisingly dangerous – and never more so than in summertime, when the harvest was at its peak. Indeed, cart crashes, overloaded carts, carts driven by young boys at a time when no licensing arrangements existed, dangerous harvesting techniques, equine mishaps and windmill mangling were only a few of the perils facing the Tudor farmworker, and between 1558 and 1560 almost three quarters of fatal accidents were recorded in high summer. In one case, we hear of an exhausted labourer falling asleep beside a hayrick which then collapsed and suffocated its drowsy victim. Other men, meanwhile, were careless with scythes and cut themselves deeply enough to die of shock or loss of blood. There are frequent references, too, to trampling by animals – especially horses, which accounted for around 90 per cent of all such cases. Falling from trees while in quest of fruit or nuts was another familiar cause of death. Even pig farmers could suffer from such height hazards, falling out of oak trees when looking for acorns in the early autumn. Indeed, contemporary handbooks, not unlike the almanac featured here, warned about the risks involved in removing the nests of scavenging crows. Tree removal was also fraught with hazards, it seems, with more than one in ten fatal accidents involving the cutting or transport of wood.

Under such circumstances, then, was there any compensation at all to be had for the back-breaking labour and physical danger entailed by work on a Tudor farm? One at least may just be worth the passing consideration of a twenty-first-century audience. For though, as the almanac suggests, the sixteenth-century labourer awoke at dawn in accordance with the availability of sunlight, so his hours were task-led rather than time-determined, with the result that when his chores were done he returned home and thus avoided the 'nine-to-five' drudgery of modern working life. And while the months of May to September might be a time of frenzied activity, autumn and winter was an altogether slacker period when repairs and routine matters alone took up the shorter days. If, then, our Tudor forebears faced physical strain and hardship on a scale unfamiliar to most of their modern counterparts, they were nevertheless not only spared the more insidious stresses of the modern working environment but may well, ironically, have worked fewer hours overall for their daily bread.

21

Cloth seal

In 1551 Daniel Barbaro informed the Venetian senate that England was very fertile, especially in pasture for sheep, and produced excellent wool. Nor did he exaggerate, for at the start of the Tudor period, over half a century earlier, there were as many as 8 million sheep in the kingdom – almost three to every man, woman and child. So profitable was English woollen cloth trade, moreover, that the great gentlemen sheep farmers of the day owned teeming flocks that they grazed on every available area by consolidating their holdings at the expense of existing residents, irrespective of the social cost involved. In the process, 'enclosure' of farmland for the purpose of intensive sheep farming would become one of the major issues of the day as families like the Spencers of Althorp and Wormleighton expanded their flocks to upwards of 13,000. 'Your sheep, which are usually so tame and so cheaply fed,' wrote Sir Thomas More in Book I of *Utopia*, 'do now devour human beings themselves and devastate and depopulate fields, houses, and towns'.

And as the mighty sheep magnates thrived, so too did the merchants who produced the woollen broadcloth that made their vast fortunes and ensured the wealth of the towns in which they resided. The three main areas for woollen cloth-making were the West Riding of Yorkshire, East Anglia and the West Country, and since 90 per cent of England's overseas trade was wool-based, by the end of the reign of Henry VII the importance of these centres may well be imagined. Outside London, for example, only Norwich, York, Bristol and Newcastle were at that time larger than Exeter, a town which had trebled in population during the fifteenth century on the back of Devon's woollen industry. And Norwich's own wealth had derived from the same source, so that by the beginning of the sixteenth century it was yielding more in taxation for the government than any other provincial town in England. By 1550, moreover, fewer than thirty of Norwich's wealthiest citizens – most of whom had grown rich on the proceeds from the cloth trade – controlled over 40 per cent of its

wealth. Lavenham in Suffolk, meanwhile, was said to be the fourteenth wealthiest town in Tudor England, despite its comparatively small size, and its fine timber-framed buildings and beautiful church had all been proudly built on the success of the wool trade.

The standard of English cloth was therefore a matter of critical importance, and it was for this reason that seals like the one featured here were produced as a guarantee of the highest possible quality. By selecting fleece from a certain part of the animal or a certain type of sheep, the standard and texture of the resulting cloth could be radically altered, and each length of woollen cloth therefore had at least two seals attached. One carried the mark of a merchant to identify the owner. Another, like the one pictured, carried the seal of the alnager, a city official responsible for ensuring that the finished article matched the regulations determining size, length and quality. This particular stamp reads 's *alnagii pannorv in bristollia*', the 'seal of alnage of cloths in Bristol', and dates to about 1500. It was attached to broadcloth, which was both warm and waterproof and so-called because it was around 2 yards or 184cm wide. The standard unit for determining length, on the other hand, was an ell, measuring 2ft 6in or 114cm. A 'cloth', in consequence, was made and sold in standard lengths of 20 or 40 ells, which the seal confirmed.

Yet in spite of such painstaking controls, England's woollen cloth trade was experiencing steady decline by the end of the Tudor period. In Norwich, Colchester and other places, vain attempts were made to deal with foreign competition by importing Dutch, Flemish and Huguenot weavers, although the significance and influence of the woollen cloth continued to resonate in English culture long after its pivotal place in the national economy had been superseded. To this day, of course, the Lord Speaker's seat in the House of Lords remains a large square bale of wool called the 'woolsack'. However, the impact of the woollen cloth trade also took subtler, if more prosaic, forms. For an Act of Parliament of 1571 attempted to revive flagging wool consumption by stipulating that on Sundays and holidays, all males over 6 years of age, except for the nobility and 'persons of degree', were to wear woollen caps on pain of a fine of three farthings per day. And though the measure was finally repealed in 1597, the flat cap had by that time already become firmly entrenched in English culture as a curiously inverted status symbol of humble birth.

22

Miner's jacket

This extraordinary garment had lain undiscovered in mine workings dating from the late fifteenth or early sixteenth century until it was discovered by chance during open-cast coal mining in Coleorton, Leicestershire, on 26 May 1988. Among the earliest survivals of working clothing in Britain and probably dating to the mid- or late sixteenth century, it is made of tabby woven wool that bears evidence of yellow and blue dye, and the wear patterns indicate that it was actually worn by a miner of the Tudor period. The item's quality, however, suggests that it may have begun life as the possession of a person of higher standing, although this is debatable, since information about some of the few contemporary miners known to us indicates that they were occasionally individuals of some substance in their own right. Records in the West Country, for instance, tell us that a miner like a certain John Philips, who was living in Chewton near Wells during the 1540s, owned 59 acres of land and kept substantial flocks of sheep. Such men, doubling as husbandmen-cum-miners, were not uncommon in this part of the world, and even peasants who earned income as miners accumulated enough cash to purchase 'luxury' items for their efforts. Perhaps, then, the stereotype of the hapless Tudor miner scraping a paltry existence from the bowels of the earth may well require some further reappraisal.

Other fascinating evidence emerging from Coleorton, however, confirms the hardship endured by many of those who worked the mine. Parts of about twenty-five pairs of shoes were uncovered, which in most cases were badly worn out by the time they were finally discarded. Several displayed patching, including one which had been repaired with a leather jerkin, and in two cases, at least, the wearers' feet displayed deformities. One child's boot was also found – clearly cut down from an old full-size one. Significantly, too, the remnants of several tallow candles were discovered, which helps explain why fire appears to have been an ongoing problem at some of the Coleorton workings, particularly during the reign

Leicestershire County Council

of Henry VIII. In one area of the workings, meanwhile, incomplete remnants of several three-legged stools were found and it is likely that these were used by miners when working in galleries of particularly awkward height. All these items were apparently left behind when the workings were finally abandoned in the last quarter of the sixteenth century.

The evidence from contemporary documents shows that coal mining in Leicestershire dates back to at least the thirteenth century, and probably to before the Norman Conquest. Leicestershire's early miners, moreover, would have been local people working around Swannington and Coleorton and supplying coal to most of the county using packhorses and carts which travelled to Leicester across established routes. Indeed, several such routes crossed packhorse bridges still surviving to this day, including those at Anstey, Aylestone and Thurcaston, though damage done to local roads by numerous coal carts seems to have been the only environmental concern of local men and women. Other issues, including health and safety among the mining community, seem to have gone largely unregarded. For while Tudor miners generally dug shafts no more than 30m deep, coroners' reports confirm that many were already suffocating from coal damp, even at these comparatively shallow levels.

Nor did hardship, danger and loss of life stem the growth of mining during the Tudor period, helped by a buoyant demand for metal and luxury goods. Though it is an exaggeration to talk of any 'early industrial revolution', there was nevertheless a considerable increase in the production of coal, lead, copper and iron in the second half of the sixteenth century, in spite of the fact that the alluvial tin deposits of Cornwall and Devon had already begun to decline by 1500. In the decade 1551–60, for instance, coal production stood at about 170,000 tons, while over the course of the century as a whole, lead production doubled and iron production more than trebled. Copper mining, on the other hand, which had been non-existent in 1500, would double in yield between 1580 and 1600 alone. And with this expansion, predictably, came other developments. For, while the founder of the Tudor dynasty was still reigning, the first blast furnace in England had been built at Newbridge in the Weald in 1496 and in 1538 came the first recorded use of the phrase 'like carrying coals to Newcastle'.

23

Apprenticeship register

In Tudor England, craft guilds were still responsible for regulating individual trades and supervising a range of matters such as prices, wages, hours of work and quality of workmanship. If occasion demanded, moreover, they also fought vigorously to protect their interests from the competition of outsiders, or 'foreigners', as they were frequently dubbed. When London plasterers, for instance – who were considered by the capital's painters to be 'but dawbers and mud-wall-makers' – began to paint alehouses, their interference became a matter for debate in the Parliaments of both 1598 and 1601 as the painters' guild jealously protected its members' monopoly. But guilds also had a more fundamental and broader responsibility for hiring and training apprentices, and the apprenticeship register featured here demonstrates the rigour with which they performed this task. Produced by Newcastle-upon-Tyne's Incorporated Company of Tailors, this rare and unexpected survival dates all the way back to 1576 and covers the period up to 1625, detailing the names of apprentices, their fathers' names and the names of the masters to whom their training was entrusted.

A typical entry relates to a certain Frances Richeson, and is dated 29 September 1588, the year of the Spanish Armada. Written in what is known as 'secretary hand', it runs as follows:

This Indentur maied the xxixth daye of September in the xxxth yeare of the Reigne of our Sovereigne Ladie Elizabeth by the grace of god queen of England Fraunce and Irelande queen defender of the faith etc Between Fraunces Richeson laiet sonn of Robarte Richeson of harte in the Countie of Durham yoman deceased bindes

me apprentes with John Shorte of The Towne of Newcastell uppon Tyne Tayllor for the space of Seaven yeares And beinge bounde from the daye of the dayte as a foersaied untell the full end and Tearmes yeares And in the Tyme of Mr Rogger Nychollby beinge maioer Mr George Farnabe sherrefe in Anno Domini 1588.

At least 60 per cent of people in late Tudor England spent their youth as either a servant in someone else's house or learning a trade as an apprentice to a master craftsman. For many middling urban families, a few yeomen and the occasional younger son of a member of the gentry, meanwhile, this latter option was particularly attractive, and, at the age of 14 or 15, boys – and very occasionally girls – left home and gave themselves over entirely to the care and control of their master. Since apprenticeships cost money, different trades were able to charge different fees. Wealth-generating crafts such as those controlled by the goldsmiths and high-status trades like the ones associated with the capital's twelve great Livery Companies charged considerably more than others. Yet all apprenticeships remained limited to the better off or well-connected – usually urban – families, even though the number of individual crafts and trades in the larger towns was expanding considerably. Elizabethan London, for instance, had become the base for specialist luxury crafts which scarcely existed elsewhere, like jewellery, printing and clock-making, though most leading provincial towns could also support a few specialists of their own: Worcester and York each possessed a gunsmith by the 1590s, and York its own clock-maker. Leicester's own dynasty of bell founders, in its turn, was already well established by the same period.

And while many Tudor apprentices were unable to become masters in their own right as soon as they qualified, either for lack of working capital or because trade was slack, there was still the option of becoming adult hands – or 'journeymen' – for other masters. For a young trainee like Frances Richeson, of course, his term of service involved no pay, long hours, rigorous discipline, and a host of other hardships including curfew bells and limited contact with the opposite sex. Yet sixteenth-century Newcastle was a thriving town, already boasting a population of 10,000 in 1547, and where wealth resided, so too did the need to advertise it. Fine clothes were therefore an essential accessory of rank for local 'hostmen', who had gobbled up the Gateshead collieries previously controlled by the Church and now controlled the export of Tyne coal. And as they and their peers grew wealthy, so too, perhaps, did the mature Richeson, enjoying the fruits of his earlier sacrifices while guiding a new generation of eager young tailors to future success of their own.

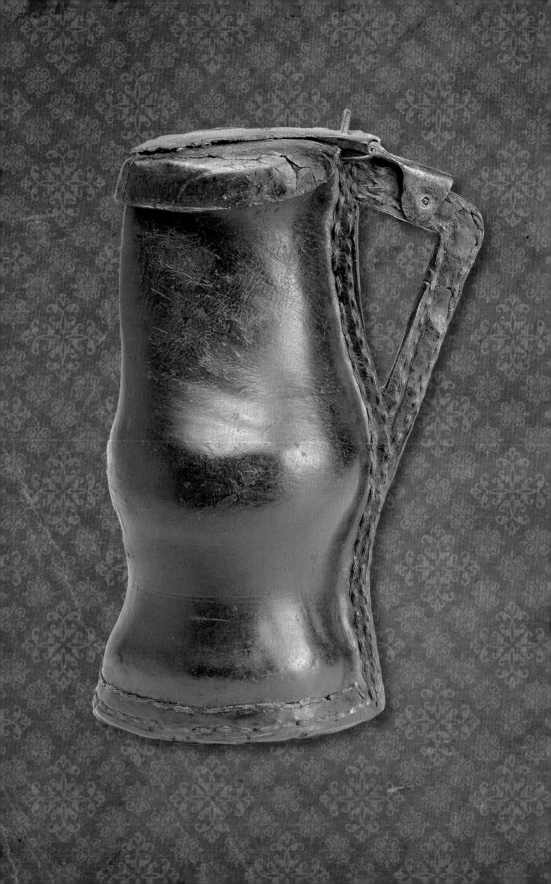

24

Leather bombard

The 'leather bottel', 'black jack' or 'bombard', as it was frequently known, was one of the most useful objects in the Tudor household. Its qualities as a robust, leakproof container for water and alcoholic beverages were widely praised in contemporary drinking songs, and the name 'leather bottel' became a popular choice for many proprietors of the kingdom's alehouses, taverns and inns. This particular example from the Museum of London has a lid attached to the handle with a metal hinge, and on the base and right-hand side of the item the leather is sewn together with a double row of stitching. Its slight constriction between centre and base, giving rise to a globose body, adds stability to the bombard, and places it firmly in the Tudor period. Constructed when the leather was wet and easier to shape, it was subsequently air dried. Air-dried leather of this kind was known as 'jack leather', which is why bombards were also referred to as 'black jacks'. The name 'bombard', meanwhile, was derived from the fact that the body shape of early examples resembled the barrel of a bombard gun.

Since leather is very light in comparison to its strength and durability, its suitability for drinking vessels was universally acknowledged and such vessels were used at all levels of society from the man in the street to royalty, the only distinction being that the bombards of higher social ranks boasted more elaborate decoration. In richer households, too, it was customary for a servant to be on hand with a larger 'leather bottel' at mealtimes, ready to supply the diners with drink. Known originally as the 'botteler', this servant would eventually be dubbed a 'butler'. And such was the prestige of English craftsmanship that leather items like these bombards, with their integral inner waterproof lining, became highly prized objects abroad. Since it had been discovered early on that the skin side of the hide is most naturally waterproof, it was used as the inside of the vessel, while the outside of the jug would be rubbed with either beeswax or boiled birch tree sap. As birch sap turns black when boiled, this became another reason for the alternative name 'black jack'.

Yet drinking vessels such as these were only one feature of the much wider spectrum of goods produced by the English leather industry, which stood out as one of the major sectors of the Tudor economy. Not only was leather the material of choice for footwear and clothing, it was of critical importance in agriculture and even for the iron-working industry in belts, buckets and bellows for blast furnaces. In London, therefore, the Leathersellers' Company had been incorporated since Richard II's time, and the capital's tanneries, with their need for ample supplies of water, became thriving fixtures on the Thames at Bermondsey and Southwark. Outside London, meanwhile, the leather industry burgeoned in the Midlands especially. The wealthiest men in Birmingham were butchers and tanners, while at Northampton, in the subsidy list of 1524, the leather and allied trades constituted the largest single group in the population. In Nottingham, over a third of all burgesses were involved in the leather trade, and even in Coventry – best known for its cloth industry – butchers, shoemakers and tanners all came in the first dozen trades in terms of numbers. Elsewhere, the major provincial towns in the north, west and east, such as York, Chester, Bristol, Gloucester, Exeter and Norwich, were well-established centres of leather manufacture in their own right.

'In most villages of the realm,' wrote one contemporary, 'there is some one worker or dresser of leather, and for the supplies of such as have not there are in most of the market townes iij, iiij or v, and in many great townes and cities x or xxte.' Leather glove-making, in its turn, maintained 'a great Number of Poor, many of which are incapable of following any other Employ'. Overall, then, as many as 8 to 10 per cent of the population may have been involved in some aspect or other of the leather trade, and in consequence only the cloth industry attracted equivalent protection from the government. Ultimately, in fact, the Leather Act of 1563, along with the Statute of Artificers of 1563 and Cloth Act of 1552, would form the legislative foundation of Tudor industrial policy as a whole.

25

Glass goblet

The craving for crystalline glassware among affluent Elizabethans was so notable that in 1577 William Harrison saw fit to mention it in his *A Description of England*. 'It is a world to see in these our days,' wrote Harrison:

> Wherein gold and silver most aboundeth, how that our gentility, as loathing those metals, do now generally choose rather the Venice glasses, both for our wine and beer ... and as this is seen in the gentility, so in the wealthy communalty the like desire of glass is not neglected.

Such were the opportunities for profit that in 1571 the Venetian maker Jacopo Verzelini had been tempted to England by Jean Carré, Huguenot owner of the Crutched Friars Glasshouse in Aldgate. Upon Carré's death only one year later, moreover, Verzelini went on to acquire the Crutched Friars works in his own right before managing in December 1574 to secure royal patronage when Queen Elizabeth granted him a twenty-one-year monopoly 'to make drinking glasses in the manner of Murano, on the undertaking that he bring up in the said art and knowledge our natural subjects'. Nor, unsurprisingly, did Verzelini look back thereafter, for during the years that followed he made much fine glass like the superb goblet pictured here – with its characteristic diamond-point engraved inscription – though only ten of his glasses have survived. All bear dates between 1577 and 1590, and all but two feature elaborate designs of foliate scrolls and hunting scenes with stags, hounds and unicorns, while this particular example from the Victoria and Albert Museum carries the inscription 'God Save Qyne [Queen] Elisabeth', accompanied by both the date '1586' and the initials 'RP' and 'MP', which probably refer to its original owners.

Certainly, the importance of Venetian glass in Tudor England and indeed sixteenth-century Europe as a whole should not be underestimated. France, Spain and the Holy Roman Empire, which encompassed almost the whole of central Europe at that time, including the Low Countries, Belgium, Luxembourg and the Netherlands, remained not only entirely captivated by it but wholly unable to match its quality domestically, since Venetian production techniques had been refined through trading links with the Orient and, above all, by contact with countries that shared an ancient tradition in glass blowing, such as Syria and Egypt. By 1299, moreover, the government of Venice had banned furnaces from the central islands of the Venetian lagoon and restricted them solely to the island of Murano. In consequence, for the next two centuries Venice's glassblowers had been quite literally insulated from contact with those in the outside world who might divulge their production secrets to potential competitors abroad. And in the process Venetian, or Murano, glass-making became the leading source for fine glassware in Europe and a major source of trading income for the Republic of Venice.

Exceptionally thinly blown, entirely translucent and worked it into a bewilderment of exquisite shapes by master craftsmen, this almost magical substance became in due course an inspiration even for Shakespeare: 'Brighter than glass, and yet, as glass is, brittle', wrote the bard of his lover in *The Passionate Pilgrim*. The secrets behind its production on the island of Murano seem only to have added to its allure. By the mid-sixteenth century, Muranese craftsmen were considered such an asset to the Venetian state that they were forbidden from emigrating on pain of assassination, though this did not prevent hefty foreign enticements from encouraging a slow but steady exodus to far-flung realms. Attempts to emulate the quality of Venetian glass in England, for instance, had begun in the 1530s, when several glassmakers from the Netherlands started a factory in Southwark on the south bank of the Thames. But in 1549, Edward VI finally succeeded in approving a contract for eight Muranese glassmakers under Josepo Casselari to establish a furnace at the House of the Carmelite Crutched Friars, which had been dissolved by Henry VIII eleven years earlier. Within twelve months, the Venetian authorities had predictably demanded their return, and the result was a full-blown diplomatic stand-off as the English government, unwilling to give up its newly acquired craftsmen, imprisoned them and forbade their release until 1551.

Even after the first Muranese had finally left, however, the campaign to produce glass of an equivalent standard did not subside, and by the time of his death Jacopo Verzelini in particular had acquired considerable wealth, not least of all because he had protected his commercial interests so resolutely. Like any successful businessman, he had, for instance, strenuously protected his patent on so-called *cristallo* and used his considerable influence to sustain a ban on imports of foreign glass, which might compete with his now local product. Indeed, the ban on Italian imports that he insisted upon lasted until 1623 and resulted, in 1581, in the demolition of a rival furnace, causing bitter anger and resentment among London's tradesmen. By the time of his death in 1606 at the age of 84 he had stood firm and prospered, acquiring numerous estates around the area of Downe in Kent, including the manor of Downe Court itself, the former home of Henry Manning, Knight Marshal. An immigrant craftsman of comparatively humble origins, Verzelini had therefore prospered against the odds, and in prospering he had provided Tudor England with some of its finest surviving material artefacts.

26

Nonsuch chest

In 1563 the Lord Mayor of London, Sir John White, estimated that a total of 4,534 'strangers' were dwelling in the City of London, Westminster and Southwark, a significant proportion of whom were German craftsmen fleeing religious persecution. And this remarkable chest, belonging to the Dedham (Massachusetts) Historical Society, is a testament to a tradition of furniture-making brought to English urban centres in the late sixteenth century by their efforts. The style of ornamentation seen on this and similar chests, as well as other examples of late Elizabethan movable furniture and woodwork, employs contrasting, and often costly inset woods, such as bog oak, holly and ebony to create architectural tableaux depicting fantastic cityscapes, and because of the resemblance between the marquetry buildings and contemporary depictions of Henry VIII's Nonsuch Palace in Surrey, chests of this type came to be known during the twentieth century as 'nonsuch chests'.

In all, immigrants appear to have constituted up to 8 per cent of London's population in the late 1560s, and while the great majority consisted of some 5,000 Netherlanders, displaced by war with Spain, German artisans were a prominent component of the social flux that was to have such a significant impact on so many areas of Tudor culture. Excluded by the City of London, along with Dutch and Flemish craftsmen, on the basis that they were not members of a trade guild, most came to settle in Southwark where their skills were put to good use in both the joinery and leather trades, and John Norden's map of London in 1593 demonstrates clearly that, although there was still only one bridge across the Thames, the area south of the river was undergoing significant development. Such, moreover, was the standard of work produced by these German artisans in particular that another 'nonsuch chest' was especially constructed in 1588, the year of the Armada, to house the parish records for Southwark. Located today in Southwark Cathedral's north choir aisle, it is a particularly fine example of its kind.

Peter Follansbee

Meanwhile, of course, the rapid rise of London's importance as a European commercial centre encouraged migration in its own right, as many small industries, especially weaving, enjoyed a period of economic boom; and trade was also expanding beyond Western Europe to Russia, the Levant and the Americas as monopoly trading companies such as the Russia Company (1555) and the East India Company (1600) were established in London by royal charter. But war and religious persecution on the continent remained the major wellsprings of immigration, especially from 1572 when the Spanish destroyed the great commercial city of Antwerp, giving London first place among the North Sea ports. As the century progressed, therefore, the ongoing traditional migration to London from all over England and Wales was supplemented by significant waves of skilled foreigners, so that the capital's population rose from an estimated 50,000 in 1530 to about 225,000 in 1605. And in other

places, too, a not dissimilar trend was occurring. In 1565, for example, the Privy Council had invited thirty families of Dutch and Flemish 'strangers' to settle in Norwich, after which their numbers would swell exponentially to some 3,000 persons in 1569, 4,000 in 1571 and 6,000 in 1579 – about one third of the city's population, and proportionately a much greater influx of alien immigrants than any other known example in English history.

But the Dedham chest, pictured here, has an even broader significance. For in years to come migration would become much more of a two-way process. Significantly, the chest's original owner, a certain Michael Metcalf, was born in 1590 in the parish of Tatterford in Norfolk, England. He had then gone on to own a cloth factory in Norwich where he employed more than a hundred men before experiencing persecution for his Puritan beliefs at the hands of Bishop Wren. In consequence, Metcalf and his family emigrated through Great Yarmouth in Norfolk to Dedham, Massachusetts, in 1637. Leaving Ipswich in Suffolk, their last port in England, aboard *The Rose* on 15 April, they arrived in Boston, Massachusetts, on 8 June 1637, having braved the rolling Atlantic Ocean and carrying their treasured 'nonsuch chest' with them.

IHS

My sonne despyse not
the poer of his Almes
and turne not awaie thei
eyre from him that hath nede
lest not they pride be wreched
Gyue to reteaue and thate when
thow sholdest powe

27

Alms box

Hewn from single piece of oak, this seven-sided alms box was made in 1600, and belonged to the 'liberty' of Norton Folgate, a 9-acre area of fertile agricultural land a short way outside the City of London's walls at what is now Spitalfields. Christopher Marlowe had taken up residence there in 1589, not long before the box came into use, and found a typical Tudor community of its kind: dutiful, God-fearing, self-reliant, but above all sternly pragmatic, and nowhere more so than in respect of those who, for one reason or another, had fallen on hard times. For this, of course, was a period when poverty was endemic, state intervention minimal and provision for the needy purely a matter for individual Christian consciences, as the inscriptions on the box clearly remind us. 'Divised' for the poor, according to the words around the rim, by a certain Frances Candell in 1600, the lid urges readers to 'turne not awaie they eies from him that hath nede', reminding them further that their hands should not be stretched out to receive, only to be shut at the time to give.

In spite of this and similar pleas, however, it is estimated that up to a third of the population continued to live in poverty throughout the Tudor period as charitable provision contracted with the dissolution of the monasteries during the 1530s and the population doubled in size during the middle years of the century. Nor, in spite of earnest attempts to distinguish between those in genuine need and the merely workshy, was it altogether surprising that government attitudes to poverty frequently involved rough justice at a time when so-called 'sturdy vagabonds' appeared to represent a tangible threat to the social order. In 1495, Parliament had ordered that 'vagabonds, idle and suspected persons shall be set in the stocks for three days and three nights and have none other sustenance but bread and water and then shall be put out of Town'. And while begging licences were granted to the elderly and disabled – the so-called 'impotent' poor – an altogether severer measure of 1536 stipulated that they, too, were to be

Alex Pink

imprisoned for two days and nights in the stocks, on bread and water, if found begging outside their parish.

Treatment of the able-bodied poor remained consistently unforgiving, irrespective of prevailing economic conditions. The Act of 1536, for instance, had stipulated that they should be publicly whipped and risk the loss of an ear for a second offence, while in 1547, as the mid-Tudor economy found itself increasingly stricken by the impact of population growth, unemployment and inflation, a new measure subjected vagrants to two years' slavery and branding with a 'V' as the penalty for the first offence, and death for the second. And while Justices of the Peace proved reluctant to apply the full penalty and parishes were required to build workhouses for the poor from 1551 onwards, the early years of Elizabeth I's reign betrayed few signs of moderation. On the contrary, another law of 1572 called for offenders to be bored through the ear for a first offence and reiterated that persistent beggars should be hanged.

Yet this very same measure also made the first clear distinction between the 'professional beggar' and those unemployed through no fault of their own. Likewise, it was made compulsory in the same year for all to pay a local poor tax, while the Poor Act of 1575 ensured that each parish had a store of 'wool, hemp, flax and iron' so that the poor could be set to gainful work. Ultimately, the Act for the Relief of the Poor gave all parishes an Overseer of the Poor in 1597 and the Vagabonds Act of the same year abolished the death penalty for vagrancy. By the end of the Tudor period, therefore, as a series of poor harvests between 1595 and 1598 oppressed the realm, the first complete code of poor relief was finally encapsulated in the famous Elizabethan Poor Law of 1601.

In reality, this measure too remained limited. Able-bodied beggars who refused work, for example, were now often placed in 'houses of correction' and frequently beaten, while responsibility for children's welfare continued to reside with parents alone. Relief for the 'impotent poor', moreover, still fell on the limited resources of the parish and now came in the form of a meagre payment, a dole of clothing or, more frequently, a portion of food – the so-called 'parish loaf'. For the more fortunate elderly, of course, there was the comparative comfort of the almshouse, like the one which existed at Norton Folgate and whose modern-day namesake is still providing housing for elderly people in London's East End. But for others there remained merely the proceeds from Frances Candell's poor box and the many others like it scattered throughout the length and breadth of Tudor England.

Food,
Drink and
Fashion

28
Pewter plate and spoon

Old men in Essex in the 1560s or early 1570s told the clergyman William Harrison how they could remember such poverty 'that a man should hardlie find foure peeces of pewter ... in a good farmer's house'. Yet now, observed Harrison in 1577, a typical farmer or husbandman had a good reserve of cash, 'beside a faire garnish of pewter on his cupboard ... three or four featherbeds, so many coverlids and carpets of tapistrie, a silver salt, a bowle for wine ... and a dozen of spoones to furnish up the sute'. Clearly, an age of comparative affluence had dawned once more in England's countryside, and in Tudor towns and villages alike the proud possession and display of pewter remained perhaps the primary domestic means of displaying the growing security and self-confidence of people of the 'middling sort'. Even poorer folk, indeed, were steadily attempting to emulate their betters and saw pewter utensils as the ideal way of advertising the fact. Among a large sample of 441 wills, taken between 1532 and 1601 – including many estates of £5 or less – 95 per cent included pewter goods, while some individuals, like the two men hanged in 1600 for stealing two dozen dishes worth 10s from the house of a certain Thomas Patch, were even prepared to risk their very lives for it.

Used in the ancient world by the Egyptians, Romans and other civilisations, pewter is composed primarily of tin with varying quantities of antimony, bismuth, copper and lead, and although much harder than pure tin, it possessed the further advantage of a low enough melting point to make it easy for casting. Such was its popularity, moreover, that by 1473 the Worshipful Company of Pewterers had been granted its first charter by Edward IV, whereupon strict standards were laid down for the finer quality, known as 'sadware', and so-called 'lay metal', which contained a higher level of lead as a low-cost bulking agent for hollow-ware

items, such as pots and measures. And in the meantime this simple tin alloy became the ultimate everyday status symbol for all but the wealthiest few, who had the means to opt for silver instead. As such, the humble plate and spoon pictured here speak eloquently of an important parallel between the Tudors and their modern-day successors – the former, in their own way, no less aspirational and materially minded, albeit on an altogether less affluent plane.

The plate's plain rim and gentle 'bouge' are typical of the period, though little Tudor pewter actually survives, since damaged or worn vessels were simply melted down and recycled. The spoon, too, is typical and another comparatively rare survivor from a time when knives and forks were still something of a rarity. When they were not eating with their fingers from communal plates, such spoons remained the cutlery utensil of choice for Tudor men and women throughout the period. They were, after all, the most flexible of utensils, with especial value when soups or stews were involved, and they came over time to adopt a special social significance in their own right. In Tudor England it became customary, for example, to give an 'Apostle Spoon' as a christening gift – a practice which was prevalent among all social classes and gave rise to a long-lasting tradition.

Cutlery knives, on the other hand, when used at all, were generally employed for spearing rather than cutting food, while forks, which were introduced from Italy during the reign of Henry VIII, were mainly used for serving and sweetmeats. First mentioned as an eating utensil for pasta in a cookbook from the reign of Robert of Anjou, who was King of Naples between 1309 and 1343, forks were actually objects of outright disapproval in some quarters and remained an oddity throughout Europe for a good deal of the seventeenth century too. 'God in his wisdom has provided man with natural forks – his fingers', St Peter Damian had written in the eleventh century. 'Therefore it is an insult to Him to substitute artificial metallic forks for them when eating.' And this particular prejudice proved surprisingly tenacious, for the first English source to mention forks did not do so until 1611 when the widely travelled Thomas Coryate noted how 'the Italian cannot by any means endure to have his dish touched with fingers, seeing that all men's fingers are not alike clean'.

But as hygiene was taking its first uneasy strides towards the Tudor dining table, was the widespread use of pewter meanwhile doing greater and rather more insidious harm to those who ate from it? Pewter's lead content is now known to leach out upon contact with acidic foods, and especially tomatoes. At least in this latter respect, however, our sixteenth-century forebears appear to have been spared the worst potential side-effects of their eating habits, though more by good fortune than sound science. For although the Spanish and Italian peoples seem to have adopted tomatoes wholeheartedly after Cortès's conquest of Mexico in 1521, they were rarely seen in England at all in the sixteenth century for fear that they were poisonous – albeit more because of their resemblance to belladonna and deadly nightshade than through any potential interaction with pewter tableware.

Chiswick Chap

29

Chafing dish

A recipe for 'fried toast of spinach' in Thomas Dawson's *The Good Huswifes Jewel* (1596) is only one of many demonstrating the importance of the chafing dish in Tudor cooking. 'Take spinach and seethe it in water and salt', the recipe begins:

> When it is tender, wring out the water between two trenchers, then chop it small and set it on a chafing dish of coals. Put thereto butter, small raisins, cinnamon, ginger, sugar, a little of the juice of an orange, and two yolks of raw eggs. Let it boil till it be somewhat thick. Then toast your toast, soak them in a little butter and sugar and spread thin your spinach upon them. Set them on a dish before the fire a little while. So serve them with a little sugar upon them.

Used both to cook and to keep food warm, chafing dishes were filled with coals and usually perforated to keep the coals bathed with air and glowing. Like the skillet they seem to have been introduced around 1480, though they were clearly not an exclusively English invention since Hernán Cortès had seen them employed by the Aztecs in Mexico and mentioned them to Emperor Charles V in 1520 when reporting the manner in which Montezuma was served meals in the Aztec capital of Tenochtitlan.

One of the more interesting recipe books to make reference to chafing dishes in this country, however, was the *Propre Newe Booke of Cookerye*, written by an anonymous author and first published in London in 1545. The recipes themselves, which include exotically named concoctions such as 'a disshe full of snow', 'pan puffe', 'a tarte of borage floures' and 'eggs in moneshine' are, of course, items of much interest in their own right, as are various instructions on how 'to make pyes' and 'the order of meates and how they must be served at the table with sauces'. Yet the book's broader interest lies not only in the fact that it was one of the first

Herbert Museum and Art Gallery, Coventry

cookery books in English aimed at a specifically female audience but that it helped generate a steady growth in other similar publications, such as John Partridge's *The treasure of hidden secrets, commonlie called the good huswives closet of provision, for the health of her household* (1596) which combined not only cooking suggestions but also a range of medical recipes, and various recommendations for removal of spots on silk, velvet, cloth 'and a fewe other curious thinges'.

In almost all such books, moreover, the chafing dish continued to feature prominently, as did that most highly prized of Tudor novelties, sugar. 'Take a dyche of rosewater and a dyshe full of suger,' the *Propre Newe Booke of Cookerye* tells us:

> And set them upon a chafyngdysh, and let them boyle, then take the yolkes of vii or ix egges newe layde and putte them therto everyone, and so let them harden a lytle, and so after this maner serve them forthe and cast a little synamon and sugar upon them.

In the 1575 version of the book, meanwhile, the reader is advised to:

> Take a dozen apples and ether rooste or boyle them and drawe them thorowe a streyner, and the yolkes of three or foure egges withal, and, as ye strayne them, temper them wyth three of foure sponefull of damaske water yf ye wyll, than take an season it wyth suger and halfe a dysche of swete butter, and boyle them upon a chaffyndg-dyshe in a platter, and caste byskettes or synamon and gynger upon them and so serve them forth.

Plainly, the ravenous Tudor sweet tooth seems to have nibbled endlessly, and it is no real surprise to find that sugar, which remained an expensive commodity long after its introduction in the Middle Ages when it was mainly used medicinally for the treatment of coughs and colds, was usually kept under lock and key by the lady of the sixteenth-century household. At the beginning of the period, when the average semi-skilled labourer was earning 4*d* a day, it cost 3*d* a pound. By the 1540s, however, it had gone up to 9*d* or 10*d* a pound – about one and a half times the daily pay of a skilled labourer such as a shipwright – at which time the courtier John Johnson is said to have paid 6*s* 6*d* for a sugar loaf for his wife Sabine. And in consequence the owner of a more humble chafing dish, like the earthenware example pictured here at the Herbert Art Gallery and Museum in Coventry, is likely to have employed it more sparingly than recipe books suggest, though imports from territories in the West and East Indies as well as from Persia, Morocco and Barbary would become more widely available as the century progressed. Used for dressing vegetables and preserving fruit, it was by then considered an aid to digestion and consumed increasingly at the end of meals, giving rise to the so-called 'sweet' and also, it must be said, dental devastation on an unprecedented scale. For, while the toothbrush is said to have been invented in China in 1498, it did not appear in England until the end of the seventeenth century.

30

Colander shard

'Mudlarking' is the wonderfully evocative Georgian term for scavenging on the shore of a river in search of anything of value. In the London of Dr Johnson and Dickens it was an occupation for the poorest of the poor, usually children, who would sift through the rubbish thrown off boats in the hope of scraping enough together to buy a hunk of bread. Now, however, it is an increasingly popular hobby for a growing army of amateur historians, one of whom was both fortunate and skilled enough to rescue this earthenware shard from the Thames foreshore. Covering an area the size of a hand, its rough texture, shiny brown glaze on the inside and traces of a thin glaze on the outside suggest that it is redware, a type of terracotta deriving its colour from the concentration of ferrous oxide, which was produced by the local potteries at Woolwich, Deptford and elsewhere that made the great majority of everyday domestic pottery used in the homes of Londoners of all classes during the late sixteenth century. The holes and, above all, the leg suggest, however, that this particular object was a somewhat more unusual item – a type of colander employed for serving fish at table in one of the capital's more affluent households, where freshwater fish, such as trout and salmon, was considered a particular delicacy. Used, too, for storing fish both before and after preparation, the holes seem to have been intended for ventilation rather than drainage.

In 1542 the physician Andrew Boorde suggested in his *Compendyous Regyment or Dyetary of Health* that different meats were suitable for different classes of person. Beef, he noted, was best for an upper-class Englishman whereas bacon was good for carters and ploughmen, 'the which be ever labouring in the earth or dung'. But Boorde noted, too, that the country was well served by 'sea-fysshe ... fresh-water fysshe and ... salt fysshe', and although meat seems to have comprised some 75 per cent of the diet of those who could afford it, fish was indeed widely consumed by wealthier Tudors, not least of all due to pressure from both the clergy and government. Meat and poultry were proscribed during Lent, for instance, as well as on the so-called 'fish days' of Fridays and Saturdays – although more imaginative gourmands were able to take some consolation from the fact that beavers were also classified as fish at this time. Queen Elizabeth, meanwhile, encouraged fish-eating on Tuesdays, too, in order to develop the skills of English fishermen, who were considered essential to national defence in the absence of a full-time navy. And in August 1596, when dearth was widespread, the Privy Council extended the ban on meat to suppertimes on Wednesday.

In consequence, fish-eating became construed not only as a form of fasting, but as a kind of patriotic duty, notwithstanding the fact that wealthier families were able to eat every bit as heartily on these occasions as at any other time. For, while primitive transport conditions raised the problem of maintaining freshness, any family of sufficient means could buy not only freshwater fish but also small quantities of sea fish such as sole, flounder, plaice and whiting. At the same time much fish, bought salted for use in stews and other dishes, was far less expensive. Carp were kept in carp ponds, and those country estates boasting rivers enjoyed ready supplies of bream, roach, perch, tench and pike. Herrings and mackerel, too, were popular, along with eels and shellfish such as mussels. Even whalemeat, served boiled or well roasted, was available as a result of the plentiful supply of whales in the North Sea at this time, and the banquets of the Tudor elite frequently featured porpoise.

Even those unhampered by the need to make a living were intent, it seems, upon landing their catch. For by the end of the Tudor period the art of an altogether more genteel type of fishing was gaining ground. William Gryndall's *Hawking, Hunting, Fouling and Fishing* (1596), for example, reflected the growing popularity of angling among both Tudor men and women of gentle birth, while William Samuel's *The Arte of Angling*, published earlier in 1577, had become only the second fishing book to be written in English, following *The Treatyse of Fysshynge wyth an Angle* (1496). *The Arte of Angling* (1653), presented in the form of a fishing lesson given by a character called 'Piscator', foreshadows much of the advice given over seventy years later, though with little acknowledgement, in Walton's *The Compleat Angler*. Nor, like his creator, were Piscator's efforts fully recognised, since his fictional wife, Cisley, became the first English-speaking woman to have her complaints about her husband's obsessional pastime committed to the printed page. 'You men say that women be talkative,' protests Cisley upon hearing the virtues of worms in 'old black dung' as bait, 'but here be such a number of words about nothing as passeth description'.

31

Apple baker

Long-established by biblical tradition as forbidden fruit, the apple assumed a special allegorical significance in Tudor England as a symbol for love, sexuality and pregnancy. It was apples, it seems, that Anne Boleyn craved upon falling pregnant, and there was no small irony either in Henry VIII's decision to encourage the planting of orchards by the royal fruiterer, Richard Harris, since the king's dissolution of the monasteries in the 1530s would result in widespread destruction of the very *pomaria* in which monks had done so much to perfect the art of planting, cultivation, grafting and pruning. Nevertheless, the new orchards established by Harris at Teynham near Sittingbourne in Kent soon took fruit production to new levels, with the introduction of pippin varieties from France and the use of scion wood from the Netherlands as grafting material for pears. In the longer term, Harris's orchards were the first step in creating the East Kent 'fruit belt' and establishing that county's reputation as the 'garden of England'.

Notwithstanding certain Tudor concerns about the effect of fresh fruit upon digestion – let alone its allegedly deadly effects upon plague victims – cooked, dried and preserved varieties continued to enjoy considerable popularity, as the item pictured here confirms. Apples, quinces and pears were all either stewed and preserved, baked in pastry or thickened with oats or breadcrumbs to make a sort of pottage. Roasted and baked apples, moreover, remained equally popular, especially as flavouring for pork, since the acid tended to counter the greasiness of the fat. In such cases, apples were usually suspended on spiked stands above a fire, though in some instances an earthenware container like the one here was used and placed directly into the flames. Excavated in Bayley Lane, Coventry, in 1988, this particular apple baker, made from Midlands yellowware which was produced from about 1550 onwards, is indeed an exceptionally rare item. Nor should the presence of some green glaze patches which

dripped on to it from other pottery during preparation be allowed to mislead, since the item was almost certainly the possession of a wealthier household willing and able to spend valuable pennies on such a gadget.

For those on the lowest rung of the social ladder, meanwhile, seasonal vegetables, supplemented with oats, bread and pulses, remained the staple. Onions, leeks, pumpkins, spinach and garlic were the most common 'worts' grown, with almost all Tudor households, including even those in cities, dependent upon their own small plot of land. Carrots, too, had become available after their introduction into southern Europe about the twelfth century, though they remained black, yellow, purple or white rather than orange until the latter colour began to predominate during the reign of Queen Elizabeth. Potatoes, likewise, were introduced in the 1580s – only to prove unpopular initially – along with Brussel sprouts and broccoli, which were being grown extensively on the Continent but largely avoided here. Much more popular, in fact, were beetroot leaves – as opposed to the root itself – and a wide variety of nuts which were harvested and stored as ingredients for pies and puddings. Available across England when in season, walnuts and hazelnuts in particular were often eaten at the end of meals, in order to 'close' the stomach.

Fruit, however, continued to gain ground as the century progressed, and besides berries of various kinds, damsons and plums – especially wild varieties, such as the so-called bullace – more unusual types, including melons and lemons, gradually became available too. The rich could also afford exceptionally expensive fruits such as pomegranates, peaches, apricots and oranges, which began to be imported from southern Europe during the Tudor period. Figs too, for that matter, were grown in increasing numbers, while gooseberries – or 'feaberries' as they were often called – were considered 'greatlie profitable to such as are troubled with a hot, burning ague'. Contact with the New World led to the gradual introduction of maize, Indian corn, chocolate, peanuts, vanilla, pineapples, red and green peppers and tapioca.

And what, finally, do we know of the varieties of apple that may have been placed in the Bayley Street baker all those centuries ago? The earliest written reference to apples in England was made in about AD 885 by King Alfred in his English translation of *Gregory's Pastoral Care*. By the thirteenth century, the 'costard' variety was being grown sufficiently extensively in many parts of England to give rise to the term 'costermonger'. In Tudor times, however, the most common kind was the so-called 'Queene', though several forgotten varieties were also popular such as the apple-john, leathercoat, pomewater, codlin, jennetting, catshead, redstreak and nonpareil, while later types were sometimes developed by accident, as was the case with the 'Bess Pool' – discovered growing wild by a Gloucestershire innkeeper's daughter of that name – and the 'D'Arcy Spice', originating by chance on a tree in the orchard of the D'Arcy family in Essex who gave modern Tolleshunt D'Arcy its name. With such an abundance of natural goodness, it was small wonder that in cider-producing regions of England, Tudor men and women customarily sang to the trees in their orchards, in hope of a plentiful harvest.

32

Christmas pie

On 6 January 1508, to mark the end of the twelve days of Christmas, Edward Stafford, Duke of Buckingham and premier nobleman of England, gave a feast for 460 people at his family seat in Thornbury, Gloucestershire. The menu, we are told, included swans, herons and peacocks, 680 loaves, 260 flagons of ale, 400 eggs, 200 oysters, 12 pigs and 10 sheep. The total cost was £7 – more than a year's pay for an average labourer. Nor was such culinary extravagance uncommon, for Tudor cooks were renowned for both the scale and inventiveness of their efforts, a fact that few dishes demonstrate better than Christmas pie. Consisting of a coffin-shape crust that enveloped a turkey stuffed with a goose, stuffed with a chicken, stuffed with a partridge, stuffed with a pigeon, it was a marvel of excess. And when it is remembered that the whole concoction was surrounded, when served, by a jointed hare, small game birds and wild fowl, the unabashed exuberance of contemporary gastronomy becomes clear – though there was method as well as madness in the recipe, since the use of open fires rather than ovens in most Tudor cooking meant that the outer meat of birds cooked on their own rather than within a pie tended to become tough and dry.

Not satisfied with merely cramming creatures into one another for the consumption of their masters and mistresses by means of what is now known as 'engastration', Tudor cooks can also be credited with physically combining animals for their feasts by a process of culinary grafting. Perhaps the most famous example of such mind-boggling creativity is the so-called 'cockentrice', which was produced by sewing a pig's upper body on to the bottom half of a capon or turkey. Born, it seems, out of Henry VIII's uncontrollable desire to impress the King of France with a huge 'meat feast' that some commentators suggest may have cost as much as £5 million in modern-day terms, the cockentrice was, in effect, the 'star turn' of a spectacle which involved the additional slaughter of no fewer than 2,000 sheep and 1,000 chickens – not to mention at least one dolphin. And there was similar experimentation with colour, too. Not content with mere quantity, the Tudor elite expected their food to be eye-catching as well as delicious. Ingredients were therefore duly embellished with green from spinach, yellow from egg yolk or saffron, red from sandalwood and blue from indigo. On special occasions, indeed, dishes were presented in rainbow stripes of colours, while sweets were adorned with gold and silver leaf.

But it was at Christmas that all classes of Tudors came into their culinary own. All but the poorest, for instance, enjoyed mince pies, which had a special symbolic significance, since their thirteen ingredients represented Jesus and the apostles, and there was Christmas pudding, too, though this was shaped like a sausage and contained meat, oatmeal and spices. Turkey, meanwhile, had first been introduced into England around the year 1523 and Henry VIII was one of the first to eat it as part of his Christmas meal, though goose also became popular after 1588 when it had been consumed by Elizabeth I upon the defeat of the Spanish Armada. Thereafter, the queen suggested that its consumption upon the most convivial feast day of the year would be a fitting tribute to the victorious English sailors.

Not altogether surprisingly, sixteenth-century customs have left a lasting mark. The tradition of the Christmas tree, for example, may well have originated with Martin Luther, who is said to have been so struck by the beauty of the stars shining through a fir tree on a homeward journey that he subsequently cut off the top of one of the smaller trees and took it home, placing small candles on the ends of the branches to resemble stars. English households, by contrast, tended in the main to decorate their homes on Christmas Eve with holly, ivy, mistletoe, box, laurel and yew. Yet the Tudors were certainly responsible for one of the most enduring of all Christmas customs, involving the so-called 'kissing bough' – a hoop or sphere woven from willow, ash or hazel wood, with a small figure of the Holy Family or a figure of the Christ child placed in the middle. Since mistletoe, as an evergreen, was regularly used to make the bough, this evolved over time into the popular tradition of 'kissing under the mistletoe'.

In 1521, meanwhile, the earliest recorded collection of carols was published, which included the famous *Boars Head Carol*. Other Christmas carols sung by the Tudors included *We Wish You a Merry Christmas, The First Nowell, The Coventry Carol, While Shepherds Watched, Angels from the Realms of Glory, Ding Dong Merrily on High* and *In Dulci Jubilo*. To complete the season of peace and goodwill, moreover, all work was halted throughout the Christmas period, except for the care of animals. Even the toil of women seems to have abated as spinning ceased and spinning wheels became surrounded by flowers. Only on Plough Monday, the first Monday following Twelfth Night, did women and men alike return to their labours.

33

Ye Olde Mitre pub

Hidden down an alleyway in London's Hatton Garden, marked by an old crooked street lamp and a small sign in the shape of a bishop's mitre, lies a tiny drinking establishment providing a direct link with the capital's beery Tudor past. The original Olde Mitre Tavern was built, as the sign above the arched alleyway entrance suggests, in 1546 for the servants of the nearby palace of the bishops of Ely. But while these bishops were among the most influential members of the English episcopacy and regularly entertained English monarchs at their London base, they were nevertheless forced by Elizabeth I in 1581 to rent some of their land to Sir Christopher Hatton, one of her favourite courtiers. The eventual result was the creation of Hatton Garden, the centre of the capital's diamond and jewellery trade, and the ultimate destruction in 1772 of both the original tavern and the bishops' palace itself, the only remaining trace of which is a stone mitre from its gatehouse still standing on the new tavern's wall to this day.

At the time of its establishment in the penultimate year of Henry VIII's reign, the Old Mitre formed part of a booming drinking culture within the capital and country at large that was an increasing cause of alarm for the Tudor authorities. Figures from Coventry in 1520, for instance, suggest that typical consumption per person was as much as seventeen pints of ale a week, although it must be remembered, of course, that this particular beverage was considered safer to drink than water in Tudor England and was even taken for breakfast. Indeed, the Tudor physician Andrew Boorde considered ale a 'natural drink' and preferable to water which, in his opinion was 'not holesome'. But binge drinking of stronger Tudor brews, such as 'mad dog', 'dagger ale' and 'dragon's milk', nevertheless remained commonplace, and in 1552 alehouses were forced for the first time to obtain licenses, since, as Parliament explained, the 'intolerable hurts and troubles to the common wealth of this realm doth daily grow

and increase through such abuses and disorders as are had and used in common alehouses'.

Even so, the measure's impact was limited and by 1560 Queen Elizabeth herself was complaining of the strength of some of the new beers on the market and especially 'a kynde of very strong bere' known as 'double' beer, which 'they do commonly utter and sell at very grate and excessive price'. On this occasion too, however, the queen's concerns seem to have had little effect. In 1588 we hear of only one case among many when fourteen residents of St Albans in Hertfordshire were brought before the local mayor for brewing beer that was too potent. And while taverns continued to be widely decried as 'nurseries of naughtiness', this did nothing to prevent Elizabeth's own court from consuming 600,000 gallons of ale in 1590 alone. Clearly, the trend was too overwhelming even for the queen to staunch, so that by 1577 there was one drinking establishment in Tudor England for every 200 people, in comparison to the modern figure of one for every 1,200.

With the unchecked flow of alcohol, moreover, came a further surge in crime and vice. A report from a hostelry in Netherbury, Dorset, talking of 'manie stolen goods consumed', was sadly far from unique, and since few alehouses had glass windows, one particular Tudor practice, called angling, saw purses and other belongings being hooked away on a line by thieves. Gambling, too, was evidently out of control, despite strenuous attempts to curb card and dice games, as well as marbles, skittles and 'shove groat', which were also played for money. Bear-baiting, cock-fighting and drinking contests, meanwhile, only added to the pandemonium, though a much greater source of concern seems to have been the inevitable incidence of illicit sex. Many taverns doubled, in effect, as brothels, while some proprietors, it seems, were ready to indulge their customers' baser urges for more than merely pecuniary gain, since we learn of one particular landlord, a certain Evan ap Rice, being arraigned in 1584 for 'lodging strange men in his bed with him and his wife'.

Not all aspects of tavern and inn life, of course, were quite so reprehensible by modern-day standards, even though the poet John Skelton complained in 1521 that the 'ale wife' Elynour Rummynge, who ran the Running Horse in Leatherhead, Surrey, which is still in existence today, was regularly using hen's dung to flavour her brews. Notwithstanding Tudor London's 7,000 tobacco shops, smoking was generally discouraged – though mainly, it must be said, on grounds of fire risk – and Shakespeare himself loved to frequent the capital's inns, whose yards sometimes doubled as theatres where his plays were performed. Even the Tudor army appears to have marched on its liver, for in 1544 an English military commander in France wrote that his soldiers had drunk 'no beer these last 10 days' and considered it 'strange for Englishmen' to do so 'with so little grudging'. Where beer was not to taste, moreover, wine, cider, perry (pear cider) or sack (a type of sherry) were always readily available to serve as further sousing agents for hardy Tudor innards. 'Every county, city, town and village and other place,' observed the Puritan Philip Stubbes in 1583:

Hath an abundance of ale houses, taverns, inns which are so fraught with maltworms [drunkards] night and day that thee would wonder to see them. Thee shall have them sitting at the wine and good ale all day long … till never a one can speak a ready word.

34

Child's knitted mitten

This child's knitted mitten, which became part of the Museum of London's collections in 1912, is a particularly rare survival from our Tudor past. It was found in the Finsbury Square/Finsbury Circus area of the capital, to the north of Moorgate, which in Tudor times was damp and prone to flooding. In such locations, organic materials like textiles and leather survive exceptionally well, and the mitten seems to have come to light during building work at some point during the second half of the nineteenth century when it was purchased by the artist Seymour Lucas. Made from soft white wool, stained brownish by iron salts and peat acids, it has a very simple pattern band of three rows around the wrist which appear, under magnification, to have been produced by lichen-dyed purple wool. The gauge is approximately 8.5 stitches per inch, and the item is knitted from the top of the finger-pouch in the direction of the wrist. Now exceptionally fragile, it remains a vivid personal link to our sixteenth-century ancestors and provides a poignant reminder, too, of the importance of warm, affordable clothing to Tudor families.

Although Roman soldiers are said to have worn knitted socks when serving in the cold outposts of the empire such as Britain, knitting does not seem to have been common in England until the sixteenth century. Prior to this, indeed, any form of more sophisticated knitting was effectively the hallowed preserve of knitting and hosiery guilds, which required long and complicated apprenticeships as a condition of membership. Master knitters, who remained in existence during the Tudor period, producing not only standard items like caps, hose and shirts but also carpets, were in fact required to complete a six-year apprenticeship. Nor was it common practice for the women of Tudor households to knit.

From the time of Henry VIII, however, fine-knit silk stockings imported from Spain were an important feature of court fashion, and by the time of Elizabeth I, a well-established and less exclusive knitting industry also existed in places as far apart as London, Kingston in Surrey, and Richmond in Yorkshire. The new fashion had received its most significant boost when ladies-in-waiting to Elizabeth I began to knit silk stockings for pleasure and, in 1561, the queen's silkwoman, Alice Montague, handed the fruits of her labours to her mistress. 'I like silk stockings so well,' responded the queen, 'because they are pleasant, fine and delicate, that henceforth I will wear no more cloth stockings.' Thereafter, even the defeat of the Spanish Armada appears to have had a further favourable impact upon Tudor knitwear, since many Spanish noblemen, for whom knitting was considered a fine and fitting recreation, were among those shipwrecked in the storms that followed their defeat in 1588, leaving a legacy in the form of the many Fair Isle patterns so closely resembling fifteenth- and sixteenth-century Spanish designs.

Yet it was the poor for whom knitting presented the greatest boon, both as a source of income and, more importantly, as a means of obtaining comparatively cheap and highly functional clothing, even though second-hand clothes were readily available to those with low incomes. The worn out or unfashionable clothes of the capital's wealthier citizens, or items that could not be altered, were frequently sold and resold, and valuable trimmings, such as buttons, might be stripped off and recycled by metalsmiths and jewellers. Town-dwellers, in particular, did not have the space, resources, or time to weave their own cloth and sew clothes for themselves and their families. And unlike today, where clothes are only a small part of a yearly household budget, clothing was a major investment which needed to be of the best possible quality for most Tudor men and women, with the result that knitting offered a viable and attractive alternative.

The price of clothing meant, therefore, that any child unfortunate enough to mislay a garment like the one featured here was unlikely to escape a severe scolding. Finsbury, where the item was unearthed, was a woodland area in the manor or prebend of Brownswood in Tudor times – part of a large expanse of woodland called Hornsey Wood that had been cut back further and further for use as grazing land during the Middle Ages. And even as late as the mid-eighteenth century, Londoners would still travel north to escape the grime and bustle of the capital and enjoy the last remains of the old wood, just as the original wearer of the mitten may have done some two hundred years earlier. Here, then, possibly while playing in the winter cold, he or she may have inadvertently left us this striking memento from across the centuries.

35

Shoe

By the early Tudor period the most popular form of footwear for men of rank was the so-called 'duck's bill' – an exaggerated style of leather slip-on shoe that in its most extreme form could be as wide as 12in at the toe, forcing its wearers to waddle like waterfowl. Not altogether surprisingly, this particular fashion had faded by the mid-sixteenth century as Mary Tudor's reign introduced a perceptible Spanish influence on fashion. In particular, narrower, slashed shoes, following the more natural contours of the foot, like the shoe pictured here, began to achieve popularity with men. Like all contemporary examples it could be worn on either foot, with the slashes enabling the wearer to display his brightly coloured stockings. It was also made, like most Tudor shoes for poor and rich alike, from leather, but is certain, as a result of its style, to have belonged to an individual of at least some substance, notwithstanding the fact that the very richest also wore shoes of silk or satin.

Wealthy women, on the other hand, wore essentially the same types of shoe as the previous century with the striking exception of a new fad, originating in Venice that quickly spread to the rest of Europe. The so-called *chopine* was a type of overshoe with a raised wooden sole, normally 2–3in high, which was meant to give the wearer added height while, at the same time, raising her feet above the mud and grime of unpaved Tudor streets. Like other shoe fashions, however, *chopines* become prone to exaggeration, and in Venice particularly, heels such as the type displayed at the Museo Correr di Veneziani today, occasionally attained 20in or more, making it necessary for wearers to enlist the assistance of a maid or cane to help them walk. And though the Church had initially approved the style on the grounds that it discouraged sinful activities like dancing, such shoes were nevertheless eventually outlawed in Italy after a number of women fell from them and subsequently miscarried. Even so, Elizabeth I endorsed a more modest versions of what she herself termed

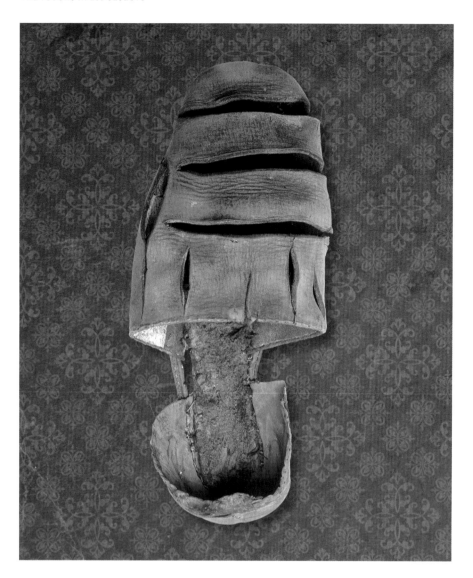

'high heels' and in 1595, at the age of 62, the queen ordered her first pair. So pleased was she that by 1599 her soft brown leather outdoor boots – or 'buskins' – had also acquired raised wooden heels.

In the meantime, the practical need for both men and women of all classes to protect their feet from rain, mud and worse remained as pressing as ever and resulted in the widespread use of 'pattens' – wooden shoes with blocks underneath which were designed to be slipped over an ordinary shoe. With the notable exception of Bristol, where some attempt had been made to deal with the problem, open sewers remained a particular hazard to both the fashion-minded and more practically inclined alike, and pattens had first appeared in the fourteenth century to keep footwear not only dry but clean. By Tudor times, however, they were worn by almost everybody across the social spectrum, surviving examples of the more expensive type demonstrating some decoration on the leather. There were numerous other types of protective overshoe, too, including leather 'startups' for working men, clogs, galoches or *galages* as they were sometimes known, and *pantofles*, which were also produced as slippers for indoors.

The specific styles available to Tudor men and women varied considerably, in fact, as did the quality of material employed in manufacture. The best leather, called 'cordwain' in England, was Spanish and those who worked with it became known as 'cordwainers', while riding and walking boots, made of smooth or wrinkled leather and fitting either loosely or tightly, came in a wide range of styles, such as the thigh length *gamache*. Pumps, on the other hand, were light, single-soled slip-on shoes, akin to *pinsons* – a thin type of shoe held in place by fit rather than fastenings – which appear in the literature from 1350 to around 1600, though without any clear contemporary description. With such a variety of footwear on offer, it was hardly surprising that shoemakers of all types abounded in Tudor England. York, for example, boasted 143 cordwainers during the second half of the sixteenth century, while Nottingham had 83 – a greater number than the total of tailors and bakers added together. Chester, in its turn, had 120 shoemakers and Leicester 53. Elizabethan Chelmsford, on the other hand, had a particularly versatile cobbler who doubled as a surgeon.

Yet by no means all contemporaries felt entirely satisfied that they were getting the best possible value for money, since even the better-quality items on offer left a good deal to be desired. Waterproofing, for example, was effectively unheard of even for the rich, and, to add danger to discomfort, Tudor shoes were generally produced without any form of grip on the sole, which may explain why examples discovered on board the *Mary Rose* were invariably removed when sailors scrubbed the decks. Almost inevitably, honesty too was an area of concern in certain circles. 'Sometimes,' wrote the irrepressible Philip Stubbes:

> They will sell you calves leather for cow leather, horsehides for oxe hides, and truelie I think rotten sheepe skins for good substantial and dureable stuffe. And yet shall a man pay for these as well as for better stuffe. And to the ende they may seeme gaudie to the eie, they must be stitched finelie, pincked, cutte, karved, rased, nickt, and I cannot tell what. And good reason, forelse would they never be sold.

36

Jerkin

The Tudor jerkin was a short leather or velvet jacket, similar to a waist-coat, which was usually sleeveless and cut low to the waist in front to reveal the snug-fitting buttoned shirt, known as a doublet. Doublets, in fact, had originated as a stitched and quilted lining, or 'doubling', worn under armour to prevent chafing and bruising, and jerkins, too, under-went a similar stylistic evolution as the sixteenth century progressed. From the 1530s, mainly as a result of Spanish influence, a narrower sil-houette became fashionable for men, and in consequence collars were cut higher and tighter, very like this particular example. At the same time, shoulders lost their padding and developed a slight slope, as exposed doublet sleeves became fuller. Other adaptations also ensued. On the one hand, jerkins made of leather were increasingly punched with holes both for decoration and to improve the fit, and like other contemporary garments, they were frequently 'slashed' – a fashion begun by German *landsknecht* mercenaries who were renowned throughout Europe for their military prowess and turned the tattered look of the battlefield into a widely imitated fashion statement. By the end of the century jerkins were being donned by women, though the dark brown example pictured here belonged to a youth. Embellished with vertical and diagonal scored bands and diamond, heart and star pinking, it is fastened with decorative pewter buttons that imitate ones made from worked silk or gilt thread over a wooden core.

And imitation of every kind, especially of one's betters, lay at the very heart of contemporary fashion, since clothing, no less than diet, was a sen-sitive indicator of wealth in Tudor England and finely fashioned garments of all descriptions were prized status symbols. Many poor people, after all, had no change of clothing whatsoever, and even urban craftsmen and their wives would often bequeath their 'workday' or 'holyday' gowns to relatives or friends. Richly bedecked noblemen like Robert Dudley, Earl of Leicester,

Museum of London

were therefore striking and much-envied exceptions to the general rule. In 1588, for example, seven doublets and two cloaks belonging to the earl were valued by his executors at £545, though the will of a Worcester barber from around the same time valued his entire wardrobe at no more than £1.

Men of the 'middling sort', meanwhile, varied considerably in terms of their sartorial assets. George Byrche, vicar of Wibley, seems to have owned no more than two gowns, a coat, a doublet, a pair of hose and a single hat in 1569. Some three decades later, however, John Brownewend, rector of Long Ditton in Surrey, was boasting two gowns, three cloaks, two doublets, two coats, three pairs of breeches, six pairs of stockings, two hats, two belts, seven shirts, six nightcaps, eight ruffs and a total of six handkerchiefs, which appear to have gained increasing popularity during the sixteenth century. Not all Tudor men were apparently so fastidious, however, for William Kitchener, yeoman farmer in the same county, seems to have possessed no such item in 1586, though he did own one cloak of 'London dye', a grey russet cloak, a mandelion (a hip-length pullover), three doublets, two pairs of boot hose, a pair of boots, a pair of stockings, two pairs of breeches, two hats, four nightcaps, four shirts, an old frieze gown, a scarf and a black frieze jerkin. And like Brownewend, significantly, he also possessed two ruffs, which by the middle of the century had become standard neckwear for both middle-class men and women, as well as children.

The ubiquitous Tudor ruff had begun as a small fabric ruffle at the drawstring neck of the shirt or chemise that could be laundered separately while protecting the wearer's doublet from soiling at the neckline. Before long, however – especially after the discovery of starch – ruffs evolved into extravagant fashion statements, advertising the rank and pretensions of the wearer. And while royalty alone might wear clothes trimmed with ermine and lesser nobles were forced by law to make do with fox and otter fur to avoid emulating their betters, there was still, it seems, no stemming the demand for fashionable clothes as the century progressed, so that when James Backhouse, a shopkeeper of Kirkby Lonsdale in Westmorland, met his end early in Elizabeth I's reign, even he left stock that included Spanish silks, French garters, Norwich lace, Oxford gloves and Turkey-work purses. 'Never have people been at such pains to tell from the habit where the highest honours belong', wrote one contemporary. 'For today we see not only gentlemen but people of low degree wearing embroidery and other adornments which were formerly the prerogative of princes or at least the most noble lords'. And for those of even lower rank who could not come by fine garments honestly there was always the option of theft, as John Stooe found in 1554 when his fine 'jerkyn of buckes leather' was stolen from his Tottenham home by a certain John Porter.

37

Codpiece

A codpiece – from the Middle English 'cod', meaning 'scrotum' – is a covering flap or pouch, usually held closed by string ties, that attaches to the front of the wearer's crotch, accentuating the genital area. Always especially associated with Tudor fashion, the codpiece has in fact a much longer history and there are numerous depictions of its use surviving from the art of the ancient world. At Minoan Knossos in Crete, for example, archaeologists have uncovered various figurines thus attired. However, most of what is known about the cut, fit and materials of Renaissance clothing has been gleaned from portraits, clothing inventories, descriptive receipts for payments, or tailors' cutting guides. For few contemporary examples actually survive, making the particular item depicted here especially interesting.

Codpieces were worn across Western Europe by men and boys from the age of 8 upwards and, in spite of their later extravagance, were anything but lewd in terms of their original use and purpose. In the fourteenth century, men's hose had consisted of two separate legs worn over linen drawers, leaving a man's genitals covered only by a layer of linen. But by 1380 men's hemlines had risen, the hose becoming longer and joined at the centre back while remaining open at the centre front. The shortening of the cote or doublet thus resulted in over-exposure of the genitals, so that the codpiece began life as nothing more than a triangular piece of fabric enclosing the gap for the purpose of concealment. As time passed, however, codpieces became shaped and padded, with a view to emphasising the phallus, reaching their peak of size and decoration in the 1540s, after which the increasing puffiness of canions and venetions seems to have precluded the necessity for codpieces as a means of 'covering the sinful parts'. And though this brash advertisement of male virility continued in fashion until about 1580, it seems thereafter to have disappeared by stages into the ever more voluminous folds of the trunk hose.

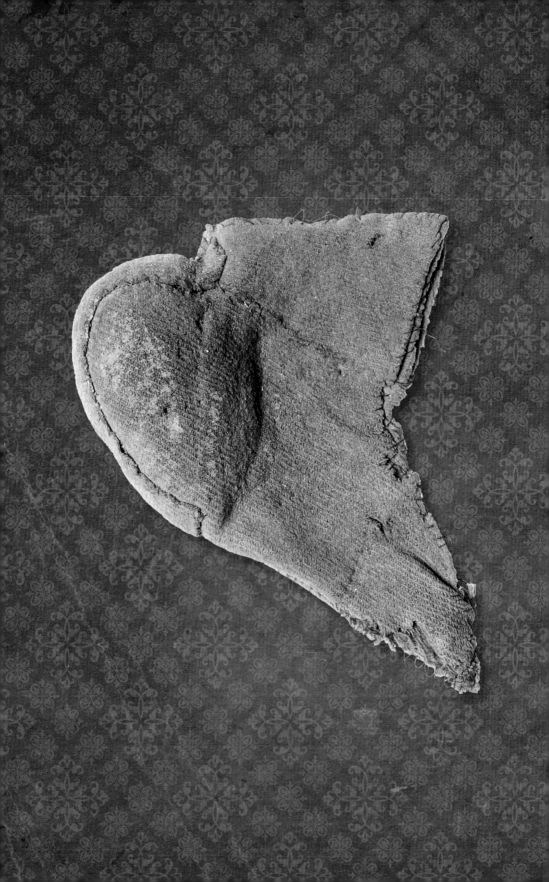

Later, indeed, the codpiece became an object of the derision showered upon all outlandish attire. The French humourist François Rabelais, for example, jokingly referred to a book entitled *On the Dignity of Codpieces* in his foreword to *The Histories of Gargantua and Pantagruel*.

Yet in its heyday the codpiece had enjoyed extraordinary popularity and its later incarnations evolved into a marginally less eye-catching padded sheath. At the same time, wearers chose increasingly to decorate their pieces with metallic thread, satin tufts, bows and other trimmings, though the item had in any case already evolved into rather more than an object of everyday display. Sixteenth-century armour, for instance, followed civilian fashion, and for a time armoured codpieces became a recurring feature of knights' harness. Moreover, in addition to serving as a private, protected penis space – keeping swords, daggers, hard purses and other belt accessories from accidentally striking the genitals – some owners also seem to have used them as pockets to carry around whatever small objects might be useful. More intriguingly still, it has even been suggested that their use may have borne some relation to the incidence of syphilis – the so-called 'Great Pox'. Since one of the treatments consisted of an ointment made from mercury and animal grease, which sufferers applied with a coated fabric that they wore at all times, it has been suggested that in a few cases at least the codpiece doubled as a fashionable way of concealing the necessary dressing under the guise of high fashion.

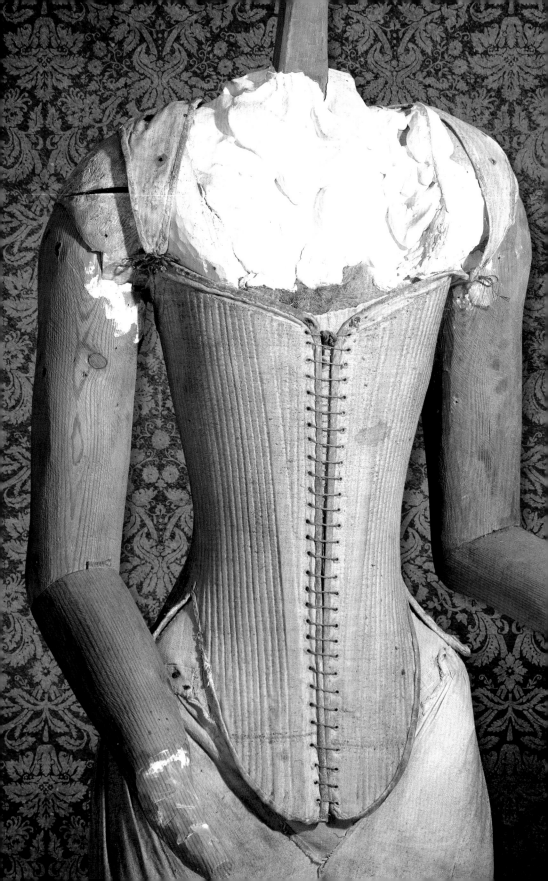

38

Effigy corset of Elizabeth I

At her funeral on 28 April 1603, Elizabeth I's coffin was taken to Westminster Abbey in suitably solemn splendour on a hearse drawn by four horses hung with black velvet. In the words of the chronicler John Stow, the surrounding area was:

> Surcharged with multitudes of all sorts of people in their streets, houses, windows, leads and gutters, that came out to see the obsequy, and when they beheld her statue lying upon the coffin, there was such a general sighing, groaning and weeping as the like hath not been seen or known in the memory of man.

The statue to which Stow referred was, in fact, a fully clothed funeral effigy designed to represent as realistically as possible the actual image of the queen as she had appeared in life. So when the effigy, which has been residing ever since at Westminster Abbey, was unclothed for study and repair to its garments in 1995, the resulting interest was intense. Indeed, once the gown and hoopskirt – dating from the mid-eighteenth century – were finally removed, the effigy's corset and drawers became visible for the first time since the 1930s. Much to the surprise of all concerned, they appeared to date not to around 1760 as had been thought, but to the very year of the queen's death or perhaps slightly earlier. Prior to this the only other contemporary corset available for detailed study, dating to 1598, had belonged to the German noblewoman Dorothea von Pfalz-Neuburg.

Comprising one back section and two front/side sections, the queen's corset has therefore been the focus of particular interest. The back section has slightly curving seams and two straps, wide at the base and narrowing

Westminster Abbey

to points, which start from the centre back and radiate out at a 30-degree angle from vertical. This angled cut and the high, boned back served as a firm base for pinning in standing ruffs and their wire under-props. The low, angled front and slightly curved front seam, meanwhile, provided sufficient support for the bosom while still allowing the low necklines of the period. Edged around the bottom, top and straps with fine leather that was originally apple-green in colour, the corset is made of fustian, woven in a twill pattern. Never exposed to human sweat and daily wear and tear, it is also in excellent condition, having been lovingly preserved at its Westminster home for more than four centuries.

Although the corset itself is almost unique, garments just like it are frequently mentioned in written sources of the time. Originating in Italy and introduced into France by Catherine de Medici in mid-century, the corset may well have evolved, in fact, from the masculine *cotte* or *gambeson*, a stiff torso garment worn by men in the later fifteenth century. It may possibly have evolved, too, from the so-called 'kirtle' – a chemise or smock worn underneath dresses – with the bodice stiffened by means of buckram or eventually reeds or bent grass. In any event, the initial purpose of the corset was not so much to constrict the female waist as to emphasise the contrast between the rigid flatness of the bodice front and the curving tops of the breasts emerging from it, and by the 1550s such garments had become the norm, attaining their classic form in the last quarter of the century, by which time, as Jérôme Lippomano, Venetian ambassador to France, made clear in a report of 1577, women had 'inconceivably narrow waists'.

The development of the corset is, then, well documented. But what do we know with regard to other items of female underwear? Did Elizabeth I wear drawers, for instance? Certainly her funeral effigy sported a narrow pair, and while it has been claimed that these were not added until as late as 1760, the 'Accounts of the Great Wardrobe' for the period 1558–1603 record that John Colte was paid £10 to provide 'the Image representing her late Majestie ... with one paire of straite bodies', i.e. a bodice, and 'a paire of drawers'. There is a reference, too, to 'six pairs of double linen hose of fine hollande cloth' made in 1587, which may, according to some commentators, have been drawers rather than stockings. And if the queen was indeed a wearer of such underwear, the implications are more intriguing still, for she will have been ignoring a strong body of contemporary opinion, which frowned upon what was considered a somewhat indecent new Italian fashion – a feeling encouraged, too, by Pietro Bertelli's *Costumes of Different Nations* of 1594 which shows only Venetian courtesans clad thus.

Petticoats, meanwhile, were not only already well established but normally red, since this colour was closely associated with health-giving qualities until well into the nineteenth century. We find, therefore, in the Royal Wardrobe Accounts of Mary Tudor in 1554 a clear reference to 'a peticoate of scarlet, the upper bodyes of crimson tapheta', while Elizabeth I's household accounts also mention 'vallopes all of fine hollande clothe' listed by the dozen. These, it seems, may well have served as sanitary pads, and it has also been suggested that three 'gyrdelles of blak Jeane silk made on the fingers garnished with buckelles hookes and eyes whipped over with silke' were intended to serve as belts to hold the pads in place. Whether, like other contemporary women, she also used pessaries made from shorn wool and stored in linen or silk bags containing herbs is, however, unknown.

39

Sun mask

This mask, worn by a Tudor gentlewoman to protect her pale complexion from the sun, was found during the renovation of an inner wall of a sixteenth-century stone building in Daventry, Northamptonshire. The wall was approximately 4ft thick, and the mask was found concealed within the inner hard core, which consisted of soil, straw and horse hair for insulation. Folded in half, lengthways, and placed within a small rectangular niche behind the face of the wall, the mask still has an amount of soil and straw adhering to one half, although the opposite half has the velvet outer material in relatively good condition prior to further conservation work. The mask is oval in shape, measuring 195mm in length and 170mm in width, and possesses a silk lining, which is strengthened by a pressed-paper inner. On the silk lining, just below the centre of the mouth, is a loose thread of white cotton which would have held a black glass bead, found at the same time as the mask itself. In the absence of holes to allow string or elastic to be put around the head, the mask would therefore have been kept in place by the wearer holding the black bead in her mouth.

In his *Anatomie of Abuses*, published in 1583, Philip Stubbes plainly looked askance at the popularity of such 'vizards', as they were known to contemporaries. 'When they use to ride abrod', he observed:

They have invisories, or masks, visors made of velvet, wherwith they cover all their faces, having holes made in them against their eyes, whereout they look. So that if a man, that knew not their guise before, should chaunce to meet one of them, he would think hee met a monster or a devil; for face hee can see none, but two brode holes against her eyes with glasses in them.

In the next century, however, the scholar Randle Holme explained precisely why such items were so popular with Tudor ladies. Covering 'the whole face', with 'holes for the eyes, a case for the nose and a slit for the mouth', they were employed, he tells us to 'keep them from sun burning', adding that they were 'taken off and put [on] in a moment of time, being only held in the teeth by means of a round bead fastened on the inside ... against the mouth'. In *Omnium Poene Gentium Habitus*, published by Abraham de Bruyn in 1581, the statement that 'in this fashion noble women either ride or walk up and down' is accompanied by an image depicting a lady wearing just such a mask with holes cut for the eyes.

While very few original masks have actually survived, both the Daventry mask and the Lady Clapham doll's mask in the Victoria and Albert Museum, as well as a cruder example in Norwich Museum, confirm their use in England. And in spite of Philip Stubbes's obvious disapproval, the wearing of this type of facial protection made obvious good sense for any self-respecting, fashion-conscious Tudor lady, for in sixteenth-century England, as elsewhere in Europe, the faintest suntan suggested base birth from an apparent need to work in the open air. Only gentlewomen, therefore, were deemed able to maintain their fair complexions, and for this reason Tudor women resorted to all sorts of cosmetic expedients, including white lead powder, lemon juice and sulphur to achieve the desired effect, though the best way to maintain a reputation as a lady of distinction remained, it seems, the practical expedient of covering one's face in the first place.

The explanation of why the Daventry mask was discovered within the walls of a sixteenth-century house remains, however, as intriguing as ever. Certainly, the practice of concealing artefacts in contemporary buildings was commonplace, and it is hard to dismiss the possibility that this mask too may have been left hidden as a 'witch deposit' with a view to warding off evil or deflecting a curse or other negative circumstance, such as illness or economic blight. Alternatively, the objects may have been viewed as 'lucky things', perhaps heirlooms from an ancestor considered to be spiritually powerful, or, more prosaically and rather less convincingly, there is always the possibility that the builders involved in constructing or altering the house may simply have wished to leave their 'mark'. In any event, masks like the one which had lain concealed at Daventry over the centuries eventually passed out of vogue, as Samuel Pepys explains in his diary:

They were commonly used by ladies in the reign of Elizabeth, and when their use was revived at the Restoration for respectable women attending the theatre, they became general. They soon, however, became the mark of loose women, and their use was discontinued by women of repute.

40

Tablets of Venetian ceruse

'Have you not noticed how much prettier a woman is when she makes up,' wrote Baldassare Castiglione in his *Book of the Courtier* (1528), 'if she does so with so little that those who see her cannot tell whether she is made up or not?' Some, however, 'are so bedaubed', he continued:

> That they seem to be wearing a mask and dare not laugh because they fear it will crack. Such women never change colour except when they dress in the morning, and must spend the rest of the day like motionless wooden images.

The excessive use of cosmetics was not uncommon, even in the early sixteenth century, though the use of heavy make-up by women at the English court was frowned upon during the reigns of Henry VII and Henry VIII. Instead, there was a decided preference during this earlier period for more natural good looks attained by creams containing honey, beeswax and sesame seed oil – a clear example of the influence of the Middle East – and the sparing use of ochre to redden the lips and cheeks slightly. Imported perfumes usually made from roses, water-lilies and violets were popular, too, for both men and women. Yet the Tudor ideal for feminine loveliness was already firmly set: sparkling green, grey or blue eyes, set far apart, and pale skin, unblemished by freckles and highlighted by ruby lips and rosy cheeks, were highly regarded by both sexes. And only as the sixteenth century progressed did the use of much heavier make-up predominate, reaching a peak under Elizabeth I who, at the age of 29, had undergone slight scarring from an attack of smallpox and later became increasingly inclined to conceal the ravages of time.

Following the queen's own example, therefore, a compound of white lead and vinegar called 'ceruse' began to be more and more lavishly employed by high-born Elizabethan women, along with various plant roots and leaves, to whiten their complexions. The most prized type of ceruse came from Venice and was mixed with water or egg white to form a paste, which was then plastered on to the skin with a damp cloth. And since the combination of ceruse with egg white, in particular, resulted in make-up cracks when the wearer smiled, it seems likely that ladies in general, and especially the queen, did indeed go to great lengths to maintain an impassive appearance at all times – something which also explains why ceruse was not applied to the neck, since even the most diligent of image-conscious women were bound to turn their heads from time to time. After a few hours, moreover, the lead turned an unsightly grey colour, and in the longer term created a much more serious depilatory effect upon both the hairline and especially the eyebrows, which would frequently fall off altogether and necessitate replacement in some cases by artificial ones made from mouse hair.

But even this last side-effect was still by no means the worst consequence of prolonged use, for ceruse's lead content was absorbed into the blood stream and resulted in further symptoms of poisoning, such as tooth loss, muscle paralysis, impaired short-term memory and ultimately dementia. Furthermore, its corrosive effects rendered the skin increasingly unattractive and necessitated the application of ever thicker layers over time. Nor, for that matter, was ceruse the only harmful cosmetic in use at this time. The ideal milky, porcelain-white complexion of a Tudor lady was highlighted, for instance, by the application to the lips and cheeks of an expensive rouge made from cochineal, a dye derived from a compound of Mexican beetle blood and corrosive nitrous acid. Madder and cinnabar, otherwise known as vermillion, were also used to achieve this reddening effect, notwithstanding the fact that cinnabar – a cheaper alternative to cochineal – was a sulphide of mercury and therefore highly poisonous in its own right. Kohl, on the other hand, was used to darken the eyelashes, along with droplets of poisonous belladonna juice to bring about 'eye-brightening' by dilating the pupils. When it is remembered, too, that some high-ranking women were prepared to undergo bleeding in an effort to achieve the necessary pallor, and that ceruse was applied to children, the health toll taken by Tudor fashion sense may well be imagined. Indeed, the deadly Italian cosmetic was almost certainly responsible for the short lifespans of many boy actors during Shakespeare's lifetime.

It was not, of course, the only age of opulent self-advertisement. Nor, for that matter, was it the only period when the link between fashion and

Bibi Saint-Pol

health risks went unheeded. Yet there were still those in Elizabethan England who warned about the harm entailed by plastering the skin 'unnaturally' – albeit for reasons that fully reflected the medical limitations of the day. Poisoning by lead and mercury, not to mention the dangers of belladonna and the acid content of cochineal, were of course matters completely outside the parameters of contemporary medical science. But, in perceiving the world through the misapprehensions of their day, some Tudor authorities nevertheless attempted an explanation of why so many women were ill and haggard before their time – giving due, if misguided, warning that the current vogue for cosmetics was blocking 'vapours' and preventing the proper circulation of energy.

Home,
Hearth
and Travel

41

Fuming pot

Contrary to popular misconception, the Tudors were by no means a universally pungent people. Nor were they uniformly tolerant of filth and noisome odours. Sir William Petre's Ingatestone Hall in Essex, for instance, was fully equipped with taps and running water, as well as drains in sealed underground pipes, which removed the waste from five separate privies. Yet in 1575 it required a team of twelve men to dig out 16 tons of excrement in an average household latrine over the course of two nights at a cost of £2 4s – the equivalent of 132 days' wages for a typical labourer – and in such circumstances, it was hardly surprising that the prevalence of stinking cesspits was much remarked upon, especially in the poorer quarters of contemporary towns and cities. For this, of course, was a time when the entire remit of civic government was altogether narrower than today, resulting in rotting piles of filth and refuse that lingered undisturbed amid tightly packed houses purposely built to overhang the pavement, since Tudor property tax was levied only on the ground floor area. When it is remembered, moreover, that Andrew Boorde, a contemporary health writer, saw fit to discourage his readers from the habit of 'pissing in chimneys', the problem of noxious fumes – both without and within – requires little elaboration.

Perhaps it is small wonder, then, that the humble 'fuming' or 'stink' pot, as contemporaries referred to it, was considered such a valuable item in any household. Handmade out of clay and measuring around 17cm in height, the pot pictured here is typical, with its green and yellow glaze, of so-called 'border ware', which was produced in considerable quantity in the border region between north-east Hampshire and western Surrey. It is hollow, with a shelf inside, and on the base there is an aperture for a lump of burning charcoal. On the shelf above the charcoal, meanwhile, there is room to place a piece of scented wood, or a handful of herbs or spices. The heat from the charcoal was intended to warm up the scented

Museum of London

material, which then released its aroma through holes in the side, and since the pot became too hot to touch after hours of use, there are also loop handles on either side to allow it to be moved.

Commonplace in sixteenth-century homes, objects like this one from the Museum of London nevertheless remained popular well beyond the Tudor period, not least because they were believed to serve a broader purpose in warding off infection. From the Middle Ages right up to the 1700s perfumed balls called pomanders were either carried on chains or girdles, held directly to the nose, or suspended in rooms to neutralise offensive smells. The Tudors, moreover, also scented their homes with herbal bouquets known as 'tussie mussies', on the grounds that a suitable concoction of sweet-smelling herbs and spices could supposedly protect the wearer from the 'bad air' or miasma that was thought to have resulted from the improper alignment of the planets. Ultimately, even the Privy Council would see fit in November 1578 to issue a series of plague regulations or 'advices', based on recommendations from the College of Physicians, emphasising the importance of air cleansers, and listing specific recommendations on possible types.

'Take rosemary dried, or juniper, bay leaves, or frankincense', suggests one such instruction, before urging its readers to 'cast the same on a chafing dish, and receive the fume or smoke thereof'. Another explains how to 'better correct the air of the houses' by burning wood, and by making fires 'rather in pans, to remove about the chamber, than in chimneys', while there is also a reference elsewhere to the efficacy of vinegar in purging foul odours. 'Take a quantity of vinegar very strong', the recommendation runs:

> And put to it some small quantity of rosewater and ten branches of rosemary. Put them all into a basin, then take five or six flintstones, heated in the fire till they be burning hot. Cast them into the same vinegar, and so let the fumes be received from place to place in your house.

Nor, it seems, was the plague the only disease associated with infected air, for the contraction of influenza was explained in the same way as was the incidence of a particularly virulent form of it known as *Sudor Anglicus*, or the 'English Sweat', which first visited the country in 1485, causing widespread panic at regular intervals among high and low alike until its final appearance in 1578. The very term 'influenza', indeed, is derived from the Tudor belief in the celestial 'influence' upon the atmosphere – not at all unlike the other disease most obviously connected with bad air and known, appropriately enough, as 'malaria'.

42

Prince Arthur's hutch

This well-known cupboard, which became the subject of various copies in the early twentieth century, was found at a farmhouse in Shropshire near Tickenhall Manor where Prince Arthur, eldest son of Henry VII, lived with Catherine of Aragon before his death in 1502. The Prince of Wales ostrich feathers flanking the lower door and the carved initial 'A' on the upper door were regarded for some time as indicators of personal royal ownership, with the result that the cupboard is sometimes known as Prince Arthur's 'hutch', or food cupboard. In view of the comparative crudity of construction, however – not to mention the late Victorian market for furniture with colourful historical associations – doubts have been raised about the item's authenticity. There is little doubt, for instance, that equivalent church fittings or wainscot from the same period frequently display greater consistency, economy and neatness of construction and finish. And it has been suggested that some of the carved panels could have been added after the cupboard was constructed or that plain panels were embellished with later carving. Yet by no means all palace furniture in the early Tudor period was especially sophisticated and the cupboard's authenticity or otherwise is further obscured by the overall sparsity of similar furniture from about 1500 with which to compare it.

Made of oak and standing at a height of 164cm, the hutch, or 'livery' cupboard as such items were sometimes called, is certainly a sturdy enough structure, and with a width of 126cm and depth of 61cm, it offered plenty of space for its intended purpose. As a food cupboard, moreover, it was sensibly raised above the floor by stiles, in order to keep out vermin. And if Prince Arthur did not actually own it personally, there is firm evidence, nevertheless, not only to identify the cupboard as a contemporary object

but to suggest that it was intended for a person of rank. The mason's mitre joints employed to hold the cupboard's panelling in place are indicative of a date before 1600, and the large side panels, formed with vertical planks, are another feature usually associated with Tudor joinery. The extensive worm damage may be indicative of sapwood, suggesting perhaps that the object was expected to be painted ornamentally – something which is consistent with the size and plainness of the panels and the use of an angled joint to make the artist's task easier.

Yet the real fascination of this piece of furniture remains not so much its origins as its purpose, since the Tudor 'hutch', 'livery', or 'dole' cupboard opens up an intriguing tale not only of our ancestors' eating habits but also their sleeping routine. Uunlike their modern counterparts, who, under pressure of the 'nine-to-five' day, most frequently consume their main meal in the evening, sixteenth-century men and women usually ate it in the middle of the day and took only a light repast before bed, with the result that night-time snacking became routine. More interestingly still, perhaps, the notion of the solid eight-hour sleep also appears to have been foreign to them. It was common for the Tudors not only to remain in bed longer – particularly in winter – but to sleep in two distinct phases, with a so-called 'first sleep' being followed by a waking period of one to two hours and then a second sleep. The 'hutch', therefore, seems to have been a highly valued item of bedroom furniture, enabling its owners to satisfy their dead-of-night cravings at leisure prior to resuming their slumbers. Significantly, the term 'livery' derives from the French *livrée*, a contemporary term associated with the distribution of items at specific times, and in 1596 Edmund Spenser duly noted how 'liverye is sayd to be served up for all night', adding that this included the 'nyghtes allowance of drinks'.

Eating, however, was not the only pastime of restless Tudor slumberers, unencumbered as they were by those time constraints accepted as 'normal' in modern industrial societies. During their nightly waking periods people appear to have been quite active, not only getting up to relieve themselves but frequently smoking tobacco and sometimes even visiting neighbours. Those who preferred the comfort of their beds, meanwhile, tended to read, write or, in some cases, pray, which explains why numerous prayer manuals from the late fifteenth century include special prayers for the hours in between sleeps. And these same hours were rarely entirely solitary, of course – so that Tudor men and women routinely chatted to bed-fellows or engaged in sex. Indeed, a doctor's manual from sixteenth-century France even advised couples that the best time to conceive was not at the end of a long day's labour but 'after the first sleep' when 'they have more enjoyment' and 'do it better'.

43

Leaded window

By 1559, when this splendid bay window was installed in the east wing of Little Moreton Hall in Cheshire, leaded glass was still a rarity in the houses of all but the very wealthiest. Forty years later, however, as the reign of Elizabeth I began to draw to a close, such windows had emerged as the ultimate status symbol for any townsman with enough disposable income to import them in pre-constructed frames from Burgundy, Normandy and Flanders, if English glass was not available. But nowhere more than at Little Moreton perhaps was the new fad more extravagantly articulated as Richard Dale, master carpenter and window designer extraordinaire, gave the freest possible rein to his imagination. One of a pair, the double-storied window pictured here fronted the so-called 'withdrawing room' or 'bower' – a place where women frequently gathered to play music or attend to their needlework – and although the second half of the century, with its increased emphasis upon domestic privacy, had witnessed the building of numerous small bedrooms and private apartments of similar kind, the fact that so much care and craftsmanship had been expended upon such a room speaks for itself.

By no means though was Little Moreton's east wing the only area to be treated to its owner's passion for leaded windows. The south wing's famous Long Gallery, installed by William Moreton II in 1562 and measuring some 20m in length, became what is arguably the defining feature of the whole house. Yet while similar galleries were growing in popularity, the engineering implications of such structures - particularly when extensively glazed and leaded – remained highly problematic. Little Moreton's crowning glory, which was apparently conceived as an afterthought during the construction of the gatehouse on which it sits, was loaded directly onto the first-floor ceiling joists, regardless of the flimsy foundations beneath, and the result was the lopsided appearance of the house, which has gradu-

Robert G.

ally become one of its most distinctive features. Indeed, only the insertion of iron tie rods at the end of the nineteenth century prevented the entire edifice from collapse, though even these could not rectify the bowed windows and crooked floors and beams that continue to impart a vague sensation of sea-sickness to many modern-day visitors.

Notwithstanding the considerable technical problems involved, however, effective insulation against the elements and the transmission of light remained key priorities for Elizabethan builders. The English word 'window' is derived from the Old Norse *vindauga*, meaning 'windy eye', since the openings in walls that were so necessary for illumination also let in the weather, and it is easy to forget that until the arrival of cheap fossil fuels and improved technology during the Industrial Revolution, glass was not only extremely expensive but could only be produced in very small pieces, making the production of window panes a painstaking process. In fact, most Tudor builders employed the type known as 'muff', 'broadsheet', or 'cylinder', which was made by swinging a bubble of glass to and fro on a blow pipe until it became a long cylindrical vessel. Thereafter, it was opened up at each end, split along the middle and allowed to uncurl on a flat surface within an oven to form a flat sheet, typically measuring a maximum of 15cm square. As a result, almost all windows of the Tudor and Jacobean periods were made up of leaded light panels, often with diamond-shaped panes called 'quarries', although there existed countless other patterns that became more complex as time went on.

Ultimately, of course, the glazing craze of the second half of the sixteenth century would generate not only a design revolution in the homes of the wealthy but also a range of ingenious building techniques to facilitate it. And with typical self-confidence, the Elizabethan elite were therefore able to advertise their status ever more exuberantly as the period progressed. 'Hardwick Hall, more glass than wall' ran the contemporary description of Lady Arbella Stuart's great house in Derbyshire, though the arrangements made by common folk in their humble wattle and daub dwellings, however ingenious, remained altogether less grand. Oiled parchment or cloth, waxed paper, split horn and mica were all used as translucent window coverings, but glass would not grace the majority of homes until the nineteenth century, by which time glass technology had allowed window panes to increase considerably in size. Almost fifty years after the construction of the Crystal Palace in 1851, agricultural workers in the East Riding of Yorkshire were still using coarse sackcloth for the windows of their cottages, while in County Donegal in the west of Ireland, strips of sheepskin were being used for precisely the same purpose – both expedients that would have seemed fully familiar to Tudor men and women.

44
Oak chest

The will of John Tytmarche, husbandman of Over Norton, Oxfordshire, makes interesting reading. At the time of his death in 1590 he lived in a small dwelling consisting of a hall, a chamber containing a single bed, and a 'backside' in which lay corn, hay, two 'beasts' and twelve sheep. In all, the dwelling's movables, which included some brass and pewter ware, were valued at £7 13s 8d, while the hall, which contained a hen pen, was furnished by no more than a small table and a bench. In this last respect Tytmarche's home was no exception to the general rule, since furniture was never a high priority for humble Tudor folk. Indeed, one English 'vocabulary' of the fifteenth century made reference to only five different types of movable furniture – beds, trestles, chests, stools and benches – while another slightly fuller work of the same period added only two more: screens, on the one hand, and so-called 'settles', which were seats with high straight backs and panelled storage space built into the bottom. When it is remembered, too, that chairs of any kind were not even moderately common until the end of the Middle Ages and did not become familiar features of household furniture until well into the seventeenth century, the difference between Tudor homes and their modern-day equivalents are even more apparent. Where they were found at all, in fact, chairs were usually reserved for the owners of homes when presiding over meals, while other members of the family and guests, too, usually made do with stools, perhaps with cushions as a passing concession to comfort.

Chests, by contrast, probably ranked second only to beds in the hierarchy of household necessities and may well have ranked highest of all from some perspectives, since most Tudor men and women slept on crude straw pallets or rough mats covered with a sheet. Serving alternately as seat, storage space, strong box, side table and even bed, the household chest was therefore a central item in any sixteenth-century home – all of which makes the one pictured here, dating from around 1500, an item

of particular interest. Decorated with whorls and perpendicular tracery and a lock plate to fit above two gothic leaves, it is English, made from six boards of oak nailed together at the sides and ends; it belonged at one time to the collection of the American newspaper tycoon William Randolph Hearst before being acquired by a private collector. And although its precise functions will remain unknown, two conclusions, at least, can be drawn with some certainty from its design. On the one hand, at 60cm in height, 130cm in width and 40cm in depth, it will clearly have served as a seat. And the fact that it is raised above floor level on so-called 'slab' legs to protect its contents from damp, grime and vermin suggests that its other primary purpose was the storage of items of some importance.

Even so, the comparative crudity of its construction is apparent and accurately reflects the limitations of everyday English craftsmanship at this time. Usually made from hewn planks doweled together to form the box, early Tudor chests of this kind had only recently – around 1450 – begun to benefit from the invention of the mortice and tenon joint, and it was not until 1520 or so that such 'joyned' items began to supersede clamped ones. Moreover, though chests of drawers were also making their appearance, and chests themselves were beginning to evolve into panelled settles – the forerunners of settees and sofas – it remains one of the distinctive features of even wealthier Tudor homes that they contained so much cumbersome, uncomfortable and crudely functional furniture. Though the walnut tree was imported into England by the Earl of Pembroke in the 1560s and other furniture, fashioned from elm, ash and beech, may well have been at least slightly more popular than the surviving items suggest, the emphasis was upon durability. And it was hardy oak, often imported from the Baltic since English stocks of suitable wood were surprisingly low, that predominated at all levels.

On the whole, then, English furniture had remained starkly functional, and heavily reliant upon a teeming underclass of sparsely skilled practitioners – as many as ninety-nine unlicensed joiners were recorded in the capital in 1563, mainly in Westminster, St Katherine's and Southwark. And the humble Tudor chest, for all its stylistic limitations, continued to have its consolations, as a story in the autobiography of Thomas Whythorne, a sixteenth-century itinerant music teacher, illustrates. The mistress of one house where Whythorne lodged appears to have used his chest to extend their relationship beyond the purely professional, causing the item:

> To be removed out of the chamber where before that time I was accustomed to lie, and to be brought into a chamber so nigh to her own chamber as she might have come from one to the other when she list without any suspicion.

'This chamber,' Whythorne noted, 'I was then placed in', so that the night's rest which a man of his status would almost certainly have otherwise taken upon his chest was subsequently enjoyed in altogether cosier circumstances.

45

Floor watering pot

Floors made of flattened earth, or earth mixed with straw or rushes, were common not only in the Tudor period but well into the eighteenth century, mainly in areas outside the south-east of the country. They long remained a feature, too, of homes in many parts of Europe, as well as Virginia and parts of New England. Dampness, of course, was the main problem with such floors for much of the year, but dust was another major inconvenience, exacerbated by the prevalence of draughts, which scattered the smoke and ash from open fires, not to mention candle soot, dried mud, disintegrating straw and a host of other domestic detritus, into every conceivable nook and cranny. Long before the advent of electrical appliances, therefore, the Tudors had adopted their own ingenious approach to dust management, which involved the gentle sprinkling of their floors with water, thereby containing it in one place by making it damp enough to stick among the reed or straw floor coverings, and preventing it from flying around when eventually swept away.

Watering pots, like the glazed redware example featured here, were used not only to nurture young plants but to refresh floor coverings and keep down dust. Indeed, the short nozzle on this particular item suggests that its primary function is likely to have been the latter. Standing 29cm high, it is oviform in shape, with a generous pierced rose pouring bulb, a rubbed neck and splash guard. The foot rim and edge of the bulb, meanwhile, are modestly embellished with a waved band of clay. And though some doubts remain about aspects of the pot's provenance, it is certainly English and was probably manufactured, like so much other glazed redware of its type, in London during the last quarter of the sixteenth century.

Other aspects of Tudor housework were altogether more onerous. Since household items such as plates and bowls were generally made from wood, the task of keeping these items clean without the assistance of commercial cleaning agents was itself a considerable task, especially

when it is remembered that the process of fetching and disposing of water would have to be conducted manually – the waste water being carried outside to a 'sink', which, as the name suggests, meant literally at that time a hole in the ground. Scouring, in its turn, required even more intensive activity as sharp river sand, or sometimes the plant known as 'horsetails' (*equisetum telmateia*), was vigorously applied to the surface of the dirty item.

Yet it was the lot of the washerwoman in a wealthy household that probably left most to be desired, since high-ranking Tudors took particular care to safeguard their respectability by ensuring that their linen was scrupulously clean. In his *Heptameron of Civil Discourses*, a contemporary manual on how to achieve a happy marriage, Richard Jones, for example, warned that a woman who does not wear clean linen 'shal neither be prazed of strangers, or delight her husband', and most women of means would therefore attempt to change their linen daily, while the wealthiest sometimes changed their under-smocks several times per day. Tablecloths and sheets were also cleaned regularly by the same strenuous process of 'bucking', which involved carefully soaking items in a large buck tub before applying a strong alkaline solution of 'ley' – made either from the ashes of dried ferns or by making water pass through clean wood ashes – and conducting further soaking, stirring and rinsing until all dirt had painstakingly been removed. Furthermore, since unbleached linen was a greyish-cream colour, it was usually then bleached in the sun and wind by laying it on the ground or over a bush, and wetting it repeatedly with a mixture of lye – another strongly alkaline substance composed mainly of potassium hydroxide – and urine.

Finer items of clothing, on the other hand, had to be washed with 'black-soap', which had a jelly-like consistency and was made by boiling up fat with lye, while woollen items had to be brushed weekly and shaken out to expel moths. More luxurious fabrics like silk, velvet and cloth of gold required even more elaborate cleaning procedures, of course, and extra problems were posed by the fine wall hangings that decorated homes of the wealthy and the fur that lined winter garments. Such, indeed, were the complexities of the Tudor washerwoman's task that in 1585 Leonard Mascall saw fit to publish *A profitable boke declaring dyvers approoved remedies, to take out spottes and staines, in Silkes, Velvets, Linnen and Woollen clothes*. Among other things, Mascall recommended that grease spots be removed by the application of Castille soap and a clean feather, though other authorities suggested that the best effects were obtained by using water in which peas had previously been soaked.

Understandably, then, the daily chores of domestic life in Tudor England were a subject of much interest. But while innumerable hard-working women made do with floor watering pots and other simple gadgets to lighten their labours, a few, at least, earned a worthwhile wage for their grind and toil. Anne Harris, laundress to King Henry VIII, earned no less than £10 a year for washing the king's tablecloths and towels and keeping his drapery 'sweet', though even she, as the royal accounts make clear, was forced to bear the cost of her own soap.

46

Garderobe

A garderobe was a toilet, or bank of toilets, sometimes connected by pipe to the building that housed it, so that the waste emptied directly into a pit, moat, or river outside. Like the example pictured here, which has been carefully preserved at the Weald and Downland Open Air Museum in Sussex, garderobes usually projected out from the first floor or higher storeys and were often exposed to the elements. Although garderobes are a common feature of castles and other surviving stone structures, this example from a late medieval farmhouse is much rarer. The farmhouse itself, which consists of four ground-floor rooms and two first-floor rooms, was originally built at Idle Hill in Kent before being dismantled and relocated to its present site in 1968. It is comparatively typical of dwellings owned by early Tudor yeoman farmers, who, as minor landowners, would enjoy increasing wealth as the century progressed, though their everyday lives, as this item demonstrates, remained comparatively Spartan by modern standards. For while some, as William Harrison suggested in his *Description of England*, were sleeping in feather beds by the 1570s, their wealth was on the whole vested in their farms rather than their dwellings.

Yet stereotypes about contemporary sanitation need to be treated with at least some caution. John Russell, for example, in his *Book of Nurture*, which was written around 1460, recommended that privies have a ewer and basin for the washing of hands after a visit and that small strips of 'blanket, cotyn or lynyn' should also be provided 'to wipe the nether end'. At least some of his advice was heeded, it seems, since archaeological digs in London and Worcester have found examples of all three fabrics plus moss and wool scraps deposited underneath old garderobes. Certainly, William Horman, headmaster of Eton during the first nine years of Henry VII's reign, was one of the converts to the new fastidiousness. 'See not,' he instructed imperiously, 'that I lack not by my bedside a chair of easement with a vessel under and a urinal by'. And by 1547 the Privy

Council was also exerting its influence to protect the king from 'nuisance at court' by proclaiming that 'no person of what degree soever shall make water or cast any annoyance within the precinct of the court, within the gates of the porter's lodge, whereby corruption may breed and tend to the prejudice of his royal person.'

By around 1530 the garderobe was already falling out of favour with builders, though Henry VIII's courtiers continued to share an oak plank, accommodating twenty-eight seats each 60cm apart, at Hampton Court's 'Great House of Easement'. Even here, however, as a result of Cardinal Wolsey's original instructions, the waste fell straight into brick-lined culverts where it was washed away under the moat and into the Thames by water brought to the palace in lead pipes from Coombe Hill in Kingston, some 3 miles away. The task of cleaning all royal sewers and the garderobes within a 20-mile radius of London fell, meanwhile, to the king's personal band of 'gong scourers'. Paid 6*d* a day during the reign of Elizabeth, these hardy individuals worked exclusively at night between 9 p.m. and 5 a.m., and having undergone the very real risk of asphyxiation from the so-called 'night soil', they were also subjected to predictable social stigma and permitted to live only in certain areas.

At least the king did not add to their task personally. Instead, his own waste was deposited in a specially designed box or 'close stool' tucked away in a private room off the state bedchamber. Lavishly covered in black velvet, its lid opened to reveal a padded and beribboned interior covered in the same material, with a hole in the centre, beneath which a pewter bowl was placed. The task of attending the king fell to the Groom of the Stool – a prestigious post reserved only for high-ranking courtiers who were worthy of such intimate acquaintance with their ruler. Ever ready to assist at any hour, one groom recorded in 1539 how the king had taken laxative pills and an enema before sleeping until 2 a.m., whereupon 'His Grace rose to go upon his stool which, with the working of the pills and the enema His Highness had taken before, had a very fair siege'.

On small Tudor landholdings, by contrast, there was perhaps the most imaginative arrangement of all, involving a marvel of recycling, derived from a simple fact of nature: namely, that pigs consume not only leftovers but human waste as well.On one side of the Tudor peasant's pigsty, therefore, frequently stood 'the midden' or human toilet, with a gentle slope into the pigs quarters, whereby the swine not only gained nutrition but made extra manure, helping to make the vegetables in the typical Tudor garden grow ever more abundantly. Even this arrangement, however, could rarely surmount one time-honoured drawback, it seems: 'Beware of pissing in draughts,' warned Andrew Boorde earnestly.

John Bolnton

47

Hot water cistern

Numerous Tudor tile fragments from stoves used to heat royal bathrooms have been found in a variety of excavations of contemporary palaces, but this particular object, dating from around 1530, is probably the only surviving hot water cistern of the period and demonstrates the level of sophistication to which the Tudor court and nobility aspired. Made of white earthenware, moulded in relief with a copper-green lead glaze, it is another example of Surrey–Hampshire border ware and bears the arms of Henry VII and his wife Elizabeth of York, along with their initials HR and ER and the royal motto *dieu et mon droit* (God and my right). Though both monarchs were dead by the time of the cistern's manufacture, this type of embellishment is far from unusual, since the Tudors, as self-conscious newcomers to the English throne, were invariably keen to emphasise the continuity of their dynasty and therefore took an almost obsessive interest in their ancestry and claims to the English throne, allowing their coat of arms to be used in a wide range of decorative contexts.

Somewhat surprisingly, perhaps, Edward III's luxuriously appointed bathroom at Westminster had already been equipped over a century earlier with two 'large bronze taps for the king's bath' to bring in hot and cold water. But by about 1500, wood-fired ceramic stoves, fabricated entirely from deep concave moulded tiles originating in Germany, were already widely used in Northern Europe, and these stoves could be integrally linked, as in this case, to a hot water cistern. With both stoke-hole and flue outside the room, they were clean and efficient, and eminently suitable, therefore, for application to bath chambers, so that in 1529 Henry VIII duly ordered a new bathroom to be built on the first floor of the Bayne Tower at Hampton Court, along with a bedroom, private study, library and jewel house. Equipped with deep window-seats, beneath which lay cupboards, and a ceiling richly decorated with gold battens on a white background, the king's bathroom, as might be expected, was a testament

Victoria and Albert Museum

not only to the finest Tudor taste but to the most up-to-date technology available. The baths, which were made by a cooper and attached to the wall, were supplied by two taps, one for cold water and one for hot, while directly behind the bathroom, in another small room, was a charcoal-fired stove, or boiler, fed from a tank on the second floor.

By the 1540s, moreover, the king's bathroom at Whitehall seems to have exceeded even the luxury and sophistication of its equivalent at Hampton Court. Indeed, the old-fashioned bathtub used earlier in his reign could not offer a greater contrast to the luxury sauna-bath arrangement introduced during the final decade of his life. Complete with another green-glazed stove – classically designed with pediment and entablature – and steps leading down into a sunken stone pool in his privy quarters, it epitomised Henry's wholehearted embrace with the finest aspects of a full Continental Renaissance lifestyle, though we are still uncertain how often the king actually used his baths. We hear, in fact, only that he took 'medicinal herbal baths' each winter and avoided bathing altogether when the sweating sickness made one of its regular appearances in his realm. Yet bathe he certainly did and the widespread inclusion of recipes for soap and 'hand or washing waters' in contemporary household instruction manuals suggests that his habit was not as unusual among contemporary men and women as popular myth might tend to suggest.

As early as the fourteenth century, indeed, Hugh Plat's *Delightes for Ladies* had given directions for preparing washing water with 'sage, marjoram, camomile, rosemary and orange peel as possible ingredients'. Soft soap, made from mutton fat, wood ash and soda, was another popular cleansing agent, while hard soaps consisted of olive oil, soda, lime, herbs and flowers. On the other hand, 'dry' washing with clean linen appears to have had a number of advocates and it should be remembered, too, that ear scoops and manicure sets made from bone, as well as lice combs, were sufficiently common in Tudor England to be found among the possessions of sailors on board the *Mary Rose* at the time of its sinking. Nor, for that matter, do contemporary coroners' reports neglect to make frequent reference to labourers who had died while bathing in streams and rivers after a hard day's work. If the mother of Mary Queen of Scots was advised not to wash her hair more than once a week during pregnancy, this reflected not so much a disregard for hygiene as a fear of catching cold, in much the same way that a law of 1550 banning pictures of the baby Jesus being bathed was merely intended to emphasise the Son of Man's innate purity.

48

Bee skep

When Charles Butler, author of *The Feminine Monarchie* – the first full-length book on beekeeping – was born in 1560, the honey bee was already a long-established and familiar feature of many Tudor households. 'Among all the creatures which our bountiful God hath made for the use and service of man,' wrote Butler, 'the Bees are most to be admired', and he then went on, over some ten chapters, to advise his readers on all aspects of the finer points of apiary, including 'the nature & properties of Bees & of their Queene', 'the fruit, and profit of Bees', 'the breeding of Bees and of the drone', 'the removing of Bees', and 'the Bees enimies'. He wrote extensively, too, about the construction of straw hives or 'skeps', which, he believed, were much preferable to wicker ones or those made of privet or hazel and daubed with 'cowcloome', a mixture of manure and clay. Skeps, Butler suggested, should be constructed during the dead of winter and should be made from 'betweene a bushel and a halfe, as the time of yeare and quantities of the swarme doth require' with a diameter of approximately fourteen inches (35cm). As an additional refinement, small strips of willow called spleeting were also to be fitted inside to reinforce the dome, after which the skep was to be protected from the weather within an enclosure or 'bole'.

In an age where the value of the humble honeybee was already universally acknowledged, such information did not, of course, fall on deaf ears. For bees, which in Tudor times were black rather than striped, not only provided their owners with valuable honey and beeswax, but also pollinated the fruits and flowers of the garden. Free at the point of origin, unlike the exorbitantly expensive luxury of sugar which was beginning to grace the tables of the high and mighty, honey was used in all manner of recipes as well as in the making of mead, a sweet alcoholic wine much loved by Queen Elizabeth, whose favourite tipple was a flavoured variant known as metheglin, containing ginger, tea, orange peel,

nutmeg, coriander, cinnamon and cloves or vanilla. Beeswax was not only employed in candles, sealing wax and the production of unguents and salves for medicinal purposes, but in bow-making and the production of wax writing tablets. Used, too, to strengthen and preserve sewing thread and to coat hemp strands for making wick, it even served as a sealant or lubricant for bullets in early firearms and as a tried and trusted form of dental filling.

It is not altogether surprising, therefore, that boles and skeps featured no less prominently on the estates of the high and mighty than they did on the altogether humbler plots of labourers like William Baule from Bishopton just outside Stratford-upon-Avon, whose will of 1599 left 'two stalles of bees' valued at 4s to his daughter Elizabeth. Lady Margaret Hoby, for example, recorded in her diary entry for 1 September 1599 how she 'went to take my beesse' and later 'went to se my honnie ordered'. The evidence of such devotion to bee-keeping can be seen, moreover, on a variety of surviving sixteenth-century estates. The Tudor garden at Thornbury Castle in Gloucestershire had twenty-six bee boles; three still survive in a south-facing late Tudor wall behind Quebec House, Westerham. At Packwood House in Warwickshire, meanwhile, thirty line a south-facing garden wall, and at Titchfield Abbey, Hampshire, four alcoves can still be seen in two rows along the boundary wall which have long since been bricked up.

For good measure, bees and their wax were even beneficiaries of the Church's official stamp of approval, though the serried ranks of candles surrounding worshippers in pre-Reformation churches, some weighing as much as 14kg, were hugely superior to the humble rush-candles used in the houses of common folk, which were made by dipping a rush into 'tallow', a congealed sheep or pig fat collected during cooking. Unlike their much more expensive beeswax counterparts, most dipped candles of this kind were usually made from the lowest grades of tallow and produced a considerable amount of evil-smelling smoke, while even the more expensive candles employed in the houses of the gentry would more often be made only from higher-grade tallow rather than beeswax, which was utilised only for special occasions. As such, the beeswax candles of early Tudor churches served, aptly enough perhaps, to provide the congregation with one more link to heaven itself. 'The origin of bees is from paradise,' the *Gwentian Code* had formerly declared, 'and because of the sin of man they came thence and God conferred His grace upon them'. 'Therefore,' the code concluded, 'the Mass cannot be sung without the wax'.

49

Chimney

When Edward Stafford, Duke of Buckingham and High Constable of England, went to the block on Tower Hill on 17 May 1521, he left behind him his glorious castle at Thornbury in Gloucestershire, which he had built only ten years earlier to affirm his status as the premier nobleman of all England. An imposing gatehouse, towering crenellated roofs and magnificent oriel windows – one containing 720 panes of glass – were only some of the castle's more striking features, each one emphasising the duke's exalted rank as a direct descendant of Edward III, while above them all towered two intricate red-brick chimneys, built in 1514, which remain the oldest of their kind still functioning today. Similar to those built at Hampton Court Palace, they were a testament not only to the duke's undoubted grandeur but to the 'new technology' of enclosed fireplaces, which would come over time to revolutionise house design in Tudor England.

The word chimney comes from the Latin *caminus*, meaning a furnace, and by the sixteenth century the word had also come to encompass the flue itself. Traditionally, the main chamber or hall of any house, great or small, was heated by burning logs on a central hearth, and until the fourteenth century chimneys were rare. Instead, the smoke escaped through a hole in the roof, which sufficed more or less satisfactorily for a large single-storey building but was useless for buildings of two or more storeys. As towns grew in the fourteenth and fifteenth centuries and multi-storey buildings began to proliferate, so chimneys became more common. Equally important was the increasing adoption of coal as fuel, which produced more smoke than wood and required more of a downdraft for lighting purposes.

In consequence, the spread of chimneys rapidly became one of the most striking features of the urban landscape, and by the 1570s they were clearly making their mark in the countryside, too. According to William Harrison, 'the multitude of chimneys lately erected' was one of several things 'marvellously altered' in the village of some old men he encountered while compiling his *Description of England*. Observing how 'in their young days there were not above two or three, if so many, in most uplandish towns of the realm', now, it seems, there were many, and the days when 'each one made his fire against a reredos in the hall, where he dined and dressed his meat' were all but gone. Though still something of a luxury item, the use of brick, which had spread from East Anglia, where it had been introduced from the Low Countries in the late medieval period, was also making its impact, as Thornbury Castle's ornate chimneys plainly demonstrate.

Yet many early chimneys remained structurally unsound, constructed from highly inappropriate materials such as timber and wattle and daub, and the inevitable chimney fires resulting from this period of experimentation and makeshift building represented one of the main household hazards of Tudor England. The most serious calamity on record to befall the Suffolk town of Beccles, for instance, occurred on 29 November 1586 when a fire broke out in the chimney of one of the town's smaller houses. Fanned by a violent gale blowing at the very time that the River Waveney was hard frozen, it gutted the church of St Michael's, leaving the lower half of its steeple blackened with smoke for more than two and a half centuries, and consumed some eighty houses, causing loss and damage amounting to the enormous sum of £20,000 – a small part of which was attributed to theft conducted by opportunists in the ensuing confusion.

Clearly, the occurrence of such a calamity which, as all contemporaries knew, could strike at any time and any place, had resonated far and wide, and it was therefore no small wonder that many Tudor men and women should have sought less conventional protection from such misfortune. There is plentiful evidence, for instance, that some individuals resorted to supernatural means, carving ritual symbols on and around fireplaces and especially chimney lintels, while similar Christian symbols, representing Christ and the Virgin Mary, were also common even after the Reformation. And as England's heathen past and Christian present mingled around the Tudor fireside, so other types of superstition abounded, too. Flying cinders, for instance, suggested to many Tudor folk that a birth was imminent, while in some areas of the kingdom it was customary to spit on cooling cinder in the hope that it might crackle and thus portend that wealth was on the way – all of which may have served in its own innocent way to divert attention from the more ominous features of the household hearth and the lurking threat that glowed within.

50

The bridge at Great Mitton

This bridge over the River Hodder at Great Mitton in Lancashire was built in 1561 by the Catholic Sir Richard Shireburne to help the parishioners of 'Mytton Church' attend the Protestant services introduced by Elizabeth I some two years or so earlier. In view of Shireburne's own beliefs, not to mention the more general allegiance of Lancastrians to the old religion, it was an unexpected gesture of compliance at a time when many Catholics were still smarting from the reimposition of new doctrines after Mary Tudor's death. Before long, however, the bridge was mainly serving as a packhorse trail and transit point for riders intrepid enough to brave long journeys along Elizabethan England's treacherous road system. Known today as Cromwell's Bridge, after a Roundhead army crossed on their way from Gisburn to engage the Royalists at the Battle of Preston in 1648, it was an uncharacteristically sturdy construction for its day. Consisting of three segmental circular arches, which at the time of its creation measured around 2m in width, it was also equipped eventually with low parapets to allow the transit of animals carrying large panniers. And though the Statute of Bridges of 1531 had empowered local magistrates to levy a special rate for the upkeep of such structures, its survival to this day is no small surprise. For, at a time when money was short and government interest limited, transport and travel routes of any kind in Tudor England were routinely neglected.

'The highways be cried out upon,' wrote one of Thomas Cromwell's agents from Lincolnshire in February 1539. 'Every flood makes them impassable.' And though fenland was notoriously difficult to cross, other areas, too, presented similar problems to hard-pressed Tudor travellers. 'Many common ways in Kent,' noted an Act of Parliament of 1523, 'be so

deep and noyous, by wearing and course of water, that people cannot have their carriages or passages by horses upon or by the same, but to their great pains, peril or jeopardy.' At Keynsham near Bristol, meanwhile, the fine six-arched stone bridge was 'all in ruin' when the antiquarian John Leland visited it on his travels. Signposts, moreover, were non-existent and habitations few and far between, so that travellers frequently became lost and sometimes perished. 'Hinky punk', a diminutive sprite assuming the appearance of wispy blue, grey or white smoke, specialised, it was said, in luring travellers off their paths at night into treacherous bogs or wetlands under the guise of a helpful, lamp-bearing being, and it is no coincidence that his image remains carved to this day into one of the pew panels at St Peter's Church in Tawstock, Devon. Nor, of course, was it only mythical ne'er-do-wells that threatened wayfarers. An Italian visitor in 1500 was convinced that 'there is no country in the world where there are so many thieves and robbers as in England', and wooded areas such as Sherwood and Epping were particularly notorious danger spots for anyone making their way at snail's pace along lonely Tudor roads.

Slowness, indeed, was one of the major banes of travel in its own right. Although an Act of 1555 authorised Justices of the Peace to forcibly co-opt labourers for work on the highways, and subsequent Elizabethan laws

Ian Greig

required parishes to carry out at least six days' repair work on roads each summer, the measures were rarely enforced. Henry VIII had set up the first royal post-horse service in 1511, and the main 'post-roads' – from London to Dover, Holyhead, Milford Haven and Truro, and the 'Great North Road' from London to Berwick-upon-Tweed, with a branch to Carlisle – were better maintained than most. Richer travellers on these roads could, for instance, change horses at set points and journey 'post-haste', while the new light 'coaches' which began to appear early in Elizabeth I's reign proved considerably faster on good roads than their predecessors. Yet most travellers on foot still achieved only 12 miles a day, and even horse riders normally no more than three times as much.

One notable exception was Robert Carey, who set out from London on Thursday 24 March 1603 to announce to James VI of Scotland that he had just inherited the throne of England after the death of Queen Elizabeth. Leaving at mid-morning, Carey had covered 162 miles before he slept that night at Doncaster. Next day, moreover, further relays of horses, carefully prepared in advance, guaranteed that he covered another 136 miles along the ill-kept track known as the Great North Road linking the capitals of the two kingdoms. In all, Carey's dash of nearly 400 miles was eventually undertaken in about 60 hours. But even this record, predictably enough, was only won at the cost of a 'great fall by the way', which resulted in both the rider's delay and 'a great blow on the head' from one of his horse's hoofs 'that made me shed much blood'. Ultimately, therefore, as the tireless messenger himself related, he would kneel before the new King of England, 'be-bloodied and bruised'.

Culture and Pastimes

51

Shakespeare's signet ring

One of the most prized possessions in the collection of the Shakespeare Birthplace Trust is this gold signet ring, dating from the late sixteenth or early seventeenth century. Predictably, the reversed inscription, 'WS', has invited much speculation about its possible owner and for many people it remains the most significant surviving object to be owned and used by England's most revered playwright. The term 'signet' derives from the Old French word *signe*, meaning signature, and in the sixteenth and early seventeenth centuries rings of this type were used to imprint a red resin called 'shellac', which was applied to documents with the signer or sender's symbol in the form a monogram, coat of arms or any other recognisable design. In Shakespeare's day even quite ordinary people possessed their own seal, and a signet ring was often the most expensive personal item that a person possessed. The bard's mother, for example, is known to have possessed one depicting a rearing horse, as did his son-in-law, John Hall.

Significantly, the ring associated with Shakespeare himself displays remarkably little wear, suggesting that it was relatively new or little used when it was apparently mislaid all of four centuries ago, though its design accords entirely with equivalent items from the same period. It is large and quite heavy – amounting to about 18g of solid gold – and in the middle of the face, or bezel, are the owner's initials, reversed to give a positive impression when pressed into hot shellac. Meanwhile, the crossing of the central lines of the 'W' with the oblique direction of the lines of the 'S' conforms exactly to the style of the day, and the letters themselves are intertwined with a tassel known as a 'Bowen' or 'true lover's knot', the upper bow or flourish of which forms the resemblance of a heart.

Shakespeare Birthplace Trust

Interestingly, on the porch of Charlcote House near Stratford, which once belonged to the very Sir Thomas Lucy who is said to have attempted to prosecute Shakespeare for deer stealing, the letters TL are surrounded in precisely the same manner.

But whether the ring did indeed belong to Shakespeare personally remains a matter for speculation. The ring's provenance is complicated not only by the fact that the actor David Garrick displayed a similar one in his Temple to Shakespeare in the 1750s, but by the very nature of its discovery. Unearthed in March 1810 by a female labourer named Mrs Martin in a field adjacent to the church of Holy Trinity at Mill Close where Shakespeare is known to have worshipped, the good lady at once saw fit to test its composition by having it dipped in nitric acid – much to the dismay of local historian and solicitor, Robert Bell Wheler, who was swiftly informed of the object's existence and, in his own words, 'purchased it upon the same day for 36 shillings'.

Notwithstanding its rough treatment, however, there remains a good deal of circumstantial evidence to support the ring's authenticity. Not least of all, the only other person living in Stratford at that time with the same initials appears to have been a draper named William Smith. Yet Smith is known to have had a seal inscribed with a skull and bones, and while there are no surviving documents bearing Shakespeare's own seal impression, there are nevertheless several other interesting links between Shakespeare and the site where the ring was discovered. Holy Trinity Church, close to where the ring was found was, after all, Shakespeare's own church, and the playwright is also known to have owned 107 acres in the open fields of Old Stratford, where Mill Close is located, together with a farmhouse, garden and orchard, and 20 acres of pasture. Most significantly of all, perhaps, it would seem that Shakespeare had originally intended to endorse his will by attaching his seal to the document, though he later crossed out the word 'seal' at the bottom and merely signed the document when he amended his will on 25 March 1616 shortly before his death.

Clearly, then, the playwright had possessed a seal at some point and it seems perfectly plausible that this particular signet ring may have been lost just prior to this date – even, it has been suggested rather tantalisingly, when his daughter Judith was married at Holy Trinity Church at the end of January. The truth, of course, remains as elusive as ever and will no doubt continue to exercise many an imagination across centuries to come, though for the time being at least, the ring's wanderings are now over, and have been since it was finally presented to the Shakespeare Trust by Wheler's sister, Anne, in 1868.

52

Thomas Tallis keyboard

Although the components of this organ console at St Alfege's Church in Greenwich belong predominantly to the eighteenth century, there is one feature at least that defies the general rule. For experts believe that the middle keyboard is almost certainly from Tudor times and would have been played not only by Thomas Tallis, whose influence was invaluable to the development and flowering of the golden age of Tudor music under Elizabeth I, but by the Princesses Mary and Elizabeth while they lived at Greenwich Palace and received musical tuition under the composer's guidance. When the palace chapel's roof collapsed in 1552 one of the keyboards was saved and eventually found its way to St Alfege's, which was built by Sir Nicholas Hawksmoor between 1711 and 1714, and there it resides today, complete with its curious arrangement of reverse colour keys, some of which are split to achieve sharps, and a Middle D which is for some reason noticeably more worn than the usual Middle C. Nor was the roofing collapse of 1552 the keyboard's only narrow escape, for in 1941 it survived a direct hit on its current home from a German bomb.

Like Thomas Tallis's own music, then, the keyboard has proved a survivor against the odds. For while Tallis today occupies a primary place in anthologies of English church music, and is considered among the best of England's early composers, it was only with the publication in 1928 of his collected works in the series *Tudor Church Music* that easy access to his compositions became possible at all. Probably born about 1505, nothing is known of his parents, place of origin, or early education, and the date of his birth can only be conjectured from the fact that one of his works was copied into a music manuscript (British Library, MS Harley 1709), apparently in the later 1520s. What we do know, however, is that Tallis was a

direct beneficiary of the musical tradition established at the English court by Henry VIII and that he not only composed and performed for the king but taught all three of his children after his appointment as a Gentleman of the Chapel Royal in 1543. In riding out the tumultuous religious changes of the reigns of Edward VI, Mary I and Elizabeth, moreover, the composer would prove infinitely adaptable in tailoring his musical repertoire to suit the prevailing climate at any one time, notwithstanding his own allegiance to Roman Catholicism.

Perhaps it was hardly surprising that Tallis should have secured so firm a place at the English court throughout such a period, for his talent was manifest, and patronage of the arts was universally perceived as the hallmark of any truly accomplished Renaissance prince. 'A prince,' wrote Niccolò Machiavelli in 1513, 'should show himself a lover of the virtues, giving recognition to virtuous men, and he should honour those who are excellent in an art.' So while Edward IV had employed only five musicians, his grandson, Henry VIII, increased the total to fifty-eight – and this was no mere exercise in empty posturing, since Henry's personal interest in music was apparent from an early age. He had, after all, received a thorough musical education and was accomplished at both the lute and organ, as well as the virginal. As a young man, too, the king composed a good deal of music, including songs such as *Pastime with Good Company* and motets like *O Lord, the Maker of all Things* – though, contrary to popular belief, there is no evidence to substantiate his connection with either the melody or the words of *Greensleeves*.

If Tudor monarchs valued music, however, the lot of their musicians did not always altogether reflect this. For while musicians attached to the privy chamber enjoyed the status of quasi-gentlemen or grooms, and were thus probably lodged in the royal household, instrumentalists ranked considerably below singers, and it was foreign *virtuosi* rather than native Englishmen who commanded the highest regard. Certainly Thomas Tallis, in spite of his gifts as an organist, seems to have made little financial gain from his talents, notwithstanding the fact that he and his business partner, William Byrd, held the Crown Patent for the printing of music and lined music paper for twenty-one years. Indeed, in June 1577 the two patentees petitioned the Crown for a lease in reversion, claiming to have 'fallen out to our great loss and hindrance to the value of two hundred marks at least'. In the event, only one book of music was actually printed according to the terms of their licence – a collection of Latin motets entitled *Cantiones quae ab argumento sacrae vocantur* – and even this was published at a financial loss. In the meantime, Tallis made little money from his tuition of Henry VIII's daughters either, and there is therefore no small irony that the musician's mortal remains should reside today in the same chancel of St Alfege's Church as the single keyboard upon which he once taught them.

53

Misericord depicting a chained bear

A misericord, or 'mercy seat', is a bracketed ledge affixed to the underside of a choir stall, forming a secondary high-level support when the stall is tilted upwards and thereby providing a measure of comfort for weary choristers who were technically required to stand throughout the Mass. But since misericords were wholly out of sight when the seats were turned down, the carvers who fashioned them were at liberty to give free rein to their imaginations, with the result that these objects provide a tantalising wealth of information about the pastimes, myths and popular culture of the day. And few are finer or more revealing than those in the Tunstall Chapel of University College, Durham. Slightly older than the chapel itself, they were made in the early sixteenth century for the Bishop's Castle at Auckland, before their transfer by Bishop Cuthbert Tunstall who plainly prized them as artistic works in their own right. The chained bear depicted here, moreover, is arguably one of the finest and most significant of all, demonstrating not only the considerable skill of the carver but also the Tudor obsession with a 'sport' that thrived in all parts of the kingdom on a scale that is likely both to surprise and appal modern observers.

Until its prohibition in 1835 by the Cruelty to Animals Act – an event which provoked one Member of Parliament to proclaim that 'the British constitution must stand or fall with the British bear garden' – bear-baiting had remained a common form of entertainment, and such was its popularity in Tudor times that from around 1540 onwards purpose-built arenas, some holding more than a thousand people, were being constructed for the spectacle in London. By far the most famous of these was the Paris Gardens at Bankside, lying to the west of the liberty of the Clink in

Southwark, which stood outside the city boundaries and therefore beyond the supervision of the municipal authorities. Notorious as a location for loose living and excess, ambassadors met their spies and agents there, it was said, and on 7 September 1601 Sir Walter Raleigh was also present among the baying crowds to witness the drama and agony in the company of his guest, the Duke of Biron.

The carefree cruelty involved has lost nothing of its impact across the centuries. Within the high fenced area of the pit and amid the raised spectator seating, the bear was chained by either the leg or neck to a post, after which its muzzle was removed and it was subjected to frenzied attack by a number of well-trained hunting dogs – usually 'bandogs' (mastiffs), or Old English bulldogs – which would be replaced as they became tired or were wounded or killed. At a length of some 5m or so, the chain allowed the bear enough movement to threaten the dogs, but it was common for the tormented animal to be blinded or to have its teeth filed down in advance of the conflict. The whipping of blinded bears, such as the renowned 'Harry Hunks', who was scourged 'till the blood ran down his shoulders', was another feature of the entertainment, and rosettes were often affixed between the animal's eyes, which became a primary target for the attacking dogs.

'It was,' wrote Robert Laneham in 1575:

Jeffrey Veitch

A sport very pleasant, of these beasts, to see the bear with his pink eyes leering after his enemies' approach, the nimbleness and wayt of the dog to take his advantage, and the force and experience of the bear again to avoid the assaults.

But a few lone voices were raised nevertheless against the practice, particularly among Puritans who condemned it as a distraction from pious observance. Indeed, when a stand collapsed at the Paris Gardens on 12 January 1583, resulting in the deaths of seven people and injury to countless others, it was viewed by the godly minority as a sign of divine anger, though not so much for the cruelty involved but rather because the bear-baiting was taking place on a Sunday. Certainly, according to the Reverend John Field's account of the event, there was little doubt regarding the tragedy's cause. 'The yeard, standings and galleries being ful fraught' and the crowd 'being now amidest their joilty, when the dogs and Bear were in the chiefest Batel,' he wrote, 'the mighty hand of God' came 'uppon them'.

And there were, it seems, other occasions when the bears themselves delivered retribution without recourse to the Almighty's intervention. In 1563, for instance, an unfortunate widow called Agnes Rapte was killed by Lord Bergavenny's bear when it broke loose at his house at Birling, Kent, while on another occasion wretched Agnes Owen from Herefordshire was done to death in her very own bed by a runaway. Nor were the offending creatures always made to pay the ultimate price for such misdeeds. For when one bear saw fit to bite a man to death in Oxford in 1565, it was taken into royal custody rather than punished, no doubt because it was worth all of 26s 8d – some six months' wages for the average labourer.

54
Hawking vervel

Of all those who made up the boisterous community of 'henchmen' and 'boon companions' that surrounded the young Henry VIII, one in particular would exercise a lifelong influence upon him. Charles Brandon was seven years older than the king and in all respects the kind of dashing, reckless individual whom any hot-blooded boy with a showy streak was sure to follow. Tall, broad-shouldered, black-haired, spade-bearded, extrovert and glamorous, Brandon's gifts of mind were, it is true, few, but he more than made up for this by sharing to the full his royal companion's marked physical exuberance and headstrong delight in tilting, jousting, soldiering and, last but not least, hunting. 'By God's Body', declared an anonymous gentleman of precisely Brandon's temperament in 1517:

> I would rather that my son should hang than study literature. It behoves the sons of gentlemen to blow horn calls correctly, to hunt skilfully, to train a hawk well and carry it elegantly. But the study of literature should be left to clodhoppers.

And the hawking vervel pictured here, from both front and reverse, could not provide a more poignant or appropriate link with both Brandon and the entire noble class he typified.

Vervels were used to confirm the identity and ownership of birds of prey, and this one, discovered by a metal detector enthusiast in December 2012, is of particular rarity and interest. Made of silver-gilt and weighing 2g, the 23mm ring was worn around the bird's leg, and was unearthed in the Colney area of Norfolk just outside Norwich. Curiously, it carries not only the arms of Brandon on one side but those of the king on the other, and even more intriguing is the question of how it came to be deposited in its final resting place at all, since birds of prey were usually recovered when they died during a hunt. One explanation is that the unfortunate

hawk came to grief in full flight and fell into a bush or a well wooded area, so that it rotted away, leaving the vervel to find its way into the soil of the ploughed field where it was eventually discovered almost five centuries later. Whatever the answer, it has subsequently arrived at the British Museum pending a report to be prepared for a treasure trove inquest by the Norfolk coroner.

Unlike today, of course, hunting of any kind was considered a wholly appropriate pastime for any Tudor gentleman, and despite the protests of a few well-intentioned humanists like Sir Thomas More, an immense body of chivalric literature depicted it not only as a worthy pursuit in its own right but as an implicitly moral one embodying the highest virtues of knighthood and nobility. 'Idlenes', declared Henry VIII, was 'the ground of all vyce' and, as such, hunting allowed him 'to exercise that thing that shal be honourable and profitable'. Equally, hunting was justified by contemporaries as a training for warfare, which was still regarded as the gentleman's principal calling. 'Knightes', wrote Ramon Lull in a book brought to the early Tudor reading public by William Caxton, 'ougt to hunte at hertes, at bores and other wyld bestes, for in doynge these thynges the knyghtes exercyse them to armes'.

Meanwhile, of course, if any further reason were needed, there was also the obvious connection between exercise and health to justify the sprees of casual slaughter to which the Tudor ruling class found itself so addicted. The pursuit of animals on horseback or on foot, more than other type of hunting, was, in the view of Andrew Boorde, especially important because it provided 'valiaunt motion of the spirites' by which all thinges superfluous be expelled, and the conduits of the body clensed'. Even young children were encouraged to develop their bodies, as well as their moral fibre, by vigorous participation in the chase. In 1525 Henry VIII was informed that his 6-year-old son, the Duke of Richmond, though ill and travelling in a litter for some miles, had shot a deer by himself in Clyff Park in Northamptonshire, while the king's chief minister, Thomas Cromwell, was kept regularly informed of his son Gregory's progress at hunting, as well as his studies at school.

And if Tudor gentlemen valued their sons above all else, their hunting dogs may well, in some cases, have come a close second. Though greyhounds in particular had nearly suffered extinction during times of famine in the Middle Ages, they had been saved by members of the clergy who bred them for the nobility, and they had by Tudor times attained an almost iconic status. Employed as emblems, often on tombs, they lay at the feet of the effigies of dead gentlemen, symbolising for posterity the knightly virtues of loyalty and bravery, and encapsulating in the process the ideal of the aristocratic way of life. At a time, too, when ladies' tombs were duly embellished with little lapdogs, representing marital faithfulness and domestic virtue, what, perhaps, could have been more appropriate?

55

Dice and shaker

Sometimes the most innocent and humdrum of objects assumes a function and significance far outside its original intended purpose, and this bird seed pot, found on the Thames foreshore, is undeniably a case in point. For it was found with a set of twenty-four false dice inside, and had clearly come to serve as a shaker for one of the many dishonest gamblers who thrived in Tudor England. Dating from the late fifteenth century, the pot itself is pewter and decorated on the front with an eagle and a lozenge pattern, but it is the small bone dice that hide the most intriguing secrets of all, since x-rays show that some had been weighted with drops of mercury to ensure that they would fall the same way every time. Eleven of them were 'loaded' in this way to show five or six, others the numbers one or two, and this was not the only crooked trick in the former owner's repertoire, for three other dice have the numbers one to three repeated so that they always fall on low numbers, while a further three display only the numbers four to six. Such dice were known as low or high 'despatchers', and could be skilfully deployed to fool any sufficiently gullible punter that the 'professional' had singled out in advance. And if contemporary accounts of cheating and fighting over the use of counterfeit dice are any guide, their use was exceptionally common. Indeed, such dice even had their own distinctive nickname, 'fulhams', which appears to suggest that the modern-day London borough, which was then an inconspicuous Thames-side village, was probably notorious as the haunt of villainous sharpers.

However, it was by no means only hucksters and credulous half-wits who shared a consuming passion for what contemporaries termed 'gaming'. 'Girls', wrote the scholar Erasmus in 1529, 'today take up dice, cards and other masculine amusements', and his disapproval was enough for him to devote an entire section of his *Colloquies* to a dialogue on 'knucklebones, or the game of tali', which was particularly popular at that time. In 1495, moreover, Henry VII's Parliament saw fit to decree that:

> No apprentice, agricultural worker, labourer or employee in a craft shall play at the tables from 10 January next except for food and drink only, or at tennis, closh, dice, cards, bowls or any other illegal game in any way other than at Christmas.

Yet, as the privy purse accounts make clear, this did not prevent the king himself from gambling heavily throughout the year, not only on traditional games of chance but also on tennis and archery. And the same was no less true of Henry VIII or his daughter Mary who was also inclined to bet on games of bowls. In 1540, for example, during one particularly engrossing game, she even resorted to asking servants for stake money, only to be refused, whereupon she wagered a free breakfast the next day. 'Payed for a brekefaste loste at Bolling by my lady maryes grace', her accounts duly recorded after her defeat.

Predictably, perhaps, heavy bets were also placed on horse racing; and billiards, or 'balliards' as it was known to contemporaries, was another favourite game that frequently involved wagering. Certainly, Mary, Queen of Scots appears to have been an enthusiast, for only a month before her execution, she complained that her table had been taken away, while the accounts of the Duke of Norfolk make it clear that in 1588 he, too, owned 'a billyard bord covered with a green cloth ... three billyard sticks and eleven balls of yvery'. Likewise, a type of ten-pin bowling, known as 'clash', where skittles were knocked down with a ball, was often played for money, as were board games like 'merrills' – a crude form of backgammon – and draughts, which was commonly known at the time by its French name of 'dames'. A merrills board was found carved into a barrel lid by sailors on the *Mary Rose*, while others, more surprisingly still, have also been found scratched into cloister seats at Westminster Abbey and in several cathedrals.

But it was dicing, and in particular the game of hazard, that provoked the most widespread social concern. Played long before and after the Tudor period, the game was mentioned in Chaucer's *Canterbury Tales*, but appears to have followed no clearly defined rules beyond attempting to throw a specified number in order to win or 'nick' the game outright. Beyond this, complex computations were involved in gaining further throws until the game was eventually won or lost. Utterly addictive to those who came under its spell, it seems, indeed, that the etymology of the modern term 'hazard' may well be traced to the Spanish *azar*, meaning an unfortunate dice roll, or the Arabic word for dice, *az-zahr* (الزهر). In any event, the modern expression 'at sixes and sevens' certainly appears to be related to it, for it was first employed by Chaucer in relation to an entire fortune being 'set upon six and seven'.

56

Playing cards

These playing cards, dating back to the time of Lady Margaret Beaufort (1443–1509), the mother of Henry VII, were found in the Muniment Room at Christ's College, Cambridge, during renovation works in the 1960s and now reside in the college library. Lady Margaret established the college in 1505, and the knave pictured here, like the other three 'face' cards of royal characters in the pack, wears a costume consistent with those worn at her son's court. The other cards, however, are thought to date from around 1515. As coloured woodblock printing was not yet widespread, such cards were hand-painted and therefore only available to the wealthy, and since card-playing was a comparatively new pastime, the names of the cards and even the total number in a pack varied, although the suits, which may well have originated with French card-makers such as Valery Faucil of Rouen, do appear to have been standardised by this time. Certainly, references to card-playing are few and far between before the late fourteenth century and it was not until almost a hundred years later, in 1495, that Henry VII forbade servants and apprentices to play cards other than at Christmas, which suggests that in England at least, they did not appear until the 1400s.

One of the first English references to 'card-playing' is made in a letter from John Paston to his wife Margaret around 1459. She had enquired as to what entertainments a recently widowed neighbour might reasonably enjoy, to which he responded that 'although lowde dysports' such as dancing should be avoided, chess, tables and cards might be not be inappropriate. And while the Franciscan friar and future saint, Bernardino da Siena, preached so successfully against gaming in Bologna that the people threw thousands of cards on to a great bonfire in the public square, recreational play continued to grow in popularity, so that when the fifteenth-century artist Antonio Cicognara painted a set of tarot cards, which at that time were used for gaming rather than divination, and presented

them to Cardinal Ascanio Sforza, the cardinal evidently felt no qualms in asking the artist to make similar packs for his sisters, who were nuns in the Augustinian convent in Cremona – though not, perhaps, without certain long-term consequences. For women often became particularly avid card players, and Mary Tudor was only one of a number to run up substantial debts 'for the playe at cardes', while the pious archduchess Johanna of Austria in her turn would establish a sturdy card-sharping reputation upon the popular French game of piquet.

Queen Mary was by no means the only Tudor monarch to develop a weakness for wagering with her privy purse. During the reign of Henry VII (whose wife Elizabeth of York was also a keen gambler and became the standard image for the queen on playing cards), there are several notices of money issued to cover their majesties' losses. In the ninth year of his reign, on 26 December, for instance, there is a record relating to a payment of 100s made for the purpose of playing at cards, and games of chance were eventually to become so popular at court that the Knight Marshall of the Household even acted as a bookmaker at tournaments. At a banquet of 1511, moreover, it was Henry VIII's turn to engage in a particularly heavy spell of wagering, apparently egged on by a group of Italian bankers. Having lost a considerable amount of money, however, and feeling that he had been cheated by his Italian playmates, he then proceeded to ban them from the palace.

The king's weakness for 'primero' is likely to have done the damage on this occasion and the game's notoriety was soon a watchword for the dangers of gaming in general. 'I never prospered since I forswore myself at Primero', declares Falstaff, and it was not without good reason that Shakespeare depicted the king playing the game with his brother-in-law Charles Brandon, Duke of Suffolk, though if Tudor monarchs regularly played and lost at cards, one at least, with an eagle eye for opportunity, saw other possibilities in making money from them with rather more certainty of the outcome. For in 1598, in return for an appropriate payment, Elizabeth I granted Edward Darcy a twenty-one-year monopoly on the import, manufacture and sale of both cards and dice. Following his predecessor's example, James I would impose a tax on cards that had the curious side-effect of stipulating that an ornate insignia be displayed on the ace of spades as proof of payment by the manufacturer. The result was a change in the card's appearance, which has remained with us to this day. Indeed, until 4 August 1960, all decks of playing cards printed and sold in the United Kingdom continued to be subject to taxable duty and were made to carry a similar indication of the name of the printer.

57

World's oldest football

This ball, which is made from leather on the outside and a pig's bladder on the inside, was found at Stirling Castle in the 1970s, snugly tucked up in the rafters of a bedroom that had once belonged to Mary, Queen of Scots. Lying concealed since it had been accidentally kicked there some time before the 1540s when the ceiling was enclosed with wooden panels, it has a strong claim to be the oldest object of its kind ever found anywhere in the world and confirms the antiquity of football itself. Certainly, manuscript accounts from King James IV of Scotland show that he had paid 2s for a bag of 'fut ballis' as early as 11 April 1497, and records also suggest that Queen Mary was a keen spectator of the game. The diary of Sir Francis Knollys, who was ordered by Queen Elizabeth I to hold Queen Mary under house arrest in Carlisle when she fled Scotland after being forced to abdicate amid civil rebellion, contains an account of a game played before her in 1568, where players competed with a ball using only their feet 'very strongly, nimbly, and skilfully'. Played at Carlisle Castle on a pitch half the size of its modern equivalent, the game had twenty players and lasted two hours – the same duration as that of the first official association football match in Scotland between Queen's Park and Thistle FC in 1868. And there are further accounts of another game in the early 1580s at which a foul quarrel between the 5th Earl of Bothwell and another man on the pitch ended with demands for a duel to the death.

South of the border, meanwhile, accounts of early football matches were appearing as early as 1514. The poet Alexander Barclay relates how 'they get the bladder and blowe it great and thin, with many beanes and peason put within'. 'It ratleth, shineth and soundeth clere and fayre,' he continued, 'while it is throwen and caste up in the eyre' and 'eche one

Smith Art gallery & Museum, Stirling

contendeth and hath a great delite, with foote and hande the bladder for to smite'. The first record of a pair of football boots occurred when Henry VIII placed an order from the Great Wardrobe in 1526, at which time the royal shopping list for footwear included forty-five velvet pairs of shoes for everyday use, as well as one leather pair 'for football'. Naturally enough, the fact that Henry's son, the future Edward VI, would eventually ban the game in 1548 on the grounds that it encouraged riots, makes this particular entry all the more curious.

And football's reputation for violence would persist in England throughout the sixteenth century, notwithstanding the few lone voices raised in its defence. In 1534, for instance, Sir Thomas Elyot was prepared in his *Castell of Helth* to acknowledge the virtue of the game as a means of 'vehement exercise', though only three years earlier in *The Boke named The Governour* he had roundly condemned it, noting that, unlike archery, there was 'nothinge but beastly furie and exstreme violence' in the game. In concluding at that time, moreover, that football should therefore be 'put in perpetuall silence', Elyot was echoing the universal censure of 'responsible' opinion. And when in 1582 Richard Mulcaster, headmaster of Merchant Taylors School in London, chose football to emphasise the importance of physical as well as academic education, he was nevertheless only condoning an organised, umpired version of the game conducted by small teams playing in formation.

It was in Italy in 1580 that the first official rules of what natives called *calcio Fiorentino*, or 'Florentine kick', were first recorded. Involving teams of twenty-seven kicking and carrying a ball in a giant sandpit set up in the Piazza Santa Croce in the centre of Florence, the object was to aim for a designated point on the perimeter of the sandpit. But the game, it seems, had been developing in this area of Europe long before, so that in 1555 Antonio Scaino found a ready audience for his treatise *Del Giuoco della Palla*, or 'On the Game of the Ball'. According to Scaino, the game was popular with students and could be played with any number of players. Yet the only rules mentioned in his account were that the ball could not be thrown by hand and that weapons could not be brought on to the field.

And so, in spite of the best efforts of more refined souls, the game's reputation for mayhem continued. Certainly, football, or *pila pedalis*, had been strictly forbidden at St John's College, Oxford, in the 1550s, and similar decrees followed swiftly in other colleges at both Oxford and Cambridge. Moreover, when Richard Hakluyt suggested that, in 1586, men from a ship commanded by English explorer John Davis had gone ashore to play a form of football with the Inuit people of Greenland, one can only guess at the likely casualty rate among the unsuspecting natives.

Health
and
Healing

58

Medicine chest

Made for Vincenzo Giustiniani, the banker, art collector and last Genoese governor of the island of Chios in the eastern Aegean Sea, this medicine chest, which dates from the mid-1560s and measures nearly 1m in length, still holds 126 bottles and pots for drugs, some of which appear to contain their original sixteenth-century contents, including rhubarb powder, ointment for worms, juniper water and mustard oil. On a box from the middle drawer is painted the device of Chios – a black eagle above a three-towered castle – and although the painting on the inside of the lid is from a later date, the chest itself, which was acquired by Henry Wellcome in 1924, provides a fascinating and unique window upon the kind of medicines known not only to Italian doctors but to distinguished Tudor physicians, such as Thomas Linacre, who had studied at the University of Padua some years earlier and was instrumental in the creation of the College of Physicians by royal charter in 1518.

Like all Tudor physicians, Linacre distanced himself from the more practical aspects of his craft, and especially surgery. Indeed, most contemporary practitioners, unlike their barber-surgeon counterparts, rarely deigned to touch a patient, save for taking a pulse or checking a fever, relying instead upon the examination of excrement and urine in order to render a diagnosis and prescribe treatment. The latter especially was considered essential in framing an accurate diagnosis, and an accomplished physician could identify more than a score of different colours and densities, and describe the significance of each. There were, for instance, five designated shades of yellow alone, four of red, and five of green – from pistachio to rainbow to verdigris to emerald through to leek – not to mention two near-black, while the liquid iself might prove thick or thin, turbid or clear, musty or semen-like, or resemble poor wine or chick-pea water. Even the sediment could be broken into ten distinct types, from flaky to fleshy to mucoid. To the trained eye – and indeed nose – such nuances might indicate dispersion of vitality, the presence of an atrabilious humour, deficient digestive power, or, when white or slightly reddish, duly herald the advent of dropsy.

Similar diagnoses were deduced from the tint of the skin. A lemon-yellow colour suggested a blockage of the liver, while a brown complexion denoted obstruction of the spleen. A black tongue, in its turn, was associated with an ardent fever, just as red cheeks betokened peripneumonia and hooked nails, phthisis. In all cases, however, the Tudor physician's first and only resort was his medicine chest. Head pains were treated with sweet-smelling herbs such as rose, lavender, sage and bay, and stomach pains and sickness with wormwood, mint and balm. Lung problems were alleviated by liquorice and comfrey. Vinegar was used as a cleansing agent to kill disease, along with a variety of purgatives designed to restore the natural balance of the so-called 'four humours' – yellow bile, black bile, blood and phlegm – upon which good health depended.

And since illnesses of virtually all kinds were thought to derive from blockages or obstructions, it followed that treatment hinged largely upon the restoration of a healthy flow of the humours by means of purgation of various sorts. Above all, the violent purging of the bowels or the stomach could be expected to create a 'sympathetic' chain of unblockings, as stagnant, corrupt, or poisoned humours were made to flow away. Bloodletting, in its turn, was believed to remove over-heated, excessive blood, and allow congested veins to 'breathe', while'diaphoretics' encouraged copious sweating and aimed to remove deep-seated poisons to the outer parts of the body, which could then be evacuated as sweat. In the meantime, cordials could be employed to strengthen the patient and lift the spirits – not least because most were liberally laced with alcohol.

The administration of such 'physick', however, was no random matter, since it was intimately linked in contemporary medical theory to the influence of the zodiac upon the humours. A diagnosing physician in Tudor times would therefore invariably wish to know the 'birth time' of the disease – namely, the precise moment at which the patient took to his or her bed. And just as astrology was vital to diagnosis, so it also affected treatment and prognosis. Was the patient strong enough, for example, to survive his ailment until the life-giving influence of the Sun or Jupiter counteracted the currently malign configuration of the zodiac? In the process, the sixteenth-century doctor came to look as intently upon the daily movement of the heavens as he did upon the anatomy and physiology of those unfortunates he treated. 'A calendar, a calendar!' declares Bottom in Act 3 Scene 1 of *A Midsummer Night's Dream*. 'Find out moonshine, find out moonshine.' And in doing so, he could well have been echoing any physician of his day, whether in a London back street or the royal court itself.

59

Urethral syringe

'If I were asked which is the most destructive of all diseases,' wrote Desiderius Erasmus in 1520, 'I should unhesitatingly reply, it is that which for some years has been raging with impunity.' The malady to which the Dutchman referred was the 'great pox' or *grande verole*, which would finally be dubbed syphilis by Girolamo Fracastoro some ten years later. It had made its sudden and terrifying impact upon Europe in 1495, wreaking havoc among Charles VIII's French army during the invasion of Naples at the time of the First Italian War, and its reputation as a ruthless and harrowing killer of its victims was soon vividly imprinted on contemporaries of all nations and classes. 'On their flippant way through Italy', Voltaire would declare later, 'the French carelessly picked up Genoa, Naples and syphilis. Then they were thrown out and deprived of Naples and Genoa. But they did not lose everything – syphilis went with them.' Nor did the French keep the disease to themselves, for by the end of 1495 the epidemic had spread to Switzerland and Germany before reaching England and Scotland two years later. By 1500, moreover, the Scandinavian countries, Hungary, Greece, Poland and Russia had also been infected, along with Calcutta, Africa, the near East, China and Japan, all of which found themselves stricken by yet another unwelcome side-effect of European exploration.

One contemporary sufferer, the German knight and scholar Ulrich von Hutten, described the effects in a work of 1519, entitled *De Morbo Gallico*, before dying from the disease four years later on the island of Ufenau on Lake Zurich. He spoke of terrible abscesses and sores, nocturnal bone pains – *dolores osteocopi nocturne* – muscle disease, excruciating ulcers in the bladder and various other effects upon the internal organs. Some victims, meanwhile, were stricken by unsightly skin ulcers, paralysis, gradual blindness, dementia and 'saddle nose', a grotesque deformity which occurs when the bridge of the nose caves into the face. The early

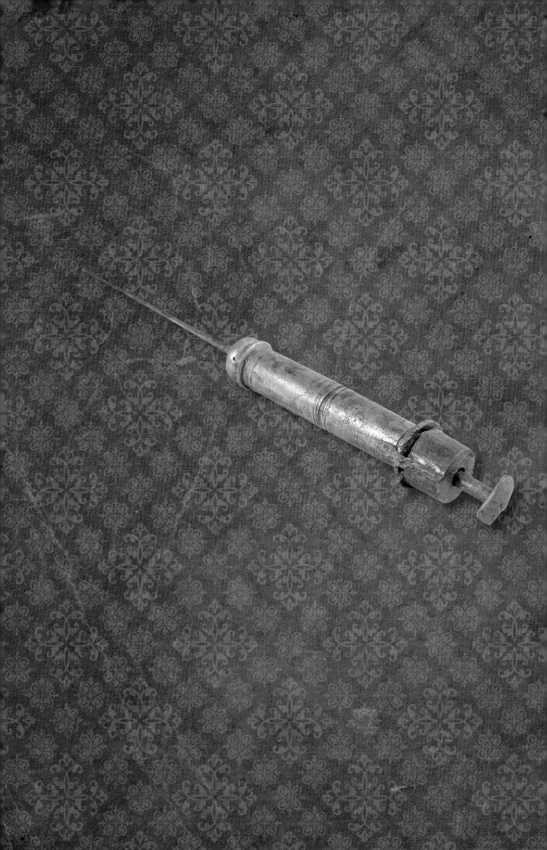

signs were genital ulcers, followed by a fever, a general rash, and joint and muscle pains, which culminated weeks or months later in large, painful and foul-smelling abscesses and sores, or pocks, all over the body. Sores became ulcers that could eat into bones and destroy lips and eyes, and often extended into the mouth and throat. It appears, from descriptions by scholars and from woodcut drawings at the time, that the disease was not only much more severe than its equivalent today, with a higher and more rapid mortality, but also more easily spread, possibly because it was a new disease and the population had no immunity against it.

Until the development of the drug salvarsan by Paul Ehrlich in 1909, the disease remained every bit as incurable as it was terrifying, though this did not prevent contemporaries from employing a number of medicines. The Spanish priest Francisco Delicado, for instance, who was himself a sufferer, favoured the use of *guiaicum* or 'holy wood' in his treatise of 1525, *El modo de adoperare el legno de India*, while Nicholas Culpeper recommended the use of heartsease (wild pansy), a herb with antimicrobial agents. But the most commonly prescribed remedy remained mercury, administered in various fashions, whether by mouth, by application to the skin, or by means of suffumigation, which involved enclosing all but the heads of patients in sealed boxes heated by fire, so that their bodies could be exposed to the vaporising liquid metal within.

Last but not least, mercury was also administered by means of syringes like the one pictured here, which was retrieved in remarkable condition from the wreck of the *Mary Rose* and whose function requires little explanation. Inserted directly into the urethra, an object of this kind could deliver its payload straight to the primary location of the infection, for if contemporaries had little or no knowledge of effective treatment, they had every appreciation of how sufferers came to contract the disease in the first place. Jacques de Bethencourt, in his work of 1527 entitled *Nouveau Cartme de Penitence* or 'New Litany of Penitence', had first introduced the term 'venereal disease', on the grounds that syphilis was 'the malady of Venus', arising from 'illicit love'. But if the term itself was new, the link between sexual intercourse and infection was already common knowledge. 'One night with Venus,' ran the contemporary saying, 'a lifetime on Mercury'.

A lifetime on such a toxic substance, moreover, was unlikely to be a long one, since kidney failure and sundry neuropathies, not to mention lesser consequences like severe mouth ulcers and loss of teeth, were only some of mercury's side-effects, though this was of small concern to a physician like de Bethencourt, whose learned treatise betrayed no compunction in considering what level of suffering a patient should be allowed to endure, in order to 'be taught a necessary lesson' for creating their own predicament.

60

Condom

Contraception, like abortion, was illegal in sixteenth-century England, though some women certainly employed it, since many of those unfortunates executed as witches at the end of the Tudor period were accused of involvement in both. However, aside from the so-called 'rhythm method' and prolonged breastfeeding, which was widely known to reduce fertility, women also resorted to various types of vaginal inserts, or pessaries, including small knots of wool soaked in vinegar or small bundles of herbs. Female folklore, meanwhile, encompassed more unusual methods, including the insertion of beeswax, small stones, or even wooden blocks, while other sources advised the wearing of amulets, such as the testicles of a weasel, the dried liver of a black cat, and the anus of a hare around the neck or thigh.

For Tudor men, however, who often regarded female physiology as mysterious and potentially threatening, any interference with the natural process of conception was akin to witchcraft, and as late as the eighteenth century Daniel Defoe was comparing such activity to infanticide. In consequence, though glans condoms made of oiled silk paper, lamb intestines, tortoise shell or animal horn had been known in Asia prior to the fifteenth century, their use for birth control in England and, for that matter, Europe as a whole appears to have been minimal. Indeed, the first indication of their employment for contraception is not recorded until the publication in 1605 of *De iustitia et iure* – 'On Justice and Law' – by the Catholic theologian Leonardus Lessius, who condemned them as immoral. Furthermore, the first explicit suggestion in literature that *un petit linge* (a small cloth) might be profitably employed to prevent pregnancy does not occur until 1655 with the work attributed to Michel Millot and Jean L'Ange, entitled *L'Ecole des Filles*, although the oldest condoms ever excavated in England date to slightly earlier. Made from animal and fish membrane, the one pictured here, for example, was found with others of the same type in 1985 in a cesspit located in the Great Tower of Dudley Castle, where it had been deposited some time before 1646, when the castle was surrendered to the Parliamentarians during the English Civil War.

A similar condom, discovered at Lund in Sweden and dating back to 1640, is now generally considered the oldest surviving item of its kind in the world. Its original instruction manual, written in Latin, suggests, moreover, that it was not only reusable but intended to be immersed in warm milk prior to use, as a means of countering infectious diseases. And in this last respect especially, it is directly related to earlier examples beginning to be popularised across much of Europe in the previous century. For, while condoms had been widely condemned as contraceptives, their use for the purpose of disease prevention was certainly known to Tudor men and women.

As early as 1564 Gabriele Fallopio's *De Morbo Gallico* had attempted to popularise their function. Published two years after its author's death, the book described linen sheaths soaked in a solution of salt and herbs which had been allowed to dry before they were attached to the glans of the penis by means of a ribbon. By using such sheaths, Fallopio contended, the risk of contracting syphilis from intercourse could be effectively eradicated: a claim which he reinforced by reference to one of the earliest experimental trials on record. 'I tried the procedure on 1,100 men and I call immortal God to witness that not one of them was infected.' The ribbon, meanwhile, was to be coloured pink, in order to appeal to the female involved.

This is not to say, of course, that contraceptives of this kind were common. On the contrary, the apparent absence of condoms or any other effective or socially acceptable form of contraception was continuing to make itself felt in England particularly where, as Richard Hakluyt rightly observed, 'wee are growen more populous than ever heretofore'. From a manuscript in the Bodleian Library (MS Ashmole 765, fo. 19v), we learn that Cheshire women were considered both 'frutefull in bearing of children after they be married, and sometimes beffore', while in seven local parishes analysed over the period 1550–99 nearly one third of the children born to newly married couples arrived after less than nine months – a trend broadly in keeping, it seems, with the country at large.

As the sap rose, however, so too, in some quarters, did interest in how it might be managed by illicit means. It was no coincidence that Edmund Spenser's *Fairie Queene* made reference to a list of herbs with allegedly contraceptive properties, and no real surprise either that a vicar – from Cheshire, predictably enough – should have stood accused in 1590 as 'an instructor of young folks how to commit the syn of adultrie or fornication and not to beget children', though in the second respect at least, his counsel was plainly wanting.

61

Apothecary jar

This cylindrical, tin-glazed earthenware jar, known as an *albarello*, was designed to hold apothecaries' ointments and dry drugs. Produced in Faenza, Italy, around 1480, it is typical of large numbers of similar items that became common in England not only during the Tudor period but until well into the eighteenth century and beyond. Since such jars served both a decorative and functional purpose in traditional apothecary shops, they were often colourfully painted like this one, and common design themes included floral motifs against a white background, as well as more elaborate designs such as portraits of cherubs or priests. Florence, Venice, Gerace and Palermo were also main production centres, each exhibiting their own distinctions, and similar variations in height, ranging from 10cm to 40cm, can also be seen according to region. More often than not, however, the jars were sealed with leather, or alternatively a piece of parchment tied with a piece of cord, detailing what was inside.

In this case, the contents are described as *syrupus acetositatis citriorum*, or 'syrup of lemon juice', which was used to treat inflammation, calm fevers, quench thirst, and counteract drunkenness and dizziness. Not all jars were filled with such innocuous substances, however, for many early modern apothecaries, like their predecessors in antiquity, made extensive use of human faeces, urine, saliva and ear wax. Inflammation of the throat was treated by a mixture of dried children's excrement and honey, while a combination of mud and ear wax was employed to cure migraines. Saliva – preferably that of a 'fasting young man' – was recommended for dog bites and itchy rashes, and lepers were encouraged to soak their limbs in human blood, which was also drunk by patients suffering from any kind of debilitating weakness. Dysentery, in its turn, advised one contemporary text, was to be tackled by crow droppings dissolved in wine, and jaundice by the chopped meat of geese and 'well-nourished kittens', roasted and distilled.

Plainly, the gulf between the Tudor apothecary and the modern pharmacist was considerable. 'Take a half measure of earthworms and cold

wash them diligently in white wine', began one standard prescription for 'comforting cold nerves' and joint pain, and the remedy of 'the powdered skull of a man killed in war' as a cure for malaria, or 'tertian fever' as it was known, was hardly more promising. Yet aniseed was certainly effective for gastric wind and coughs, and the spiders and cobwebs which also featured so frequently in Tudor apothecaries' potions and lotions are now known to contain antiseptic properties. As the sixteenth century progressed, moreover, exotic herbs and spices from all over Africa and the Far East – many with genuinely therapeutic qualities – found their way on to apothecaries' shelves from Spain and Portugal in particular. And the prescription of colchium for gout still persists today.

Nor should it be imagined that all apothecaries were entirely untrained. On the contrary, they were expected to undergo an apprenticeship lasting seven years, which enabled them to fulfil a role not unlike that of the modern general practitioner, irrespective of the fact that overall control of medical practice was retained by the College of Physicians. In 1600, interestingly enough, apothecaries' charges ranged from 8s to 20s in comparison to physicians' rates of between 10s and 13s, and though by 1617 there was widespread recognition that 'very many empiricks and unskilled and ignorant men' were active in the field, William Bulleyn's *Government of Health*, published in 1558, had readily acknowledged the value of those apothecaries who saw it as their duty to 'first serve God', 'pity the poor' and 'delyte to reede' the work of experts in their field. Above all, wrote Bulleyn, it was the apothecary's main duty to 'invent medicines', and in this respect especially, he would not be disappointed. Indeed, the Tudor apothecary, untrammelled by formal supervision of any kind, was ever susceptible to every conceivable fad and fancy, not the least of which was an unquestioning advocacy of the health-enhancing virtues of tobacco.

Hailed for its beneficial effects upon the memory, for curing cataracts, and for mitigating headaches and asthma, tobacco was also used for dealing with toothache, worms, lockjaw, bad breath and even cancer. Tobacco oil, in its turn, was used on pimples and administered in ear drops to cure deafness, while tobacco salt, it was said, whitened teeth and tobacco syrup arrested colds. Indeed, Thomas Hariot, a friend of Sir Walter Raleigh, wrote that tobacco smoke was the surest remedy of any kind for sores, wounds, throat and chest infections and the plague. Tobacco, he declared after his visit to America in 1585, 'purgeth superfluous fleame & other grosse humors' and 'openeth all the pores & passages of the body'. True to his principles, therefore, he became an avid smoker, only to die of a cancerous ulcer in his nose, becoming probably the first person in England to die of a smoking-related disease.

J. Paul Getty Museum

62

Arrow remover

Like many of his contemporaries, the Protestant bishop and martyr Hugh Latimer had been taught to use a longbow from an early age by his own yeoman father. 'For men,' he observed, 'shall never shoot well unless they be brought up to it.' And this, predictably enough, was a sentiment fully endorsed by the government of the day. In 1514, indeed, Henry VIII's Act for the Maintenance of Archery had stipulated that all males over the age of 11, 'not lame nor having no lawfull impediment', were to undertake regular training with the deadly longbow, with a view to sustaining a force of archers that had been feared and renowned throughout the Hundred Years War. For, in the hands of an expert, an arrow could be shot through a solid oak door 8cm thick, and inflict deadly wounds over considerable distances; the furthest target on the London practice grounds of Finsbury Fields in the sixteenth century extended some 345 yards (315m).

Not altogether surprisingly, therefore, the problem of arrow removal from wounded victims had been a pressing concern for surgeons over many years; bows were commonly used for hunting as well as warfare and accidents were frequent. During the late medieval period specialised tools had been developed to deal with arrows lodged in places where bone prevented them from being pushed through the surrounding flesh in the usual manner. The royal physician John Bradmore, for instance, left a famous account of how he dealt with the facial wound of the future Henry V at the Battle of Shrewsbury in 1403. The arrow had penetrated to a depth of 15cm, fixing in the bone at the back of his skull, and necessitated the insertion of specially designed tongs, complete with a screw mechanism to assist their operation. Having cut through the prince's face to the depth of the wound, Bradmore then 'put these tongs in at an angle in the same way as the arrow had first entered ... [moving them] to and fro, little by little (with the help of God)' to extract the arrowhead. Almost three weeks later, after the insertion of new probes to deliver a cleansing ointment of bread sops, barley, honey and turpentine oil, the wound was found to be 'perfectly well cleansed'.

Hector Cole

211

The precise design of Bradmore's tongs is uncertain, but his description is reminiscent of similar implements dating to the sixteenth century, which closely resemble the modern reproduction pictured here, with one or two minor refinements. One instrument, made in 1540, possessed sharpened edges facing outward, which could be carefully expanded after insertion into the wound by means of the screw mechanism attached to the scissor-like handles. Thereafter, the function of a central shaft was to grip the arrowhead as the tongs were withdrawn. And though we have no evidence beyond Bradmore's account of the efficacy of such a procedure, if infection was avoided, as in Henry V's case, there is little reason to believe that successes rates would have been anything other than good.

Indeed, a subsequent and equally impressive example of late medieval surgery, involving a soldier killed at the Battle of Towton in 1461, confirms that battlefield surgeons in Tudor England had a substantial amount of previous good practice to call upon. The victim had, it seems, already suffered a frightful maxillo-facial injury some years before, probably from a sword-slash down the left side of his face, smashing skull, jaw, teeth and perhaps eye socket, inevitably severing several major muscles and blood vessels. Nevertheless, the man's bleeding had been staunched and his bones skilfully reset, enabling him not only to recover but to fight again another day at Towton, where he finally fell for good.

As the Tudor period progressed, the best English surgeons were learning of a range of new techniques originating mainly on the Continent. In 1550, the first and only known kidney operation of the sixteenth century was conducted when Cardan of Milan opened a lumbar abscess and discovered eighteen stones in his patient. The surgeon Gaspare Tagliacozzi would gain such fame in Italy as a restorer of amputated noses by means of skin-grafting that patients flocked to him from all over Europe, each going away 'with as many noses as he liked'. And while English surgeons remained generally less innovative, some, at least, showed signs of not only absorbing but applying the new medical wisdom emerging in Europe. Some time before 1588 – when he first published his account – William Clowes had performed an extraordinarily dangerous thigh amputation upon an unnamed 'mayde of Hygate' in London. Using the latest techniques for haemorrhage control, Clowes and his assistants removed one of her legs above the knee, after which she made a full and rapid recovery. At the start of the century, surgery of this kind would have been little short of a death sentence.

Taboos against such surgery, though, would continue to linger after the Tudor period had come and gone. For, as John Woodall made clear in 1617, there were still those who considered it 'no small presumption to dismember the image of God'.

63

Lithotomy dilator

This harrowing array of sixteenth- and seventeenth-century surgical instruments, now in the possession of the Wellcome Trust, bears ample testimony to the rigours of early modern medicine. It includes, moving clockwise from the top left-hand corner, a double-headed bistoury, forceps for removing arrow heads, a bullet extractor, a surgical saw, two pairs of dental forceps, separated by a trepan, and the sole item dating to the Tudor period, snugly lodged at the bottom left: a lithotomy dilator. 'The cure itself is something horrible, grave, and perilous', wrote one anonymous contemporary, who had witnessed this last item in operation. 'The mind recoils at the thought of so frightful a remedy,but what remedy seems frightful when it carries hope to people in peril of death?' Nor was the commentator's observation wrong on either count, since bladder stones, which were commonplace as a result of increased water impurities, could block the flow of urine into the bladder from the kidneys, or prevent the flow of urine out of the bladder through the urethra. And in either case the results were potentially lethal. In the first instance, the kidney was slowly destroyed by pressure from the urine; in the second, the bladder would swell to bursting point, leading to infection and finally death.

Yet, at a time when medical knowledge was so restricted, the chances of successful surgical intervention still stood at no more than 10 per cent at the very most. For Tudor physicians, such stones or 'gravels' were thought to be caused by excessive build-up of humours within the urine, which in 'hot' individuals would lead to 'baking' and hardening, and result in obstruction, pain and bleeding. But while all other major operations involving incision into the abdomen or other cavities of the body were altogether beyond the capabilities of contemporary surgeons, lithotomies – from the Greek *lithos* (stone) and *tomos* (cut) – had been conducted since classical times. A medical text by Celsus, written in Rome in the first century AD, describes the operation, and even before this, the ancient

Hippocratic Oath had made reference to the procedure, albeit by way of forbidding doctors from performing it. 'I will not cut for stone,' runs the oath, 'even for the patients in whom the disease is manifest'. Instead, the operation was to be performed by 'practitioners', i.e. surgeons, whom Hippocrates clearly considered inferior in learning and status, and therefore more apt for the high-risk and altogether cruder task of probing the perineum at a time when the absence of anaesthesia merely added to the ghastliness of the whole process.

For centuries to come, the practice of removing stones continued to be disdained by university-trained physicians, whose more academic approach to their craft rendered knife-wielding the sole preserve of so-called barber-surgeons, many of whom were either itinerant or ill-qualified quacks like Chelmsford's 'shoemaker surgeon' or Worcester's 'brewer surgeon'. And while the operation itself lasted only a matter of minutes, it remained as painful, dangerous and indeed humiliating as ever, as even the briefest description makes clear. Naked from the waist down, the patient was firstly bound with straps to draw the knees up to the head, in order to ensure an unobstructed view of the genitals and anus. At which point, the surgeon would push down with his left fist into the testicles to force the bladder into place and insert the fingers of his right hand into the anus, feeling for the stone and thereafter making an incision into the perineum an inch or so above above the anus, allowing him to extract the stones through either the incision itself or the anus by means of a dilator like the one pictured here. More often than not, the prostate gland would be ripped and even as late as 1658, when Samuel Pepys underwent the ordeal in the presence of his family, the wound was not stitched. Instead, it was washed and dressed with a mixture of vinegar, egg yolks and various oils, and left to heal by scar formation, after which the risk of infection was managed by nothing more than severe blood-letting.

As the century progressed, certain advances in technique occurred, mainly as a result of the innovations of Pierre Franco (1505–78), an illiterate travelling lithotomist, who, unlike many of his peers and not-withstanding the prejudice of more formally qualified practitioners, exhibited considerable skill and imagination in executing his craft. By removing the stone through the abdomen rather than the perineum, he became the pioneer of the so-called suprapubic lithotomy procedure and, as his reputation spread, he would be employed by the republic of Berne as a fully-fledged salaried surgeon. Cataracts and hernias were other areas of specialism and Franco would go on to encapsulate his knowledge in a series of works which, while written in an illiterate style, would give the clearest surgical descriptions of, arguably, any early modern writer.

For sufferers, however, the consolations remained few, particularly when other types of stone were involved. The scholar Erasmus, for instance, was a long-suffering martyr to gallstones, the only contemporary cures for which were considered to be fennel or wine. Wisely, the Dutchman opted for the latter, though even this, it seems, posed problems during his stay at Cambridge. He was 'shut in by the plague and beset by highway robbers', as he bemoaned his situation to fellow scholar Andreas Ammonius. 'Cambridge does not agree with me', he complained in a letter dated 1511. 'The beer does not suit me and the wine is unsatisfactory. If you can send me a barrel of Greek wine, the best which can be had, Erasmus will bless you.'

64

Seal matrix
from the leper hospital of St Mary Magdalene, Mile End

Every religious house in Tudor England possessed a unique seal to validate decrees executed in its name, and this pointed oval example has an inscription in black letters – *Sigillu domus dei et sce marie magdelene iuxta myle ende* – identifying it clearly with the hospital of St Mary Magdalene, which served as one of five lazar-houses for leprosy patients in sixteenth-century London. Situated originally on the main road to Essex between the hamlets of Mile End and Stratford-at-Bow, the hospital consisted of a chapel, a group of houses with six beds and a suite of rooms for the overseer, who was appointed by the Bishop of London. When St Bartholomew's Hospital took over administration in 1549, all leper patients were transferred to rural Mile End. Long before this, however, Mary Magdalene had been venerated as the patron saint of lepers, and Jesus Christ's appearance to her is therefore depicted in the seal's centre. Standing to the right and wrapped in a shroud, Christ holds in his left hand a spade representing the burial of the body after death, while the saint herself kneels on the left, displaying the long hair with which she is said to have dried her Saviour's feet and holding the alabaster box of ointment that she subsequently applied to them. They stand on a bridge of three arches possibly intended to represent the sepulchre from which Christ arose three days after the crucifixion.

In reality, the high-water mark of leprosy in England had was already past by the time that the first Tudor mounted the throne. But in 1519 we still hear of one testator bequeathing a legacy 'to every alms house for those called lepars in the shire of Kent', while St Anne's Well at Buxton in Debyshire, a long-established healing resort for sufferers, was still func-

Museum of London

tioning until Henry VIII ordered the closure of the baths in 1538. Nine years later, Edward VI's council saw fit to instruct that all 'leprouse and poore beddred creatures' should continue in the places appointed, and be permitted to have proctors to gather alms for them. Nor, indeed, was this the sole measure of its kind during Edward's reign. In 1551 'a protection to beg' was granted to 'the poor lazars of the house of our Saviour Jesus Christ and Mary Magdalene, at Mile-end', followed two years later by a general grant of £60 to the various lazar-houses around London on condition that inmates did not beg to people's annoyance within a distance of 3 miles.

Precisely how many Tudor men and women were infected with what modern doctors would recognise as leprosy, or Hansen's disease, remains in fact a matter of considerable conjecture. Since both humans and diseases change biologically over time, it is difficult in the first place to know whether contemporary leprosy took exactly the same form as the modern strain of the disease. And to complicate diagnosis further, Hansen's disease actually takes two forms: tuberculoid leprosy, which often 'burns out' over time, and the lepromatous form, which is relentlessly progressive and results in large, disfiguring skin sores, and, ultimately, degeneration of the facial features, particularly the nose. Destruction of the nerves at the extremities of the body, meanwhile, results in loss of sensation to the fingers and toes, which consequently suffer ongoing accidental damage.

Certainly, in the Middle Ages, leprosy was the name given to many skin diseases including eczema, psoriasis and smallpox, and later references to 'venereal leprosy' are likely to apply to syphilis, since the infection is not sexually transmitted. Yet sixteenth-century authorities, like their medieval predecessors, were well versed in the works of Galen, who gave clear and precise descriptions of leprosy, and if contemporary English physicians were sometimes lacking in expertise, the same was generally less true of their German counterparts, who also recorded significant numbers of leprosy cases at this time. In the *Feldtbuch der Wundartzney*, for instance, which was published in Strasbourg in 1540, the symptoms of leprosy – most notably, distension, lesions and stinking breath – are accurately recorded, along with methods of diagnosis and treatment. Claims that leprosy had all but disappeared by the middle of the sixteenth century are therefore at least slightly exaggerated, and, quite apart from the social stigma and lifestyle restrictions involved, not to mention the expense of care for inmates, casually misdiagnosed cases of more minor disorders cannot fully explain the ongoing existence of Tudor lazar-houses. 'He shall live alone; his dwelling shall be outside the camp', the Book of Leviticus tells us, and around 2,000 years later the same injunction still largely applied to the operation and location of the hospital of St Mary Magdalene's at Mile End.

Religion

65

Portable communion set

To most contemporary observers of English affairs in 1534, the kingdom seemed firmly set on the high road to religious reformation. In March, the Act of Succession had resulted in an oath affirming the royal supremacy and one month later both Sir Thomas More and Bishop John Fisher were committed to the Tower for refusing to take it. At that time, too, Thomas Cromwell, architect-in-chief of the breach with Rome, was newly installed as Henry VIII's Principal Secretary, while in May Catherine of Aragon, whose failure to produce a male heir had ultimately triggered the entire process, found herself placed under house arrest at Kimbolton Castle in Cambridgeshire. Finally, on 17 November, the Act of Supremacy confirmed the king as 'Supreme Head of the Church of England' and in doing so granted him once more those traditional royal rights that the pope had supposedly usurped over the previous four centuries.

Yet over the next thirteen years, as Henry VIII's reign ground out its tumultuous course, remarkably little changed in the doctrine and everyday life of his new Anglican Church. And it comes as little surprise, therefore, that the portable communion set pictured here would have been fully familiar in both appearance and function to any priest of the pre-Reformation era. Consisting of a leather case, a miniature silver chalice, a silver paten or plate for the holy wafers, and a glass bottle, the set bears London marks, and the letter R on the foot of the chalice confirms that it dates from 1534–35: the very years in which Henry VIII's religious revolution was apparently reaching its climax. The wood and embossed-leather travelling case, meanwhile, contains two compartments, one for the silver-gilt chalice and paten, and the other for the bottle that originally held the consecrated wine that would be transformed into Christ's actual

Msuem of London

blood upon the priest's blessing. For convenience, the bowl and foot of the chalice unscrew, and the latter is inscribed with the initials J.H. and the maker's mark. The paten, in its turn, bears a later and cruder version of the sacred monogram IHS, representing the name of Christ, but is otherwise unmarked.

Sets of this sort had been used for centuries by Catholic priests to administer the sacrament of extreme unction to the dying, and their continued use by their Anglican successors at this time says much about the limited objectives of the so-called Henrician Reformation. For while Martin Luther, in *The Pagan Servitude of the Church*, explicitly denied the status of extreme unction as a sacrament, and John Calvin had nothing but outright contempt and ridicule for the entire ritual, describing it as a piece of 'histrionic hypocrisy', it was not finally rejected in England until the publication of Edward VI's second Prayer Book in 1552. Based as it was upon the elevated status of the priest as an intercessor between man and God, and carrying with it the additional baggage of a belief in purgatory, the practice seemed to embody the most blatant elements of 'Romish' superstition. Yet it was precisely for this reason, perhaps, that extreme unction survived so effectively for so long.

Nor was it any coincidence that the immensely influential fifteenth-century tract *Ars Moriendi*, or 'Art of Dying', retained such popularity in the century that followed. In 1522, Thomas More's *De Quattuor Novissimis* had spared no detail in conveying to readers the grisly physical minutiae of their own mortality:

Lying in thy bedde, thy hed shooting, thy bak akyng, thy vaynes beating, thy heart panting, thy throat ratelyng, thy fleshe trembling, thy mouth gaping, thy nose sharping, thy legges coling, thy fingers fimbling, thy breath shorting, all thy strength fainting, thy lyfe vanishing, and thy death drawyng on.

But More's morbid preoccupation with death was fully shared by his contemporaries and matched by an equally earnest quest for eternal salvation at any possible cost. 'Forasmoche as the lif of man in this wretched world is shorte, uncertain and transitory,' declared John Burgoyne in 1540, 'it is necessary and requisite, for every true Christen man furst to provide for the lif everlasting in hevyn.'

Yet if extreme unction was desirable, the arrival of the priest and the sight of his portable communion set is likely to have been greeted with both relief and trepidation in equal measure – not least of all since canon law made it quite clear that, in the event of the failing victim's recovery, the ceremony could not be repeated within a year, leaving them perched, therefore, on a further slippery knife edge of perpetual damnation. Moreover, despite reassurances even from the clergy themselves, many recipients still persisted in the belief that, like 'stinking Lazarus' before them, they subsequently became little more than animated corpses who could never again eat meat, or enjoy sexual relations. As such, only the prospect of hell itself was perhaps more daunting, and one of the rare prayers in English to appear in primers in the 1520s amply reinforced the agonising stakes involved as the dying lay on the verge of divine judgement. Only by 'true confession, contrycyon and satisfaction', we read, may the 'peryll of my soule' find relief from the ever-watchful 'fende of hell'.

66

Pilgrim's badge

This lead badge, which depicts St George killing a dragon, watched by the lady Una whom he is rescuing, is one of hundreds of similar items found in England, reflecting the faith and practices of pre-Reformation Christians. For the first fifty years of Tudor rule, pilgrims continued to visit shrines of the Blessed Virgin or the saints to seek forgiveness for their sins, to find miraculous cures for their ailments, or merely to marvel at the beauty of certain wonder-working objects. Such was the celebrity attached to holy relics, indeed, that one particular bishop of Lincoln was said to have bitten off and brought home part of Mary Magdalene's finger, which had been on display at Fécamp, while at Caversham, crowds still flocked to see the head of the lance of Longinus, apparently delivered by an angel with a single wing, which sat in a little chapel as fresh as the day it had pierced the Saviour's side. And as credulous men and women made their way to such sites, so many treated their journey as a form of holiday, collecting badges like this one, mass produced in moulds, as cheap mementoes of their visit. In this case, the badge was probably a souvenir of a visit to Windsor, since the royal chapel there contained relics of St George, whose cult was particularly popular during the reign of Henry VII. Usually attached to clothes and hats or worn around the neck to show where they had been on pilgrimage, such items are found most often in or near rivers, because people thought it brought good luck if they threw them into water.

It is no small irony, of course, that the man ultimately responsible for the destruction of England's shrines should himself have been such a devotee of pilgrimages and the cult of saints earlier in his life. Every year, the young Henry VIII had sent 20s to the shrine of St Thomas at Canterbury and when in 1511 a male heir was born, alive but sickly, the king sought to insure his son's life by going on a secret and barefoot pilgrimage to the shrine of Our Lady at Walsingham on the north Norfolk coast – a round trip of some 200 miles taking all of ten days to make –

British Museum

where he said his prayers, kissed the relic of the Virgin's milk and made offerings of £1 13s 4d.

Few, therefore, could have predicted what lay ahead, even though the medieval heyday of pilgrimage had already passed. In 1498 Henry's own grandmother, Margaret Beaufort, had toured the shrines of East Anglia, making a generous bequest of silver to Walsingham only five years later. But by the end of 1538, Walsingham's famous statue of the Virgin Mary had been burned, its sub-prior hanged for his resistance and the site's wealth confiscated to the royal coffers. The Slipper Chapel, meanwhile, where the king once so reverently left his shoes, would soon become a farm building. In the same year, even Becket's shrine at Canterbury, the most famous and lavishly beautiful of all English pilgrimage sites, was ruthlessly desecrated, as the king employed twenty-six wagons to remove each and every precious item, and as a parting gesture not only burned Becket's bones but mingled the ashes with earth and blew them heaven-wards from the mouth of a cannon.

Yet in this very same year, notwithstanding such intense intimidation by the government, five or six hundred pilgrims a day were still visiting the shrine of St Asaph in Flintshire, while at the shrine to Our Lady at King's Lynn, a new double staircase was installed to deal with the vast numbers of visitors. Nor, of course, was such devotion to the old observances altogether surprising, particularly when the most common miracles associated with shrines around the country were health-related, involving apocryphal cures of cripples and lepers, the restoration of sight to the blind, the granting of fertility to barren women and even the revival of dead children, which was widely believed to have been achieved at the shrine of St Mary in Thetford before its eventual closure in 1540. At Ipswich, Worcester, Cardigan, Doncaster and a host of other resorts, the tradition of pilgrimage would be no more lightly abandoned than the time-honoured custom at Arden's Benedictine nunnery whereby women made such sincere offerings to St Bridget for their sick cows.

And, as some shrines were closed down even with the faithful still kneeling before them, so the badges, medals, crosses, ribbons, wax discs, holy papers, and other emblems that pilgrims had gathered on their travels to such places assumed perhaps an even deeper significance. For as well as being mementoes, they served as a continual reminder to their wearers of the divine blessing they had received by making their journey, offering consolation in sickness and hope in the face of death itself – which has, of course, its own particular irony when it is remembered that, according to at least one authority, Henry VIII's own final wish was for his soul to be offered up to the Virgin at Walsingham.

67

Reliquary

Discovered by a 4-year-old boy, minutes into his first ever attempt at metal-detecting with his father, this locket, designed to hold a holy relic, came to light in 2010, 20cm below the surface of a field in Hockley, Essex. Only three other reliquaries of this particular kind are known to exist and experts have not only dated the item to the early sixteenth century but have gone on to speculate that it may well have belonged to a member of the royal family. Certainly, its exquisite design would suggest as much. On three sides of the diamond-shaped pendant, which measures approximately 2.5cm² and weighs 8.6g, are inscribed the names of the three Wise Men – Iaspar (Caspar), Melcior (Melchiore) and Baltasar (Balthazar) – in a fine Lombardic script commonly employed during the reign of Henry VIII. Much more significantly still, the front is engraved with the image of a female saint, probably St Helena, the mother of the emperor Constantine the Great, who is traditionally associated with the discovery of the True Cross while conducting a pilgrimage to the Holy Land between ad 326 and 328. Predictably, therefore, she is depicted holding the cross upon a checkerboard pattern tile floor with floral tendrils on either side of both her and the cross itself. Most significantly of all, a series of dashes along the length and width of the cross are meant to represent wood grain: an indication that the object may well have contained what was thought at the time to be a splinter from the actual cross itself.

On the back, meanwhile, there is a shower of blood droplets falling out of and over four incisions, and a cut heart symbolising the five wounds of Christ, again reinforcing the theme of the crucifixion. This rear panel was intended to slide out along grooves cut into the sides, thus revealing the relic within, though at the time of its discovery the bottom of the panel had been pressed inwards, derailing it from its grooves and forcing it permanently shut. It was not, therefore, until painstaking work involving a microscope and miniature probe had been undertaken that the object,

which has a 73 per cent gold content and would once have been brilliantly coloured and enamelled, was finally opened. In the event, only a few local flax fibres were discovered, which electron microscopy revealed to be nothing more than root hairs of the sort that are likely to have entered at some point during the pendant's long sojourn underground.

At the same time, the sacred wooden splinter had long since disappeared, just like the belief system that had once made both it and other relics of its kind such items of deep reverence. But if the credulity of most contemporaries was already being scorned by a handful of humanist intellectuals, early Tudor England remained awash with bones, limbs, blood, teeth, clothing and all manner of wonder-working paraphernalia that characterised pre-Reformation religion. At Caversham, for example, the 'holy halter' in which Judas had hanged himself was proudly displayed alongside the dagger with which the saintly Henry VI had been slain, while the famous girdle of Our Lady at Aix-la-Chapelle was matched by another just like it at Westminster Abbey and ten more in England alone. Bath Abbey, in its turn, boasted 'a great comb called St Mary Magdalen's comb', along with other combs that had once belonged, allegedly, to St Dorothy and St Margaret, while at Bury St Edmunds, Thomas Cromwell's eagle-eyed commissioners would eventually uncover 'moche vanitie and superstition', encompassing among other things 'the coles that Sant Laurence was tosted withall, the paring of S. Edmundes naylles, S. Thomas of Canterbury penneknyff and his bootes' and, predictably, further 'peces of the olie crosse'. At Bury in Yorkshire, the same commissioners found 'reliques for rayne and certain other superstitiouse usages for avoyding of wedes growing in the corne', as well as 'divers skulles for the hedache'. And most famously of all, perhaps, there lay at the Abbey of Hailes a crystal vase supposedly containing Christ's own blood shed on Calvary, which was finally exposed in the presence of 'a great multitude' to be nothing more than an unctuous coloured gum.

By that time, in all probability, the Hockley pendant was already lost and awaiting rediscovery rather than discarded in enlightened disgust like many other items of its type at that time. Avoiding the indignity of exposure and condemnation by Hugh Latimer and like-minded reformers, it hid below ground: a compelling reminder of a bygone form of piety that belonged more fittingly in Rome than the newly fashioned Protestant England. And now, against all odds, it resides in the British Museum, having been purchased as treasure trove for £75,000, which was duly allocated to the family of its boy-discoverer and the owner of the land on which the locket was found.

68

Tyndale's New Testament

When the British Library acquired a 1526 edition for over £1 million in 1994, William Tyndale's New Testament was hailed as 'the most important book in the English language'. For, as well as being the first printed edition of the Bible in English, it was the first English translation of the Bible drawn directly from the Hebrew and Greek texts. Hitherto, vernacular translations had been strictly banned by the clergy, in order, as Tyndale vigorously maintained, 'to keep the world still in darkness, to the intent they might sit in the consciences of the people, through vain superstition and false doctrine ... and to exalt their own honour ... above God himself.' Never a man to mince his words or shrink from an unequal challenge against overwhelming odds, the Gloucestershire scholar, who was fluent in eight languages, subsequently faced exile and death in his efforts to make 'the boy that driveth the plow' as familiar with Scripture as any clergyman. And the 1534 revision pictured here, which was made by Tyndale himself, became not only the clarion call to reformation in England but a landmark in the development of the English language. Printed in Antwerp in 1534 and now housed at Chetham's Library in Manchester, the book was produced for some as yet unknown reason on yellow paper, an uncommon practice at the time, and the rear flyleaf verso carries the sixteenth-century inscription 'London the 29th May'. Among its many distinctive features, this particular edition provides the first instance of the word 'elder' used in preference to that of 'priest'.

Although the Old Testament had first been written in Hebrew and the New Testament in a dialect of Greek and, possibly, Aramaic, the official language of the Roman Catholic Church was Latin – the language of the Roman Empire, which had adopted Christianity as its religion during the fourth century – and since 1408, as a result of the Constitutions of

Oxford, it had been strictly forbidden to translate the Bible into any other tongue. For William Tyndale and others like him, however, such prohibitions were immaterial. Born in Melksham Court, Stinchcombe, at some time between 1484 and 1496, and educated first at Oxford and then at Cambridge before his ordination as a priest in 1521, he subsequently returned to Gloucestershire to serve as chaplain and tutor to Sir John Walsh and his family – work that enabled him to continue his groundbreaking study and translation of religious texts. During that time, moreover, he also translated a tract by Desiderius Erasmus, whose writings argued for a more deeply personal faith, which emphasised a direct relationship between the individual and God, rather than one mediated and controlled by the Church hierarchy.

But when Tyndale became an outspoken proponent of such views, he soon found himself in danger, and in May 1524, aided by money from Sir Humphrey Monmouth and other influential sympathisers among the laity, he made good his escape to Germany where he hoped to continue his secret work in greater safety. Basing his translation of the New Testament upon a Greek version recently completed by Erasmus from several manuscripts older and more authoritative than the Latin Vulgate version, Tyndale would complete his task in little more than a year, so that by April 1526 a pocket-sized edition of his work was circulating behind closed doors in England.

Undeniably Lutheran in tone, Tyndale's translation carefully replaced traditional terms with new ones that suggested a decisively democratic shift in the balance of religious power between clergy and laity. Now, therefore, 'congregation' replaced 'Church', 'elder' was substituted for 'priest', and 'repentance' was preferred to 'penance'. 'Love' was also emphasised over 'charity'. But in spite of its noble intentions, the explosive impact of Tyndale's challenge to both the religious and political hierarchies of the day overrode all other considerations. And the poetic quality of his writing – which made use for the first time of expressions such as 'broken-hearted', 'flowing with milk and honey', 'the apple of his eye', 'signs of the times', 'eat, drink and be merry', 'the salt of the earth', 'the powers that be', 'blessed are the peacemakers' and 'let there be light' – would do nothing to save him. Condemned as a heretic by Cardinal Wolsey in January 1529, Tyndale was eventually betrayed in Antwerp six years later by a certain Henry Phillips and condemned on a charge of heresy, from which even Thomas Cromwell's pleas could not save him.

'Strangled to death while tied to the stake' at the Castle of Vilvoorde near Brussels and subsequently burned, Tyndale appears to have met his end with characteristic resolve. 'Lord,' he is said to have cried at the last, 'open the King of England's eyes!' And the full irony of these words has not, of course, been lost upon later generations. For the ruler who had driven him into exile initially was ultimately won to his cause. Indeed, within four years of the Protestant martyr's death, four English translations of the Bible had been published in England at Henry VIII's specific behest, including the king's own official version, the so-called Great Bible of 1539, which included much of Tyndale's original translation.

Statue of the dead Christ

'I trust that there be no man so mad or woman neither,' declared Sir Thomas More in 1529, 'but that they know quick men from dead stones, and tree from flesh and bone.' Nor was More the only contemporary to appeal for moderation and common sense as Protestant zealots called out from all directions for a vigorous purge upon idolatry of any kind. An image, wrote the German painter and engraver Albrecht Dürer, 'is no more responsible for superstitious abuse than a weapon is responsible for a murder'. Yet the reign of Henry VIII and, above all, that of his young son, Edward, would witness a flood tide of iconoclasm that not only wiped out a long-standing religious tradition but also resulted in untold damage to England's artistic heritage. According to injunctions issued in 1548, 'pictures, painting and all other monuments of feigned miracles' were to be summarily destroyed in every place of worship, 'so that there remain no memory of the same in walls, glass-windows, or elsewhere within'. And the result was the wholesale demolition of baptismal fonts, the smashing of stained-glass windows, the whitewashing of depictions on walls, the painting over or actual removal of crucifixes and the unflinching desecration of statutes like the one pictured here.

A magnificently naturalistic, life-size piece, this limestone statue of the dead Christ was produced at some time between 1500 and 1520 for the monastic church and hospital of St Thomas of Acon, which lay on the north side of Cheapside before its surrender to Henry VIII in 1538 and subsequent purchase by the Mercers' Company for £969 17s 6d almost four years later. Thereafter the church was incorporated into the Mercers' Hall to serve as its chapel before both were heavily damaged in the Blitz. Only during the clearing of the bombed site in April 1954 was the statue finally unearthed and its impressive scale and minute detail brought to light once more. For it had been buried some 1.5m beneath the chapel floor on government orders, it seems, either at the time of the chapel's surrender or more probably in 1547 when the Mercers' Company accounts record an entry of 5s 6d for the removal of images in accordance with a government directive ordering the general 'purification' of churches.

Certainly, the statue had lost nothing of its power during the centuries of its interment. Lying on a slab 2m long and 70cm wide, the effect of its agonised face, with slightly open mouth and projecting tongue, is complemented by oozing wounds and exquisitely sculpted limbs, stiffened by rigor mortis and the cramps of crucifixion. On the left of Christ's neck a solitary vein protrudes and, with similar attention to detail, the artist has also included three gouts of blood between the words of a Latin inscription commemorating the Son of Man's humiliation at the hands of his tormentors. The bier, meanwhile, is covered by the royal mantle that Pilate's soldiers gave to their prisoner in mockery, and traces of colour show that this was originally painted a purplish crimson over a white undercoat. Other traces of paint also indicate that the whole body was once coloured: the tongue red, the teeth white, the hair a reddish brown, the rest in flesh tone.

Nor did the statue's disfigurement detract ultimately from its poignancy. On the contrary, the brutal attack which resulted in the loss of the crown of thorns and arms and lower legs merely served to enhance the

tragic dignity of what is now widely considered a major work of art. The face was left entirely intact, suggesting, perhaps, that even the attackers were in awe of its quality. And the fact that the object has ultimately survived at all gives it a modern-day resonance all of its own, for few similar items across the country were spared all-out destruction at the time. The churchwardens of St Mary Stamford, it is true, protected their patronal statue of the Virgin by walling in its niche, where it was ultimately discovered in the nineteenth century, and parishioners at Wakefield managed to salt away some twenty-five alabaster images in the roof of a local chapel. Much more typical, however, was the treatment of the images at St Paul's, which were entirely demolished on the night of 16 November 1547, though some of the workmen involved were injured in the process – an occurrence cited by priests as evidence of God's wrath.

Such, then, was the price of progress and the avid campaign of reformers like Hugh Latimer to rid the realm of 'the idolatrie that will neaver be left till the said images be taken awaie'. For on this and other matters Latimer was a man of deep conviction – so much so indeed that long before he became an ardent advocate of the public burning of 'idols' during the reign of Edward VI, he had already gladly presided at another such 'jolly muster' on 22 May 1538, when the papist friar John Forest was roasted over a slow fire fuelled, for extra effect, by the famous Welsh pilgrimage image of Darvel Catherne.

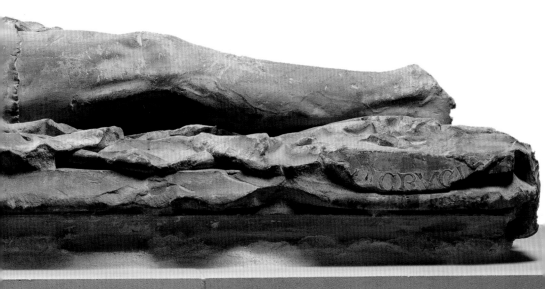

70

The Glastonbury Grace Cup

Tradition has it that this oak tankard, the so-called Glastonbury Grace Cup, belonged for generations to the abbots of Glastonbury, the last of whom, Richard Whiting, was hanged, drawn and quartered on Glastonbury Tor in 1539 for resisting Thomas Cromwell's scheme to dissolve the monasteries. Originally a supporter of Henry VIII's breach with Rome, Whiting had gone on to sign the 1534 Act of Supremacy, which made the king the head of the Church of England, before resisting the government's subsequent decision to loot his abbey and confiscate its lands. For his trouble, the abbot was executed as a traitor after a sham trial, though in one last act of defiance, the Grace Cup is said to have been smuggled out of the abbey beforehand and given for safekeeping to a Catholic branch of the Arundell family of Wardour Castle in Wiltshire. A hundred years later the tankard was in danger not only of confiscation but outright destruction when Oliver Cromwell's Parliamentarian forces laid siege to Wardour Castle in 1643. This time, however, it was Lady Blanche Arundell, left alone at the castle with only twenty-five men-at-arms while her husband was away fighting for King Charles, who fended off the attackers for nine days and managed to hide the cup before finally surrendering.

Predictably, perhaps, in light of the tankard's intriguing history, questions remain about its provenance. The decoration suggests that it may well have been carved in Germany or elsewhere in central Europe, and one theory proposes that the object was actually brought to Wardour not from Glastonbury but by Thomas Arundell, 1st Baron Arundell of Wardour, upon his return from service for the Holy Roman Emperor Rudolf II against the Ottoman Turks in 1595. Yet the very nature and purpose of

Richard Arundell

the tankard lends plausibility to claims that the tankard did indeed origi-
nate from Glastonbury Abbey. Called a Grace Cup because such items
were traditionally shared around a table after a prayer of thanksgiving
said before meals, it also contains vertical rows of pegs on its interior
that apportion an equal amount of beverage to each drinker – a feature
that is generally consistent with the practices of monastic communal
life. Given, in addition, its decoration with images of the twelve apostles
and the crucifixion of Christ, alongside birds, beasts and flowers, the
tankard's connection with Glastonbury therefore remains not altogether
implausible, even allowing for subsequent embellishment by legend.

At the very least, the object continues to provide a symbolic and highly
evocative link not only to Glastonbury Abbey itself but thereby to one of
the most momentous episodes in Tudor history. For the dissolution of the
monasteries had begun in 1536, and by January 1539 Glastonbury was the
only monastery left in Somerset. In consequence, on 19 September royal
commissioners arrived there without warning on the orders of the Lord
Privy Seal, Thomas Cromwell, in order to identify faults and thereby facilitate the abbey's closure. Finding that 78-year-old Richard Whiting was at
Sharpham, Cromwell's men hurried there and carried the abbot back to
the abbey, where they proceeded during the night to ransack his papers
and search his apartments. 'But we could not,' they wrote, 'find any letter
that was material.' And so, 'with as fair words as they could, he being but

a very weak man and sickly', they sent the old man up to London to the Tower where Cromwell would be free to work his will upon him.

In what followed, there is no evidence that Abbot Whiting was allowed a fair hearing. Indeed, a passage in Cromwell's notebook, or 'Remembrance', proves conclusively that the outcome of the sham trial held at Wells in mid-November was a foregone conclusion: 'Item. The Abbot, of Glaston to (be) tryed at Glaston and also executyd there with his complycys'. That this passage was written in advance of Whiting's trial could not speak more eloquently of the travesty of justice involved, and without due enquiry or defence Whiting and two of his monks were summarily convicted of 'robbing Glastonbury church', before being fastened upon hurdles and dragged by horses to the top of Glastonbury Tor. Here the victims were hanged, drawn and quartered, before being ritually displayed after butchery: Whiting's head, we are told, was fastened on a spike over the west gate of the now deserted abbey, while his quarters, after boiling in pitch, were exposed at Wells, Bath, Ilchester and Bridgwater.

All three monks 'took their death very patiently' and not, perhaps, without some small consolation. For while Cromwell's Remembrance also mentioned 11,000 ounces of gold plundered from the abbey, along with £1,100 'in ready money', much furniture and 'rich copes', there was no reference to the Glastonbury Grace Cup, which had already, according to tradition, made its escape. Over three and a half centuries later Whiting would receive due recognition for his bravery. Described by Thomas Wolsey upon his appointment to Glastonbury as 'an upright and religious monk, a provident and discreet man, and a priest commendable for his life, virtues and learning', he was ultimately beatified, along with his companions, by Pope Leo XIII on 13 May 1895.

71

Pilgrimage of Grace banner

As autumn approached in 1536, England's North County stirred restlessly in the wake of two consecutive bad harvests. High prices, tithes, enclosures and unpopular taxes had all added to the mix and compounded the widespread resentment also being directed at the sweeping religious changes proposed by Thomas Cromwell. The year had already seen the first onslaught on the monasteries and now there followed the first measures against those 'popular superstitions', which had been such a consolation to so many for so long, especially in the northern counties of the realm where devotion to old ways ran particularly deep. 'There can be no better way to beat the King's authority into the heads of the rude people of the North', Cromwell had written not long before, and when two tax collectors arrived at Louth on 1 October, the consequences were predictable. The lucky one was said to have been hanged, while the other was allegedly wrapped in a freshly stripped cow skin and fed to dogs. Within days, a gathering of around 10,000 peasants, craftsmen, parish priests and gentlemen was occupying Lincoln. By 4 October a group of at least eighteen local gentry was exercising a leading role in the budding insurrection.

Over the weeks and months that followed, the Pilgrimage of Grace – Tudor England's largest and most significant rebellion – underwent numerous twists and turns and at least three different incarnations as it spread northwards into Yorkshire and the surrounding areas. But there was no denying that, at its peak, under the ostensible leadership of the one-eyed lawyer Robert Aske, the rebellion shook the king and his government to the core. Styling themselves as 'pilgrims' and by and large behaving as such, singing hymns and carrying religious emblems, the rebels were soon proving capable of far more than pious tunes and righteous gestures. For when Aske finally entered York on 16 October, brimming with confidence and full of hope, he had an army rather than a mob under his command, and within three days Lord Darcy had tamely surrendered the royal castle at Pontefract in, obvious sympathy with the insurgents.

By this point, too, the 'pilgrims' had been joined by the 63-year-old gout-ridden Sir Robert Constable, carrying the banner pictured here, which resides today at Arundel Castle and illustrates so tangibly the rebels' sympathy for the old religion. The five wounds of Christ, which became the symbol of the whole rebellion, are clearly depicted, along with the crown of thorns and a central chalice, embodying what was, arguably, the centrepiece of the entire Catholic faith: the principle of transubstantiation. And the choice of such imagery could not have been more apt, for during the Middle Ages, the Cross of Jerusalem, or 'Crusaders' Cross', had evoked the Holy Wounds of Christ through its five crosses, while by the fifteenth century, the Friday following the Octave of the Feast of Corpus Christi had also been dedicated to the five wounds of Christ. Three years after the Pilgrimage of Grace had first broken out, moreover, Lady Margaret Pole would be attainted and imprisoned by Thomas Cromwell for allegedly possessing a tunic emblazoned with the same symbols, and when Elizabeth I faced her own Northern Rebellion in 1569, the insurgents once again adopted the self-same motif.

On no occasion, however, did the emblem of the Holy Wounds bring ultimate good fortune to its devotees. Aske and his rebels would be betrayed by the king after receiving 'comfortable words' and assurances that their demands would be met, and as the conservative lords rapidly withdrew their support for a further uprising led by Sir Francis Bigod, the Duke of Norfolk had little difficulty in re-establishing Henry VIII's flagging credentials as a mighty and 'puissant' ruler with a systematic campaign of vengeance in which 178 rebels were executed. 'Before you close up our said banner again', Henry now told the Duke of Norfolk:

> You shall in any wise cause such dreadful execution to be done upon a good number of every town, village and hamlet that have offended in this rebellion, as well by the hanging them up in trees, as by the quartering them, and the setting up of their heads and quarters in every town, great and small, and in all such other places, as they may be in fearful spectacle to all other hereafter that would practise in any like manner.

Sir Robert Constable, meanwhile, had been among the first of the rebel leaders to be taken. Condemned to death in June, he was butchered in Hull, where he had been briefly in command of the royal garrison, and his remains were duly hung from the Beverley Gate. Shortly afterwards, Norfolk, who was in charge of the arrangements, gloated that Sir Robert 'doth hang above the highest gate in the town, so trimmed with chains ... that I think his bones will hang there this hundred year'. Aske, in his turn, suffered a similar fate at York a month later on a market day, and when Henry learned that in Cumberland the wives and mothers of the executed were removing the bodies of their loved ones from the gibbets where they were displayed, he ordered that these women, too, be punished for their insolence.

72

Thomas Cranmer's cell door

It was not long after Mary Tudor's triumphant arrival in London on 3 August 1553, at the head of a procession which included her half-sister Elizabeth and over 800 nobles and gentlemen, that the population of England's prisons began to alter significantly in composition. Soon the vanquished Protestant supporters of Lady Jane Grey, including Thomas Cranmer, Archbishop of Canterbury, and the Protestant divines, Hugh Latimer and Nicholas Ridley, were firmly locked in captivity, while those of the new queen's Catholic persuasion, like bishops Stephen Gardiner and Edmund Bonner, found themselves not only set a liberty but restored to positions of significant influence within the new regime: Gardiner as Bishop of Winchester and Lord Chancellor, Bonner as Bishop of London.

Nor was it especially long before the lighting of the fires at Smithfield heralded a systematic campaign on the queen's part and that of her trusted adviser, Cardinal Reginald Pole, to eradicate Protestantism from the kingdom once and for all. On 4 February 1555 the biblical translator John Rogers was duly consigned to the flames, to be followed five days after by Bishop John Hooper. And just over a month later, Thomas Cranmer found himself transferred from the Tower of London to the Bocardo prison at Oxford, which lay over the city's North Gate in Cornmarket Street and adjoined the tower of St Michael at the Northgate. There he would be left to languish for seventeen months behind the cell door pictured here, awaiting trial for heresy in the company of Hugh Latimer and Nicholas Ridley after his original conviction for treason in November 1553.

'I pray that God may grant that we may endure to the end!' Cranmer wrote at the time, though his courage failed him more than once during the long process of his trial – not least of all after he was forced to witness the incineration of Latimer and Ridley on 16 September 1555 in a ditch just outside the city walls where Broad Street now stands. The latter's death had been especially harrowing, for although his brother had brought some gunpowder to place around both victims' necks to guarantee a speedy end, Ridley's pyre was composed of slow-burning green wood, which burned only his lower body without touching the upper parts. 'Lord have mercy upon me! I cannot burn. Let the fire come unto me, I cannot burn,' the hapless martyr was heard to cry until one of the bystanders finally stoked the flames to hasten his death.

Perhaps it was for this reason that Cranmer subsequently chose to renounce his Protestant beliefs after the decision from Rome in December 1555 that he should be given over to the secular authorities to face execution at their discretion. Five times, in fact, Cranmer submitted himself to Queen Mary and recognised the pope as head of the Church in an effort to save himself. Even after this, however, whether through anger at her own mother's treatment or genuine moral outrage at Cranmer's role in advancing heresy during the previous two reigns, the queen refused clemency, and on 21 March 1556, the day set for his execution, the former archbishop was told to make a final public recantation at Oxford's University church. The result was a defiant last stand of legendary proportions by a man who had thus far wilted limply before the formidable forces ranged against him. Pushed to the limit and with nothing left to lose, Cranmer delivered a withering denial of both the papacy and the Roman doctrine of the eucharist. The doctrine of transubstantiation would stand condemned, he declared, 'in the last day before the judgement of God, where the papistical doctrines contrary thereto shall be ashamed to show their face ... And as for the pope, I refuse him as Christ's enemy, and antichrist, with all his false doctrine.' He also committed himself to one final gesture when faced at last with the ordeal of his burning. Since he had written things 'contrary to the truth which I thought in my heart ... for fear of death and to save my life', the former Archbishop of Canterbury would make amends by plunging the guilty hand into the flames before any other part of his body was consumed. 'And forasmuch as my hand hath offended, writing contrary to my heart,' he affirmed, 'therefore my hand shall first be punished; for when I come to the fire, it shall first be burned'. Nor, in spite of earlier wavering, did Cranmer's courage desert him during the fulfilment of this bold pledge, as John Foxe's account of his death makes clear. 'Apparently insensible of pain, with a countenance of venerable resignation, and eyes directed to Him for whose cause he suffered,' Foxe tells us, 'he continued, like St Stephen, to say, "Lord Jesus receive my spirit!" till the fury of the flames terminated his powers of utterance and existence.'

73

Priest hole, Oxburgh Hall

'Three dayes had whollie bin spent, and no man found there all this while', wrote the Puritan priest-hunter Sir Henry Bromley to his superior in London after the successful capture of one of Tudor England's most remarkable Catholics. 'But upon the fourth day, in the morning from behind the wainscot in the Gallerie,' Bromley continued:

> Came forth two men of their owne voluntarie accord, as beeing no longer able there to concele themselves, for they confessed that they had but one apple betweene them, which was all the releefe they had received during the time they were thus hidden.

One of those captured, as it transpired, was Nicholas Owen, lay brother of the Jesuit Order, who for some twenty years previous had been at continuous risk of his life while constructing a series of supremely disguised hiding places like this one at Oxburgh Hall in Norfolk. As the activities of Elizabeth's priest-hunters, or 'pursuivants', had intensified in response to war with Spain and a string of plots between 1569 and 1587, so too, it seems, had the efforts and ingenuity of the man nicknamed 'Little John'. For, in the words of Fr John Gerard, who was himself captured by the queen's investigators on 23 April 1594, he had been 'the immediate occasion of saving many hundreds of persons, both ecclesiastical and secular, which had been lost and forfeited many times over if the priests had been taken in their houses'.

Along with others at Sawston Hall near Cambridge, Coughton Court in Warwickshire and Harvington Hall in Worcestershire, the priest hole at Oxburgh Hall is among only a handful of authentic examples of Owen's

work to survive. Situated just off the brickwork staircase in the left-hand tower of Oxburgh's magnificent Gate House, it is reached by a pivoting trapdoor which, when closed, blends in with the tiles of the floor. And such is the overall craft of its construction that no fugitive cleric was ever discovered there after the hall's owner, Sir Henry Bedingfield, had requested that the hide be built at some point after 1585 in response to an Act of Parliament proscribing the very presence of any Catholic priest in England and imposing the death penalty for anyone offering shelter or assistance.

In all, England possesses around a hundred houses with priest holes of one kind or another, many of which are of comparatively simple design. Nicholas Owen's, however, were not only more complex but also more varied, so that the discovery of one would not assist in the location of others elsewhere. Ceilings and floors were frequently raised or lowered and hides were variously concealed in roof spaces, behind panelling and walls, beneath garderobe shafts, and in or below false fireplaces. In this case, the hole contains an alternative entrance through a narrow passage leading on to a corridor in the top floor of the house where there was a room in which Mass was secretly conducted. Inside the hole, meanwhile, there is a bench, and in the masonry above, a feeding hole. The dimensions, too, are somewhat more generous than cruder examples elsewhere, which often scarcely accommodated a single priest. When Father William Weston was evading his pursuers in 1585, he described

Quodvultdeus

his 'cave-like' refuge and how 'the whole of that day I lay in hiding, and the night and day following it as well, almost till sunset', enduring the 'dark, dank and cold' in a space 'so narrow that I was forced to stand the entire time'.

Yet Owen's personal story was if anything even more remarkable than the physical legacy he left behind. Born around 1562 at St Peter le Bailey in Oxford, a centre of Catholic recusancy, Owen was in fact a master carpenter who, though only slightly taller than a dwarf, nevertheless possessed sufficient physical strength to cut through walls, floors and wooden beams in the process of fashioning his hides. Working alone, and always at night in order to minimise the likelihood of betrayal, he accepted nothing more than the necessities of life as payment, and struggled, too, with both a pronounced limp – after a packhorse fell on top of him and broke his leg – and a hernia injury that would finally kill him during torture at the Tower of London in 1606 when, in the aftermath of the Gunpowder Plot, he was subjected to agonising 'examinations' on the so-called 'Topcliffe rack'. Left dangling from a wall with both wrists held fast in iron gauntlets, his intestines distended, causing the rackmaster to strap a circular plate of iron to his stomach, so that upon his transfer to the conventional rack, the greater power of the windlass forced the hernia to be severed by the plate, resulting in an agonising death during the early morning of 2 March.

'It is incredible how great was the joy caused by his arrest,' wrote Secretary of State Sir Robert Cecil, 'knowing the great skill of Owen in constructing hiding places, and the innumerable qualities of dark holes which he had schemed for hiding priests all through England.' Yet the diminutive craftsman would reveal nothing to his inquisitors and his sacrifices were not without consolation, for in 1970, he was finally canonised by Pope Paul VI, becoming, in due course, the patron saint of escapologists and illusionists.

Superstition

74

Caul locket

A caul is a piece of birth membrane covering a newborn baby's head and face after it has left its mother's womb. Wholly harmless, it is routinely removed by modern physicians or midwives upon delivery of the child, just as it was in the sixteenth century. But since births of this kind have always been particularly rare, occurring less than once in every 80,000 cases, babies born with this distinction were considered especially fortunate in Tudor times. Often blessed, it was believed, with the gifts of 'second sight' or healing, these caul-bearers were also thought to be safeguarded against a range of dangers, including drowning – something which has always made the purchase of cauls a high priority for sailors. Such, in fact, was the supposed magical potency of a caul that even the official condemnation of the Catholic Church could not thwart the resulting superstitions as women continued to persuade priests to say blessings and masses of consecration over dried and preserved examples.

As the locket pictured here confirms, dried caul fragments were considered good luck charms not only in their own right but for the children themselves, both in infancy and later years. This English locket, fashioned around 1597, held, it seems, a piece of the caul belonging to one John Monson, and was probably bestowed upon him as a baptismal gift. In terms of Tudor folklore the owner of this particular locket was even more distinctive for being born at midnight, since this supposedly enabled him to see ghosts and spectres. Made of gold with black enamel, the object measures 5cm in height by 3cm in width, making it a substantial possession for any contemporary family of non-noble rank like the Monsons, and firmly demonstrating at one and the same time how the growing affluence of Tudors of the 'middling sort' had by no means eradicated their superstitious tendencies.

The tradition of christening gifts, which Puritans frequently dismissed as an idle distraction from the deeper significance of the ceremony, was

Victoria and Albert Museum

already in fact a well-established Tudor custom, with so-called 'apostle spoons' proving a particularly popular choice, alongside table salts, cups and other precious metal objects. Indeed, the expression 'born with a silver spoon in his mouth' relates to this particular practice. But the pervasive contemporary obsession with child mortality and security gave the gift of a caul locket an altogether profounder significance, which reflected in turn a much broader but equally curious folklore surrounding the young.

Portents of harm and harbingers of outright doom for those of tender years were discerned at the most mundane levels of everyday life. 'O Jesu bless us, he is born with teeth!' declares the panic-stricken Duke of Gloucester in Act 5, Scene 6 of *King Henry VI, Part 3*. Most Tudor men and women assumed that even the appearance of a child's first tooth in the upper jaw was a sure precursor of death in infancy. Furthermore, dental superstitions of slightly less drastic proportions were not only particularly prevalent but also displayed specific local variations. In Sussex, for instance, parents were loath to throw away their children's cast teeth, for fear that they might be found and gnawed by any passing animal, with the result that the child's new tooth would be exactly like one from the animal concerned, while in Durham it was generally accepted that when first teeth came out, the cavities must be filled with salt, and each tooth burned, in order to protect the child from occult influence.

Witches and fairies, indeed, were believed to be particularly attracted to newborn infants and inclined to steal the most beautiful and well-favoured, leaving ugly and dull-witted substitutes in their place. Such creatures, observed Edmund Spenser in *The Faerie Queene*, men 'do chaungelings call, so chaunged by faeries theft', and Shakespeare, too, makes various references of his own to this commonly held belief. 'I do but beg a little changeling to be my henchman', declares Oberon in Act 2, Scene 1 of *A Midsummer Night's Dream*, while in Act 1, Scene 1 of *Henry IV, Part 1,* the king actually professes a wish that 'some night-tripping fairy had exchanged in cradle clothes our children where they lay'. In Act 3, Scene 3 of *The Winter's Tale* too, the shepherd, after relating that he had once been told how he 'should be rich by the fairies', proceeds to demonstrate his own conviction that fairies were able and likely to intervene in human affairs if opportunity arose. 'This is some changeling: open't', he declares.

And just as children might be spirited away from their beds by fairy folk, so they might also be subject to altogether darker forces. For while cauls imparted gifts for the good, so other individuals were thought to possess more malevolent powers, like the 'evil eye', by means of which injury or ill luck could be inflicted upon the 'o'erlooked' with a single glance. 'Vile worm, thou was o'erlook'd even at thy birth', exclaims Pistol to Falstaff in Act 5, Scene 5 of *The Merry Wives of Windsor*. In such circumstances, where even a cradled babe might be 'eye-bitten', talismans of any kind were therefore bound to be of keenest interest to Tudor parents, and few were more potent than the caul, which had already guarded the child in the womb and accompanied it into the world. 'In that day', Isaiah 3:16 records, 'the Lord will take away the bravery of their tinkling ornaments about their feet, and their cauls, and their round tires like the moon'. But for Tudor men and women, high and low, the residing superstition remained firmly in place. Hamlet himself, after all, was said to have been a caul-bearer, just like Alexander the Great before him and Napoleon after.

75

John Dee's sigillum dei aemaeth

Just at that very point when the worlds of science and magic were at last becoming truly distinguishable, John Dee effectively straddled both. Alchemist, philosopher, astronomer and astrologer, Dee was also, at one and the same time, not only England's first and foremost magus but a leading mathematician of the age – a reviver of ancient arcane knowledge on the one hand and, on the other, an enthusiastic supporter of the Copernican world that was beginning to shine forth around him. It was Dee who, as court astrologer first to Mary Tudor and then to Elizabeth I, reputedly conjured the storm that shattered the Spanish Armada, and it was he, too, along with his counterpart Edward Kelly, who framed the so-called Enochian system for communing with the hierarchy of angelic entities. Yet the man who is believed by some to be the true instigator of the Rosicrucian movement was, likewise, the editor of the first English translation of Euclid's *Elements* and the recipient in either 1584 or 1585 of a doctorate in medicine from the University of Prague. More importantly still, he was also a leading expert in navigation whose training of Elizabethan explorers and support for overseas expansion played no small role in the birth of the 'British Empire' – a term that he himself was the first to use.

Few men more than Dee, therefore, encapsulate the contrasting elements of the Elizabethan age more fully, and few objects demonstrate more aptly the broad sweep of his aims than the British Museum's *sigillum dei aemaeth* or 'seal of God's truth', for Dee considered all his activities merely different facets of the same quest: the search for a transcendent understanding of the divine forms, or what he himself called the 'pure verities', underlying the visible world. 'O comfortable allurement,

Vassil

O ravishing persuasion,' he wrote in his preface to Euclid, 'to deal with a Science, whose Subject is so Ancient, so pure, so excellent, so surmounting all creatures, so used of the Almighty and incomprehensible wisdom of the Creator'. But, as he soon found, not even mathematics was apt for his ultimate quest. He had spent forty years, he told the Holy Roman Emperor Rudolf II, labouring 'with great pain, care and cost' in an effort to unravel the secrets of the universe and mankind's position within it, only to discover 'that neither any man living, nor any book I could yet meet withal, was able to teach me those truths I desired and longed for'.

In consequence, Dee had only one way to turn: to God Himself in the hope that through His angels, He might guide humanity to those eternal truths hitherto hidden from it. Thus, by a combination of divination and communing with supernatural entities, a suitably skilled seeker would learn the universal language of creation and bring about the pre-apocalyptic unity of mankind. Crucial to this enterprise was Dee's *sigillum dei*, a late medieval magical amulet that, according to one of the oldest sources, the *Liber Juratus Honorii*, allowed the initiated magician to have power over all creatures except archangels and thereby achieve the beatific vision of God Himself. Inscribing the sigil on circular wax tablets like the one pictured here, Dee would interact with the angels via his medium, Edward Kelly, and a 'shew-stone', placing one tablet upon a 'holy table', and the shew-stone upon the tablet, with four other tablets placed beneath the legs of the table. Once an angel – or demon – stepped within this configuration, they became unable to leave without submitting to interrogation. And since Dee's system of magic was heavily rooted in the number seven – a number which is also strongly connected with the seven traditional planets of astrology – this power was primarily derived from the heptagrams (seven-pointed stars) and heptagons (seven-sided polygons) inscribed upon the *sigillum dei aemeth* itself. For the same reason, the seven so-called 'angels of brightness' also feature prominently in the outer ring, since each was associated with a specific planet and allegedly possessed the ability to comprehend the seven 'inward powers of God, known to none but himself'.

Ultimately, Dee's system, as outlined in his *Mysteriorum libri Quinti*, or 'Five books of mystical exercises', written between 1581 and 1583, would be closely associated with his warmest twentieth-century admirer, Aleister Crowley, and the Hermetic Order of the Golden Dawn. But in his own day, Dee's fame and influence spread far beyond the circle of his fellow scholars and occultists. Certainly, his considerable reputation allowed him to nurture relationships not only with the queen herself but with both her key ministers, Francis Walsingham and William Cecil, and it also allowed him to enjoy the generous patronage of Robert Dudley, Earl of Leicester, Sir Philip Sidney, Edward Dyer and Sir Christopher Hatton. Yet after his return to England in 1589, after a six-year sojourn in Europe, Dee found that his home in Mortlake had been vandalised, his library ruined and many of his prized books and instruments stolen. And while the queen continued to support him thereafter, her successor was altogether less inclined to generosity. Indeed, James I's aversion to witch-craft and 'scrying' of any kind was already well established by the time of his arrival upon the throne, so that Dee's status was bound to suffer accordingly, notwithstanding the deep commitment to his own brand of Christian piety that he maintained throughout and his deeply held con-viction that only through his researches could the rift between Catholics and Protestants be satisfactorily resolved. Cared for by his daughter, Katherine, who was one of eight children borne by his three wives, Dee would die at the age of 82, bereft of the various possessions he had been forced to sell to support them both.

76

Elizabethan 'angel'

This Tudor coin, minted during the reign of Henry VIII, was found by archaeologists on the site of the hospital of St Mary Spital in Spitalfields. Since the archangel St Michael is shown on one side, such coins, which were officially called nobles, became popularly known as 'angels'. They were distributed during a special ceremony in which sufferers from scrofula – a chronic microbacterial infection in the lymph nodes, sometimes caused by tuberculosis and usually giving rise to bluish-purple abscesses in the neck – were touched by the ruling monarch in anticipation of a cure. As a consequence of the widespread belief that English kings and queens possessed the power to heal scrofula victims in this way, the disease was often referred to as the 'King's Evil', and the choice of this particular coin was no coincidence, since it depicts St Michael trampling upon a devil in the form of a dragon, at a time when the occurrence of illness was generally associated with the influence of malign forces. Approximately 3.2cm in diameter, the coin is made from gilt plate on pewter and is inscribed with the legend 'Henry by the Grace of God King of England and France'. The reverse, in its turn, bears the inscription, 'By Thy cross, save us, O Christ, our Redeemer', and depicts a ship with a cross-shaped mast.

In all likelihood, the coin belonged to a patient at the hospital where it was found, and represented a significant sum, since those put forward for healing were usually from the poorest classes of society. And although the amount bestowed as alms was originally no more than a penny, by the mid-fifteenth century recipients were presented with the new style of 'noble' worth between 6s 8d and 11s, depending upon the price of gold. First minted in 1465, these coins were much sought after in their own right, soon acquiring the nickname by which they are known to this day. So popular did the angel become, indeed, that inns and taverns all over the country, including most famously the Angel at Islington, were

Museum of London

named after it, though by Tudor times as the new dynasty attempted to establish its legitimacy by any and every means available, both the coin and the healing ceremony associated with it assumed an altogether deeper significance.

While there were intervals in which he did not perform the ritual at all, Henry VII still laid hands upon seven or eight infected people annually, while Henry VIII is known to have touched a total of fifty-nine people between early January 1530 and late December 1532 alone. And although the evangelically inclined Edward VI frowned upon the superstitious nature of the ritual, his sister Mary took her 'powers' altogether more seriously, as did Elizabeth I who resumed the practice in 1570 after the Roman Catholic Church excommunicated her and alleged that she had therefore lost the capacity to heal. Nor were her Protestant subjects, usually so wary of wonder-workings and miraculous interventions of any kind, inclined to discourage her from continuing the long tradition. On the contrary, the Elizabethan surgeon William Clowes asserted unequivocally that 'the royal touch' proved the queen's legitimacy, and claimed into the bargain that the queen was able even to heal foreigners, citing the case of a Dutchman as an example.

In an effort to reinforce their divinely ordained status, Tudor monarchs also took steps to reaffirm the sanctity of the ritual itself. As set down by Henry VII, the procedure drew heavily upon 'ancient' precedent and consisted of four elements. Initially, the monarch was to touch or stroke the face or neck of the infected person before hanging the coin – known also as a 'touch piece' – around the person's neck, where it was recommended to be retained until healing was complete. There then followed passages from the Gospel of Mark (16:14–20) and the Gospel of John (1:1–14), since the former in particular appeared to confirm not only a monarch's power to heal but also his or her immunity to infectious diseases. In the words of the evangelist, 'they shall take up serpents; and if they drink any deadly thing, it shall not hurt them; they shall lay hands on the sick, and they shall recover' – although the ceremony also involved the cleansing of the king's or queen's hands after the touch had been administered. Finally, until the Reformation at least, prayers were also offered to the Virgin Mary and saints as well as God Himself.

Coincidentally, the ritual was normally performed between Michaelmas and Easter, when cold weather made it less likely for the disease to be contracted by the healer, though Queen Elizabeth, for her part, avoided direct contact with the infected abscesses in any case, preferring instead to make a sign of the cross above the victim's head, regardless of any offence to her Puritan critics. It was believed, too, that the efficacy of the ritual was increased by its performance upon a holy day, notwithstanding the disease's tendency to go into remission naturally. Even Shakespeare was prepared, in *Macbeth*, to reinforce the widespread misapprehension that 'strangely-visited people, all swollen and ulcerous' and 'pitiful to the eyes' might be spared their sufferings by 'hanging a golden stamp about their necks, put on with holy prayers'. Such, then, it seems, was the power of an anointed Tudor monarch. 'The mere despair of surgery, he cures', as Malcolm observed to Macduff.

77

The Danny jewel

While the printing presses of sixteenth-century England were, at one level, exposing fraud and banishing ignorance, the superstitions of an earlier age were, for many, thriving with renewed vigour. Indeed, the belief in fetishes, totems, the evil eye, luck-bones, folk remedies, love charms and nefarious magic of all descriptions was prevalent throughout the realm as Christianity and paganism continued to be inextricably mingled in the minds of many Tudor men and women. This, after all, was a time when the expression 'bless you' was intended to stop the devil entering the body of a sneezing person through his or her mouth, and sailors increasingly wore golden hoop earrings to pay for their passage in the underworld if ever they should sink or drown. When jugglery and legerdemain still retained the glamour of the miraculous, moreover, and magic was used to discover lost things, bring back wayward lovers and cure disease, it was less surprising still that men should continue to seek the philosopher's stone and dabble in seemingly limitless 'alcumysticall cousenages'. Nor, when one author chose to rail in 1580 against the 'absurd, unknowne and insolent wordes' of astrologers, should we be altogether surprised that he concluded, on the strength of Scripture, with an observation that the fortunes of nations were clearly foreshadowed in the heavens.

If the so-called Danny jewel is any guide, meanwhile, this potent mix of credulity and apprehension was by no means confined to the unlettered majority, since the Campion family who owned it moved in rarefied circles as highly respected members of the upper Sussex gentry, possessing considerable estates at Danny House, Hurstpierpoint, and a sturdy reputation for God-fearing earnestness to match. Fashioned around 1550 in the shape of a ship, and acquired by the Victoria and Albert Museum in 1917, the jewel measures 8.4cm in height and contains a semi-circular section of narwhal's tusk mounted in enamelled gold, suspended by three rings from a chain. And it is the setting of the tusk itself that betrays on this occasion an altogether broader and more intriguing function for the jewel than mere ornamentation, since its owners, like other contemporaries, will certainly have taken it to be something altogether more exotic: nothing less, in fact, than a cutting from the horn of a unicorn, which was intended to serve as a sure detector of poison in food and drink.

Not altogether surprisingly, in retrospect, the threat from poisoning appears to have been a particular preoccupation of many Tudors, irrespective of background. The deadly properties of hemlock, henbane and belladonna were, in fact, common knowledge, and potential victims were quick to grasp at any prospective counter-measure. Mulberry leaves boiled in vinegar were used to combat the effects of henbane, while frankincense was considered a tried and trusted remedy for hemlock. Mistletoe and rue, meanwhile, both of which are highly toxic in their own right, were employed to ward off a wide range of potential toxins, along with other recommended safeguards such as incense, St John's wort, hassuck grass or fennel.

For many, however, the horn of the unicorn remained the most potent resort of all. Mentioned first in European literature by Ctesias, a Greek historian of the fifth century BC, and appearing too in the writings of Aristotle and Pliny, the existence of unicorns received further authentication from Latin and Greek mistranslations of the Hebrew Bible, where the word *re'em*, referring to the wild ox, is wrongly interpreted as either *unicornis* or *monokeros*, meaning 'one horn'. Indeed, even after Elizabeth I's death, the King James Bible of 1611 would continue to employ the term, making unicorns nothing less than an article of faith to most believers.

In consequence, the wealthy went to almost any length to secure their protective powers, and in doing so succumbed to a remarkable species of confidence trick, since most of the 'unicorn's horns' on the European market, like the fragment within the Danny jewel, were actually the tusks of the narwhal – a whale that grows one long, twisted tooth resembling a horn. As these creatures are rarely sighted further south than Greenland, they were hunted only by the Scandinavians, and these canny seafarers kept the secret of the strange whale's existence for nearly 500 years, protecting their supply while they sold the tusks as unicorns' horns. As a result, though many Europeans were aware of the existence of 'sea unicorns' as the sixteenth century dawned, little else was known about them, by which time a narwhal's tusk was worth several times its weight in gold. Even two centuries later, the sign of the unicorn was still hanging resolutely above the doorways of apothecary shops throughout England – a symbol of healing and the integrity of the contents inside.

78

Interrogation stool for witches

In 1566, at the Chelmsford summer assizes in Essex, Elizabeth Francis, wife of Christopher Francis, was charged with bewitching the infant child of William Auger. Hailing from the nearby village of Hatfield Peverell, she confessed, it seems, to a lengthy list of misdemeanours, which were promptly turned into a bestselling pamphlet or 'chapbook' by a certain John Phillips. According to her testimony, Elizabeth had learned the art of witchcraft from her grandmother at the age of 12 and been given a white-spotted cat named Sathan, who spoke to her in 'a strange hollow voice' and fed upon bread and milk and drops of her own blood. When a certain Andrew Byles refused to marry her, it was Sathan, she claimed, who had killed him and gone on to find her present husband, with whom she had a daughter. The couple, however, were prone, as Elizabeth herself admitted, to 'much unquietness' and 'moved to swearing and cursing', with the result that she duly ordered the cat, as her 'familiar', to dispatch the six-month-old infant and render her quarrelsome husband lame. Nor, ultimately, was Elizabeth's attachment even to Sathan permanent, for after owning the animal for some fifteen or sixteen years, she gave him to a neighbour, the elderly Agnes Waterhouse, who lost no time in employing him on a spree of hog, geese and cow killing, which culminated finally in the bewitchment and death of one William Fynne. For her exploits, Waterhouse was convicted on the evidence of a 12-year-old neighbour and became, on 29 July 1566, the first woman in England to be hanged for witchcraft. Francis, meanwhile, was merely sentenced to a year in jail and a series of bouts in the pillory, since her most recent victim had survived and, rather more remarkably, her other offences were deemed unproven beyond her own claims. She survived until 1579 when

she was finally hanged for bringing about the death of her neighbour, Anne Poole, by occult means.

In the decade that followed, some 13 per cent of assize trials in Essex were for witchcraft, or what was officially termed *maleficium*: the use of diabolical power to cause harm. Sixty-four people were tried in all, of whom fifty-three were convicted, and although outright torture was not allowed as part of the investigatory procedure, the stool pictured here provides a keen sense of the kind of interrogation to which the accused might be subjected in any number of counties up and down the country. Made from ash and oak, and inscribed with five separate circles, each with a concentric ring pattern resembling the 'witch-marks' found on the beams, door posts, lintels and mantlepieces of many contemporary houses, the object resides today at Anne Hathaway's cottage in the village of Shottery, Warwickshire. The rings were intended to neutralise the witch's occult powers while the accused – 90 per cent of whom were female – underwent questioning, either bound to the stool in a sitting position or forced to stand upon it for extended periods.

Yet while the outcome of such an interrogation might result in execution where murder or the invocation of evil spirits were proven, other occult misdemeanours, involving destruction of goods, death of animals, finding lost goods or causing someone to fall in love were often treated with surprising leniency. Even attempted murder, for that matter, carried no more than a year's prison sentence and quarterly appearances in the pillory, as Elizabeth Francis had found, while burning remained a practice conducted only in Scotland and Continental Europe. Indeed, between 1547, when Henry VIII's law of five years earlier was repealed, and the passing of Elizabeth I's Witchcraft Act in 1563, no legislation for the punishment of witches actually existed at all. Nor was the Elizabethan law employed especially rigorously in any case, it seems, for when Matilda Parke and Alice Meade of Exeter were found guilty in 1565 of practising magic upon their fellow citizens, the magistrates made every effort to avoid the death penalty. This was in marked contrast to events in Lorraine in the 1580s, for example, where the French judge and demonologist Nicholas Remy claimed to have burned some 900 witches.

At the end of Elizabeth I's reign, therefore, the excesses of the notorious Matthew Hopkins and the 'witch craze' of which he was both symptom and cause were still four decades away. In the meantime, Jean Bodin's *Traité de la Démonomie des Sorciers*, which had argued so persuasively for common sense and relaxation in the treatment of witches, had already achieved its tenth reprint. Yet while maidens continued to vomit pins and men believed their entrails infested with snakes, reason and toleration would continue to wage an uphill struggle. It would take another century and more before Voltaire would establish the link between superstition, persecution, ignorance and social misery, and until then the sorry tale of misapprehension and hysteria would continue to run its course, as women like Joan Prentice, Joan Upney and Joan Cunny, all of whom were hanged for using familiars at the third Essex witch trial of 1589, found to their cost.

79

Witch bottle

The salt-glazed 'witch bottle' pictured here provides a rare and fascinating insight into the folk beliefs of sixteenth- and seventeenth-century Britons. Unearthed in Epping more than twenty years ago, it closely resembles in both design and function an even more remarkable example found in 2004 at Greenwich, 1.5m below ground, which, when shaken, splashed and rattled. Subsequent x-ray examination showed a cluster of bent brass pins and iron nails lodged in the neck, suggesting that it had been buried upside down. Further computed topography scans showed that it was indeed half-filled with liquid, which proved to be human urine after the cork was penetrated by a long needle and the extracted brew subjected to gas chromatography and nuclear magnetic resonance tests. No less curiously, the bottle also contained a nail-pierced leather heart, ten fingernail clippings, navel fluff and hair, along with traces of iron sulphide which suggested that brimstone, the hellish substance of the Book of Revelation, had been added for good measure. The object's purpose, it seems, was to force a witch to retract a spell by means of sympathetic magic. With the urine and bulb of the bottle intended to represent the witch's bladder, it was believed that the nails and pins would so torment the enchanter that when she or he passed water they would have no choice but to comply.

Such objects were comparatively commonplace in Tudor England, but it is extremely unusual to find one still sealed, and this was the first to be opened scientifically. All too often they had been casually opened by an unwitting discoverer who then proceeded to discard the apparently insignificant contents. Prior to the discovery at Greenwich, therefore, our knowledge was largely confined to seventeenth-century documents, which suggested procedures for preparing the bottles, but provided relatively sparse detail on what precisely they should contain. Sulphur, for example, is not mentioned in any existing 'recipe', although a previously discovered bottle seemed to contain the remains of some matches. And there were

Epping Forest District Museum

other, broader insights emerging from the bottle's examination, since further analysis of the urine showed that it contained cotinine, a metabolite of nicotine, indicating that it came from a smoker, while the nail clippings were noticeably manicured, suggesting that a person of some social standing was responsible for creating the bottle in the first place.

The choice of container, on the other hand, was consistent with most other known examples of witch bottles, like the one pictured here. It is a Bartmann jug typical of those made in the Rhineland region during the sixteenth and seventeenth centuries, and so named after the German term for 'bearded man'. Bartmann jugs have round squat bodies, with short necks and loop handles, and they are covered in a brown and red glaze, which is highlighted on the front of the neck by the face of a bearded man – an image believed to derive from the 'wild man', a mythical figure popular in the medieval art and literature of Northern Europe from the fourteenth century onwards. Although created in a variety of shapes and sizes, and used conventionally for storing food and drink, for transporting goods and decanting wine, the jugs' fearsome human appearance made them particularly appropriate for use in a protective, guardian-style function in counter-magic.

But other items, too, were frequently employed to thwart the effect of evil influences. Written charms, for instance, as well as dead cats, horse skulls and concealed shoes, often children's, are among many objects frequently found imbedded in the structure of buildings, especially in East Anglia, which appears to have been a particular centre for occult activity from the reign of Elizabeth I onwards. And witch bottles themselves continued to be employed long after the queen's death, not only by superstitious homeowners, but even by apothecaries and respected physicians. In Joseph Blagrave's *Astrological Practice of Physick*, for instance, which was published in 1671, a number of remedies were proposed for curing sick victims of bewitchment:

> Another way is to stop the urine of the patient, close up in a bottle, and put into it three nails, pins or needles, with a little white salt, keeping the urine always warm. If you let it remain long in the bottle, it will endanger the witch's life, for I have found that they will be grievously tormented making their water with great difficulty, if any at all.

In a rare court document from 1682 it is recorded how one apothecary recommended that the husband of an afflicted woman should 'take a quart of your wife's urine, the paring of her nails, some of her hair, and such like, and boyl them well in a pipkin', after which the jug was to be buried on the sick person's property – saying much for the 'Scientific Revolution', which supposedly superseded the more credulous age of the Tudors.

War,
Weapons
and
Defence

80

The Flodden helm

Hanging high up on the south wall of the chancel of St Michael's church, Framlingham, is the funerary helm of Thomas Howard, 2nd Duke of Norfolk, who on 9 September 1513 'between 12 and 3 of the afternoon', led Henry VIII's troops to a crushing victory over 40,000 Scots at Flodden Field. Howard had fought his first battle in the Wars of the Roses before the Scots king, James IV, was born, and was as vigorous as ever at the age of 70 as he marched north, carrying Durham Cathedral's great banner of St Cuthbert at the head of his army, just as it had been carried to victory against earlier Scottish invaders in 1138 and 1346. When the Scots' great cannon opened fire with their 'filthey straw' from atop Branxton Hill, Howard's generalship proved every bit as decisive as that of his predecessors. Badly sited, the enemy shot harmlessly over the heads of 22,000 English troops, and as the unarmoured Highlanders then took off their shoes and staged a frenzied downhill attack, they ran straight into English archers who for the last time in history played a critical role in winning a battle. By the end of the battle King James, his bastard son, and the cream of the Scottish nobility, including eleven earls and eight lords, all lay broken on the field, waiting to be roughly plundered by dour Northumberland folk, who drove off Scottish horses in hundreds, and by armourers who swarmed over the butchered corpses for resale benefit. After this, the surviving English soldiers slaked their four days' thirst with Scots ale. They would never have believed it to be so good, they said, 'had it not been tasted ... by our folks'.

Howard himself, meanwhile, would subsequently enjoy the full flush of royal favour, notwithstanding his earlier support for Richard III at the Battle of Bosworth, which had resulted in his attainder in the first Parliament of Henry VII's reign and a three-year spell in the Tower. Within six months of Flodden he had been rewarded with the dukedom of Norfolk and, as Lord High Steward, would subsequently preside at the trial of England's premier nobleman, the Duke of Buckingham, in

May 1521, though by that time he was almost 80 and in failing health. Soon forced to withdraw from court, he would resign as Lord Treasurer in favour of his son in December of that year before retiring to his ducal castle at Framlingham in Suffolk where he died on 21 May 1524.

His funeral on 22 June at Thetford Priory was said to have been one of the most spectacular and expensive of its day. Costing over £1,300 and involving a procession of 400 hooded men bearing torches, and an elaborate bier surmounted with 700 candles, it reached its climax with the arrival of the Windsor herald, solemnly bearing the memorial Flodden helm into the chapel on horseback. Dating from around 1500, the helmet had actually been fashioned, in spite of its significance, from the chin guard and visor of two separate helmets, which were somewhat clumsily riveted together to form a commemorative funeral helm of the sort that had been hung earlier in Canterbury Cathedral for the Black Prince. And this is not the helmet's only curious feature, since the visor or 'beaver' is in reality a reinforcement visor, known as a *bouffe*, which was originally intended to strap over and reinforce the actual visor of a fighting helmet. Lacking also an occularium or vision slit, the Flodden helm was intended, therefore, entirely for ritual purposes to affirm the dead duke's status, symbolised above all by the imposing wooden lion, measuring 33cm in height, which proudly proclaims the royal descent of the Howard family.

In an age which never flinched at celebrating triumphant bloodshed, the Flodden helm could not embody more aptly both a bygone martial ethic and a rivalry between nations that still reverberates today. Yet the events at Flodden Field in Northumbria just over 400 years ago are likely to have appeared glorious only to the victors and survivors. According to Edward Hall, writing thirty years after the fray, '12,000 at the least of the best gentlemen and flower of Scotland' were slain, in return for what appears to have been some 1,500 English deaths. For Scots, therefore, the defeat would not be lightly forgotten. 'Sighing and moaning, on ilka green loaning, the flowers of the forest are a' wede away', runs the famous lament, while three centuries later even the English poet Joseph Ritson would reflect how the battle had 'made many a fatherless child, and many a widow poor' as 'many a Scottish gay lady sate weeping in her bower'.

81

Chanfron

On On 16 August 1513 a French cavalry contingent, under strict orders not to fight, misjudged its position near the fortress of Thérouanne and, when confronted unexpectedly by the English enemy, promptly turned tail and fled, leaving in its wake to be captured and ransomed a prestigious gaggle of noblemen which included the Dukes of Orléans and Longueville and that elderly military celebrity, the Chevalier Bayard. Over a hundred other noble prisoners were captured and nine banners taken, and in the process the Battle of the Spurs – so-called because these were the only sharp implements wielded by the French as they panicked and fled – swiftly secured its place in Tudor military folklore, notwithstanding the fact that contemporary accounts greatly exaggerated the numbers involved in this largely inconsequential skirmish. Plainly, the sixteenth-century man-at-arms and the chivalric ethic that was inextricably linked to him still retained significance well beyond their medieval heyday. And although the days of both were already numbered, the so-called 'chanfron' pictured here retains, perhaps, even more fascination for this very reason.

Designed to protect a horses's face in combat, chanfrons like this particular example manufactured in Italy, were only one type of equine armour in a comprehensive range which encompassed: segmented plates for the neck, known as crinieres; croupieres, made of leather, chain or plate, which protected the animal's rear; flanchards, which were attached to the saddle as protection for the sides; and peytrals for the chest. Their basic design remained consistent until the seventeenth century, when they became obsolete, and often incorporated flanges covering the eyes, hinged cheek plates and further features, such as rondels – circular pieces of metal intended for decoration, which also afforded additional protection. But like all such items they were more commonly employed in tournaments than in war, since the main English heavy cavalry force in the sixteenth century consisted of demi-lancers who rode largely 'unbarded' horses and wore only three-quarter or half-armour themselves. Carrying a lighter lance, and

eventually pistols, these men often found themselves fighting alongside German and Burgundian mercenaries, frequently striking an enemy's flank and pursuing routed troops.

But if the significance of the armour they wore has sometimes been exaggerated, horses themselves were certainly considered to be no less essential to the security of Tudor England than the men who sat astride them in battle, and it was for this reason that in 1531 Henry VIII's government forbade their export. Likewise, laws passed during 1535–36 and 1541–42 stipulated that all mares should reach 13 hands in height and stallions 14 hands, while in 1540 horses less than 15 hands high were actually forbidden from grazing on common grounds. Indeed, since horses were used for all manner of military transport, the original law also stated that smaller horses should be killed or removed to enclosed land where they could not breed with larger horses, though it is doubtful whether any widespread slaughter actually resulted, since the law was soon modified to allow that smaller animals merely be kept from breeding. Queen Elizabeth's subsequent fears about the declining numbers of horses, which in 1565 generated a six-monthly muster 'until the realm be replenished', would in any case prove unfounded, for the last major battle in which English cavalrymen were prominent had already been fought eighteen years earlier against a Scottish army at Pinkie Cleugh where the limitations of a style of warfare that had arguably reached its peak of effectiveness two centuries earlier, were all too clearly demonstrated.

At the height of the fighting, with their own heavily outnumbered cavalry easily driven off by the English horse, the Scots, it seems, duly opted to make a sudden advance with their massed pikemen, whereupon English men-at-arms and demi-lancers were thrown against the enemy's pikes, in an effort to slow the onslaught and give time for the infantry and artillery to repel the attackers. Thereafter, it was cannon that won the day and cavalrymen who paid the price, for English losses, notwithstanding ultimate victory, were heavy enough to ensure that an abiding lesson had been learned. In the longer run, moreover, even the days of the joust were numbered, for in France the death of King Henri II from wounds suffered in a tournament of 1559 had repercussions across the Channel too, where combat on horseback was progressively replaced as the highlight of court festivities by large-scale dressage displays known as 'carousels'.

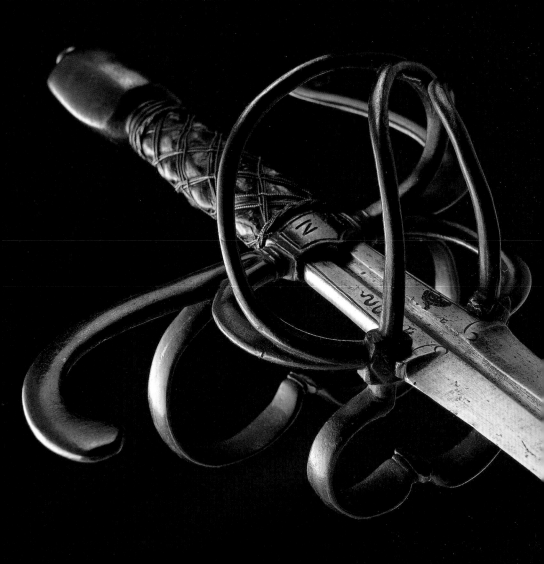

82

Rapier

Though the rapier is first mentioned in the latter half of the fifteenth century, by the 1540s it was rapidly becoming not only a lethal weapon but a must-have fashion accessory for Tudor gentlemen. Originating in Spain as an *espada ropera*, or dress sword, it was a product of improved steel-forging technology which allowed for increased lightness and strength, and its reputation and popularity spread rapidly to Italy, Germany and England, where it soon superseded the heavier, less elegant weapons of tradition. Elaborately decorated, easily slung from the belt, quickly drawn and perfectly designed for rapid long-range thrusting, it was a luxury item that symbolised the status of its owner in much the same way that an expensive watch might do today. Bladesmiths from Toledo and Milan, in particular, enjoyed an unrivalled brand image, though German weapons like the one pictured were increasingly popular by the end of the century. And if the rapier had come by then to signify 'civilised' gentry status for many a portly member of country society, it remained nevertheless in the narrow, violent streets of Tudor England's towns and cities a vastly preferable wounding and killing tool to the clumsier old longsword and small shield, known as a buckler, especially when deftly wielded in combination with a dagger.

Certainly, the rapier pictured here was perfectly capable of inflicting lethal damage, though its sleek design and finely crafted features made it every inch a thing of beauty in its own right. Designed around 1600 at Dresden by Anton Schuch, it measures 113cm in length and weighs precisely 1250g. The flattened blade, which is not Schuch's personal work but was probably purchased by his workshop at a Leipzig trade fair, displays a single short groove and bears the viper mark of Milan as well as a ducal crown and half-moon stamp, in imitation of Toledo weapons, along with a further inscription IHS representing the Greek name for Christ.

The iron hilt consists of an etched and blued grip with leather covering and copper wire, and is protected by an upper and lower side ring, both elegantly retracted in the middle and embellished with a moulded

Lennart Viebahn

swelling as an orna-
ment. Since protection
was of course neces-
sary on the inner side
of the rapier as well
as the outer, there are
also three diagonal
side rings, typical of
their kind, that origi-
nate at a common
base on the middle
shield and swing out
widely over the area
to be protected before
finally merging at the
end of the lower side
ring and the arms of
the hilt. Appropriately
enough, the hilt is also
marked with the ini-
tials SA, representing
Schuch himself, who
had become a master

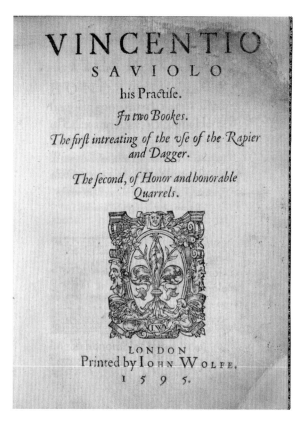

craftsman in Munich in 1577. And, as a final effect, the upper and lower
ends of the grips are decorated with Turk heads.

Yet by no means all contemporaries were entirely convinced of
the rapier's merits. On the contrary, much ink was spilt at the time in
assessing whether the traditional sword was better than these weapons.
Sir John Smythe's *Instructions, Observations and Orders Mylitarie*, for
instance, highlighted the shortcomings of the rapier from the military
standpoint, suggesting that it was too long for a footsoldier to draw in
the press of battle or a horseman to employ unless he let his reins fall.
On account of its hardness and narrow construction, Smythe argued, the
rapier's blade was also inclined to break upon striking armour. George
Silver was another critic, referring to rapiers as 'bird-spits' and listing,
like Smythe before him, their limitations in battle, including their inabil-
ity to pierce a corselet or cut through pikes. Excessively long and with
inadequate guards, they were responsible, thought Silver, for the unnec-
essary wounding of many skilled men who found themselves unable to
uncross the weapon without stepping back.

Underlying such criticisms, however, there is the suspicion that the increasing number of foreign fencing masters in London – many of whom, like Vincento Saviolo of Padua and his revered counterpart Rocco Bonetti, were doing brisk business – may well have played a part in generating at least some of the hostility towards the new weapon. In Silver's opinion the simple English ploughman was, 'without art', a far better fighter than any 'schoolman' trained in one of the new establishments, who had thereby lost 'the benefit of nature' in real combat, where 'grips, closes, wrestlings' and 'striking with the hilts' come into their own. In explaining why English fencing is superior to Italian, Silver reminded his audience, too, how:

> We like degenerate sons, have forsaken our forefathers' virtues with their weapons, and have lusted like men sick of a strange ague, after the vices and devices of Italian, French and Spanish fencers, little remembering, that these apish toys could not free France from King Henry the fifth his conquest.

Nor, ultimately, was Silver prepared to confine his beliefs to empty rhetoric, for he subsequently challenged Saviolo to a public fencing match atop a scaffold erected at the Englishman's own expense – a challenge, it should be added, that the Paduan deftly sidestepped.

83

Bollock dagger

Unlike today, the sixteenth century was a time when knives were still carried openly, albeit mainly for practical everyday purposes. It was not unusual for people to carry around their own cutlery and, when not employed in cutting and spearing food on the plate, knives doubled as scraping, etching and unpicking tools, as well as digging, opening and shaving implements. It was also fashionable for women to carry knives in wooden sheaths suspended from long belts or girdles, and in this particular regard knives sometimes served a symbolic function, since certain unmarried females carried empty sheaths at the behest of their parents, in order to indicate their virginity and availability for marriage. Frequently given as wedding or betrothal tokens, knives were universally recognised as status symbols, with well-dressed townsmen sporting finely decorated daggers from the Continent in silken sheaths with gold embroidery, while ruder peasant folk and labourers made do with blades of a single cutting edge sheathed in leather.

Predictably, however, knives also served an altogether meaner purpose as instruments of harm and violence. Although the wearing of armour and carrying of swords in the street had been banned by royal order in 1351, the law had long been ignored and Tudor men of all classes freely carried murderous blades, which they frequently deployed in anger. During Mary I's reign, for example, it was widely known that the queen's Spanish and Italian servants were at 'daggers drawn' with their English counterparts. 'Not a day goes by,' wrote one Spaniard, 'without knife work in the court', and with lethal weapons like the so-called 'bollock dagger' readily at hand the consequences of such aggression may well be imagined. Named after the oval swellings at the base of the handle, which resemble male testes, and normally measuring around 13in in overall length, cruder examples like the corroded remnants found upon the wreck of the *Mary Rose*, weighed around 7oz or so and were fashioned with boxwood

Peter Crossman, Mary Rose Trust

285

handles and single-edged blades, though in this case the blades have survived only in the form of concretions.

But various, more refined types were also common and, before its decline in the eighteenth century, the bollock dagger would enjoy one of the longest lifespans of any weapon of its type, undergoing a number of stylistic variations after its first appearance on an assortment of Continental tomb effigies between 1300 and 1350. One of the first and most common forms was a single-edged, triangular-section blade that tapered evenly from hilt to point. In some cases the blade was reinforced for piercing purposes by making it quadrangular near the point, and both styles seem to have persisted throughout the dagger's development. By 1400, however, an evenly tapered double-edge blade had also become popular and by 1450 the double-edged blade was adopting a more slender form with a thick diamond cross-section that sometimes included a *ricasso*, or unsharpened length of blade just above the hilt. This later style continued throughout the sixteenth century with the diamond cross-section becoming so thick that it could almost be considered four-sided. Often carried in a horizontal position or slipped round to the back of the wearer, these four-sided blades were the type most frequently preferred by wealthier Tudor gentlemen.

In all cases, however, the proximity of the weapon to a willing hand greatly increased its menace when tempers frayed or alcohol impaired judgement, as Christopher Marlowe found to his cost on the evening of 31 May 1593. Over the course of that day Marlowe had, it seems, eaten and played backgammon with a certain Ingram Frizer and two other men at a house in Deptford, London. Following a walk in the garden they had returned to their room when an argument broke out over the bill to be paid. Springing up from the bed on which he had been lounging, Marlowe then snatched Frizer's dagger and proceeded to hit him repeatedly on the head with the pommel – a common style of assault which has given rise to the modern term 'pummeling'. Yet when Frizer eventually managed to force the dagger from Marlowe's hand, the fray spiralled out of control. For according to the inquest, 'the said Ingram, in defence of his life, with the dagger aforesaid of the value of twelve pence, gave the said Christopher a mortal wound above his right eye, of the depth of two inches and of the width of one inch'. At a cost, then, of only one shilling and a moment's folly, one of Tudor England's most talented literary figures had been done to death in his prime – a hapless victim of poor judgement, poor company and the everyday prevalence of cold steel.

84

Elizabeth I's 'pocket pistol'

Breaker my name of rampart and wall
Over hill and dale I throw my ball

So runs the Dutch inscription upon the mighty Tudor cannon, known as Queen Elizabeth's pocket pistol, which resides today at Dover Castle. Built in Utrecht in 1544 by Jan Tolhuys, and presented to Henry VIII by Maximilian van Egmond, Count of Buren and Stadtholder of Friesland, as a gift for the king's younger daughter, it measures 7.3m in length, is decorated with figures symbolising Liberty, Victory and Fame, and once fired cannon balls of 4.75in (12cm) calibre. Before the English Civil War it guarded the cliffs of Dover and propaganda of the time suggested that it could fire a 12lb (5.5kg) ball 7 miles. Indeed, the most inflated claims even suggested that, if properly maintained, the cannon's shot could reach France, though tests done in the 1970s with similar basilisks indicate a rather more conservative range of 1,200 yards (1,100m) with a 10lb (4.5kg) ball. Mounted today on an iron stand, which was cast in 1827 at the Duke of Wellington's behest from the metal of guns brought from the field of Waterloo, it now stands indoors to prevent further damage from the Channel's salt-laden winds – an outstanding testament to contemporary military technology.

By the early sixteenth century cannon were already being made in great variety. When Henry VIII invaded France in 1513, for instance, he went fully equipped with bombards, curtows, 'Nuremberg pieces', serpentines, falconets, multi-barrelled organs and a range of other guns, heavy and light, which would together consume some 32 tons of gunpowder per day as they rained down destruction upon the fortress of Thérouanne. But

the most famous of all were the dozen heavy guns provided by Thomas Wolsey and dubbed the Twelve Apostles, each of which was drawn by twenty-four Flanders mares and could fire a 260lb (118kg) shot five times a day. Benefitting from the development of cast-iron projectiles, stand-ardised calibres and 'corned' gunpowder employing coarse grains which allowed pockets of air between the grains to allow fire to travel through the powder and ignite the charge quickly and uniformly, artillery was already becoming effectively irresistible. 'There is no wall, whatever its thickness,' wrote Niccolò Macchiavelli around this time, 'that artillery will not destroy in only a few days.'

And although castles were not made obsolete by cannon immediately, their design and function nevertheless altered rapidly. Instead of soaring towers and crenellated battlements, the new fortresses were typified by low, thick, sloped walls, and an array of earth and brick breastworks and redoubts. Henceforward these so-called star forts became dominated by their role as massive artillery platforms. Named after their characteris-tic shape, which attempted to force any advance toward it directly into the firing line of massed cannon batteries, they became a key element of Henry VIII's national defence programme against invasion from France and Spain launched in 1539 and 1540, and over thirty were built to pro-tect the harbours and estuaries along the east and south coasts, including the most impressive of all at Deal, boasting over 200 gun ports carefully designed to allow the maximum possible lines of fire.

Dover Castle

In the meantime, technological advance and innovation had continued on all fronts. At sea, for example, one of the first ships to be able to fire a full cannon broadside was the English carrack the *Mary Rose*, built in Portsmouth from 1510–12 and equipped with seventy-eight guns before an upgrade to ninety-one in the 1530s. One of the earliest purpose-built warships to serve in the English navy, she boasted a crew of 200 sailors and 185 soldiers, though pride of place belonged to the thirty skilled gunners who made her so formidable. In similar fashion, land artillery too had been making steady strides as wheeled gun carriages and trunnions became common and the invention of the limber further facilitated transportation. The use of cast-iron in place of stone projectiles also meant that even relatively light cannon could be deadly.

For monarchs like Henry VIII, however, it was always size above all that mattered, which explains why the 'pocket pistol' was so fitting a gift, particularly at a time when the king was waging his final fling against his kingdom's most bitter enemies. Maximilian van Egmond had already supported England during her 'Rough Wooing' of Scotland and his presentation of the new 'wonder' cannon after the siege of Boulogne in 1544 could not have been more guaranteed to delight, though its smaller French cousins could, it seems, be just as deadly in their own way, as Edward Carew had discovered at Thérouanne three decades earlier. Hit by a stray shrapnel fragment as he sat in Lord Herbert's pavilion, the Devonshire knight fell stone dead before the eyes of his dismayed audience. 'This is the chance of war', Herbert told those around. 'If it had hit me you must have been content; a noble heart in war is never afeared of death'. Van Egmond, meanwhile, would meet a less heroic end from sickness in 1548, but nevertheless wearing full armour and drinking the health of the Holy Roman Emperor as he took his last breath.

85

Signal station at Culmstock beacon, Devon

As the Spanish Armada approached the English coast on 29 July 1588, it is said that Cornish fishermen sailing off the Lizard gazed on impassively as it passed. The 130 ships involved, including twenty-two fighting galleons, had so far faced little opposition on their journey, as Sir Francis Drake, knowing that the incoming tide of the River Tamar in Plymouth was preventing the launch of his ships at Devonport, saw fit to play out his game of bowls at Plymouth Hoe. Even when English resistance mounted in the Channel, moreover, it had little result other than to bring about a costly waste of ammunition, since the hulls of the Spanish ships were well built and only two galleons were damaged. Yet, as these early engagements were played out, London had at least been informed of the invasion by a system of warning beacons, which, upon reaching Beachy Head in Sussex, wove inland towards the capital where Elizabeth I and her council were anxiously waiting.

As the Spanish threat mounted after the outbreak of war in 1585, the construction and hurried repair of a whole series of beacon houses had in fact been a critical government priority, although the one at Culmstock, pictured here, may conceivably date to the medieval period, since beacons have a long history in Devon – the first reference to one occurring in a document of around AD 1200 when land belonging to Torre Abbey was described as being close to the *verbecna* (fire beacon) on Woodbury Common. Built from chert and shaped like a beehive, with a circular hole in the roof for a perpendicular pole which bore two signal braziers, it

lies at the southern end of Blackdown Common and possesses a door and two narrow windows, which face in the direction of other beacons at Blackborough to the south-west and Upottery to the south-east. Outside, meanwhile, it is surrounded by a low bank of stones, with a break near the entrance, though the current structure is thought to be a rebuild of an earlier one, the remains of which seem to be represented by a circular feature to the north of the building. Certainly, in 1870 the beacon was described as being 'fallen abroad', though it was apparently intact around a century earlier when Benjamin Donn's map of 1765 referred to it as 'Blackdown Beacon'.

Somewhat surprisingly, perhaps, Culmstock Beacon is the only one of its kind to have been excavated, and the small excavation conducted in 1995 threw clear light on its design and operation. Within the interior of the stone structure, seven post-holes were identified: one in the middle for the beacon pole, carrying two braziers, which projected through the hole in the roof, and six others around the inside of the stone wall, which once held the thick wooden stakes, driven into the ground to help hold the beacon pole in position. The stakes were probably connected to struts, which radiated from the central pole like the spokes of a wheel, and evidence for these wooden struts also survives in the stone wall where small sockets can still be seen some 20cm above ground level.

Tony in Devon

From contemporary records we know much, too, about the operation of such beacons. Each was to be manned continually – two people by day and three by night – all of whom had to be wise, discreet and honest householders over 30 years of age. If the coastal watchmen saw any ships at sea, they were to judge whether their appearance, actions or course gave any suspicion, in which case, one brazier was to be lit to warn local ships and the surrounding inland districts. This, however, was not intended to lead those inland to light their beacons. For only if the coastal watchmen, whose beacon huts were topped by three braziers, saw a great number of ships giving 'vehement suspicion to be enemies' and leaving little doubt of imminent invasion, was the next stage of alert to be triggered. In this case, two out of the three beacons at shore sites and one of two beacons inland were to be lit, serving as a direct signal that every man was to 'put himself in and be ready'. Finally, when the enemy was actually in the process of landing, all three braziers were to be lit at coastal beacons and all pairs of beacons inland, at which point captains of the muster were to lead their forces to the place where the first beacon was lit, while local farmers drove all cattle, sheep, horses and victuals inland, to deny them to the enemy.

In the event, of course, this ingenious system was never called upon, for the Spanish fleet was ultimately vanquished by a potent combination of English tactical prowess and calamitous weather. But if the day of reckoning for which it was intended never actually arrived, the beacon and others like it would at least perform one other service upon the fleet's return. Over 7,000 English sailors had died from diseases such as dysentery and typhus during the time the Armada was in English waters. Moreover, those who survived were eventually given only enough money for their journey home, while some received only part of their pay. Speaking of the treatment of his sailors, the overall commander of the English navy, Lord Howard of Effingham, expressed his dismay, declaring that he 'would rather have never a penny in the world, than they should lack', before using his own money to meet their wages. In the midst of triumph, then, there was scant recognition for the men who had made that triumph possible – beyond, that is, the celebratory blazing of those self-same beacon fires that had been designed to call them to action in the first place.

Crime and
Punishment

86

Executioner's axe

This axe, belonging to the National Museum of Arms and Armour, is typical of those used by English executioners during the sixteenth century. Dating to this same period and almost certainly originating in England, it serves as a grim reminder of the fate awaiting those individuals who risked treason or merely fell foul of government displeasure at a time when the line between justice and political expediency was often blurred. Like those employed by contemporary woodsmen, axes used on Tudor scaffolds usually possessed a blade about 50cm high by 25cm wide, attached to a 1.5m handle, allowing maximum leverage. In most cases, therefore, the axe was a highly efficient killing instrument, especially when wielded by a skilled practitioner and delivered to a victim kneeling at a 'high' block, which usually measured 45–60cm in height. Prepared thus, the condemned person presented a comparatively easy target as a result of the downward inclination of the neck and the better angle at that point in the arc of the stroke when the neck received the full force of the blow. The low block, by contrast, which usually consisted of a single beam at which the victim lay flat, presented the executioner with added difficulties, since the arc prescribed by the axe in this case meant that the blade was at a greater angle to the prisoner's neck, making it more difficult to sever the head at one attempt. When Robert Devereux, Earl of Essex, lay prone to receive the axe in 1601, for example, it would take three strokes in all to dispatch him.

Yet grisly mishaps could occur in whatever position the condemned man or woman incurred the killing blow. On 28 July 1540 Thomas Cromwell was gruesomely hacked by a bungling headsman who required multiple blows to complete the task. And though he seems to have 'patiently suffered the stroke of the axe' in spite of his protracted ordeal, Edward Hall leaves us in no doubt that the execution itself was performed 'by a ragged, butcherly miser, which very ungodly performed the office'. Even uglier, meanwhile, was the death on 28 May 1541 of Margaret Pole,

Royal Armouries

Countess of Salisbury and last member of the royal house of Plantagenet. She had been falsely imprisoned in November 1539 over her alleged involvement in a plot to overthrow King Henry VIII, and by the time of her execution at the age of 67 she was both frail and ill, though this did not prevent her displaying extraordinary resistance when the time of reckoning came. Dragged to the block and refusing to lay her head upon it, the elderly countess was eventually forced down against her will with disastrous consequences, for the first blow gashed her shoulder, but allowed her to struggle free temporarily. Pursued by the executioner and finally retrieved, it would take a further ten blows before head and body were finally severed.

Swifter and smoother by far, however, was Anne Boleyn's decapitation by a two-handed sword, so that, according to eyewitnesses, when her head was raised by the executioner the lips were still moving in prayer. Nor is there any particular reason to consider this last detail fabricated, for although consciousness was usually lost within 2–3 seconds, due to a rapid fall in what is technically termed the intracranial perfusion of blood, i.e. the supply of blood to the brain, the process might take slightly longer, since the human brain itself has enough oxygen stored for metabolism to persist for some 7 seconds after decapitation occurs. Technically speaking, death from shock and anoxia, due to haemorrhage and loss of blood pressure, takes only slightly less than a full minute. And it was for this reason, it seems, that the executioner usually held up the severed head by the hair: not (as many people think) to display it to onlookers, but in fact to show the victim both the faces of those watching and, indeed, his or her own body. Certainly, when Dr Gabriel Beaurieux conducted a famous study in 1905, he observed that in the case of the executed criminal Henri Laguille, the victim opened his eyes twice over the course of 25–30 seconds in response to the calling of his name, while the German researcher S.T. Sommerling cited other reports of decapitated heads grinding their teeth and, in one case, 'grimacing horribly' when an attendant physician probed the spinal canal with his finger.

Yet for all its apparent barbarity, decapitation remains as humane a method of execution as any modern alternative, at least when conducted by an expert – something which makes the frequent employment of blatant amateurs all the more puzzling. For it was not only Thomas Cromwell who was done to death by a young and, in his case, apparently inebriated incompetent. Lady Margaret Pole, too, according to the Calendar of State Papers, was killed by a 'blundering youth'. The notion of 'professionalism' (or even rudimentary training, for that matter) was as foreign to the Tudor executioner, after all, as it was to the age as a whole in which he found himself. Indeed, next to nothing is known about the individuals employed and this itself speaks volumes perhaps for the inadequacies of the entire selection process. Though Jean Rombaud, the man who is likely to have beheaded Anne Boleyn, came from a long family line of executioners and enjoyed the rank of official executioner of St Omer during the 1530s, in England his counterparts were largely anonymous figures, masked and pulled at random in some instances from the seamier ranks of society. Moreover, while Rombaud had earned celebrity by deftly dispatching two felons with one stroke, the English headsmen at work with their clumsy woodmen's axes, weighing some 3.5kg, could not have dreamt of such finesse. Small wonder, then, that the following inscription was found on the wall of Lady Margaret Pole's cell, etched, one may assume, on the eve of her ordeal:

> For traitors on the block should die;
> I am no traitor, no, not I!
> My faithfulness stands fast and so,
> Towards the block I shall not go!
> Nor make one step, as you shall see;
> Christ in Thy Mercy, save Thou me!

87

'Scavenger's daughter'

Of all the many uses to which the Tower of London has been put, torture has attracted the largest body of myth and legend, and it has come accordingly to dominate the image of that famous landmark in the popular imagination. Yet torture has never been officially recognised in English law as a means of gaining information, and while certain inquisitors, such as Thomas Norton and the fanatically anti-Catholic Richard Topcliffe, have achieved rightful notoriety for their excesses, the overall picture was not quite as straightforward as myths and stereotypes might suggest. The reputation of 'Norton the Rackmaster', for instance, who supervised numerous interrogations at the Tower during the 1570s and 1580s, should be set alongside that of Sir Richard Berkeley, who resigned his office as Lord Lieutenant of the Tower shortly after his appointment in 1595, as a result of his reluctance to be involved. Nor, for that matter, were interrogators given an entirely free hand in their activities, for while the physical process of torture was inflicted by the warders of the Tower, under the command of the Lieutenant, questioning was conducted by two or three commissioners, at least one of whom was required to be a recognised officer of the law, such as the royal attorney or solicitor. Norton was himself a well-known lawyer and Member of Parliament, and there were even occasions, it seems, when the authorities attempted to elicit the required information by threat rather than the outright imposition of physical pain. In the case of the Jesuit John Gerard, for example, the victim was actually introduced by the clerk of the council to an individual purporting to be 'the master of torture', who eventually proved to be nothing more than a common-or-garden artillery officer.

Yet if such instances serve as useful reminders that historical reality and our more lurid simplifications of the past rarely dovetail quite so neatly as some may wish, the fact remains that the religious and political upheavals of the Tudor period undoubtedly spawned much that was not only dark and dastardly but carried out with the full knowledge and authority of the highest levels of government, including the Privy Council and the monarch. Torture, of course, could take many forms. The notorious windowless chamber in the Tower of London known as 'Little Ease', for example, measured just 1.5m square, and was designed to wear down its occupants by gross discomfort rather than excruciating pain. But outright physical agony remained, in most cases, the swiftest and surest guarantor of success, and few implements assured the desired outcome more effectively than the 'Scavenger's daughter', which, in the case of the example pictured here, was designed to compress a kneeling victim until the bones of his ribcage and spine were fractured, and the internal organs were crushed to such a degree that blood flowed from the rectum and other orifices.

Invented by Sir Leonard Skeffington, a Lieutenant of the Tower during the reign of Henry VIII, it gained its title from a corruption of the inventor's name – 'Skevington' – and though there are only six recorded cases of its use, there is no doubt concerning its operation or its effects. Consisting of an iron frame formed from a base-plate and two semi-circular bows, it was fastened tightly across the prisoner's back, holding him in a crouched position, with his arms against his sides, after which it was gradually further constricted by means of a cranking mechanism at the top. Usually requiring no more than an hour to be administered effectively, it seems to have been more efficient even than the rack in achieving its desired outcome, though, somewhat surprisingly, it never displaced its more famous counterpart as the tool of choice for most Tudor interrogators.

Certainly, for Matthias Tanner, a Jesuit historian from the seventeenth century, the infernal gadget seems to have had no rival. 'The body of the victim', he writes, 'is almost broken by this compression' in a manner 'more cruel than the rack', leaving the whole body 'so bent that blood exudes from the tips of the hands and feet ... the box of the chest being burst and a quantity of blood expelled from the mouth and nostrils'. Employed most frequently, like other devices of its type, upon Catholics, it was also used at the Tower of London on an Irish rebel called Thomas Miagh in 1581. The Irishman's ultimate fate remains unknown, though he appears at least to have survived his encounter with the torturer, for he left the following inscription upon the wall of his cell in the Beauchamp Tower where he remained imprisoned: 'By torture straynge my truth was tried, yet of my libertie denied'.

88

Rack

In 1583, just over a decade after he became Elizabeth I's Lord High Treasurer, William Cecil, 1st Baron Burghley, made the following claim about Tudor England's best known instrument of torture. 'The Queen's servants, the warders [of the Tower], whose office and act it is to handle the rack,' he claimed, 'were ever by those that attended the examinations, specially charged to use it in as charitable a manner as such a thing might be'. But however Burghley might have attempted to regulate its use, the rack's reputation remains etched to this day in popular perceptions of the Tudor period as a whole – so much so, indeed, that neither its operation nor its effects require any extended explanation. Consisting of a rectangular iron frame, with a roller at both ends and a third in the middle which was employed to turn the machine's mechanism by two levers and a system of rope pulleys, the example at the Tower of London pictured here is an accurate replica based on a diagram showing what remained of the Tower's rack in the eighteenth century when it was found in storage before being subsequently lost again. As the ropes around the victim's hands and feet tightened, his or her muscle fibres were stretched agonisingly until joints were dislocated and eventually separated – a process accompanied by the loud popping noise of snapped cartilage and ligament. 'Then they did put me on the rack because I confessed no ladies or gentlemen to be of my opinion, and thereon they kept me a long time', declared Anne Askew, a Protestant gentlewoman accused of heresy in 1545. 'And because I lay still and did not cry', she continued, 'my Lord Chancellor and Master Rich took pains to rack me with their own hands till I was nigh dead'.

In Askew's case, her interrogation was carried out by the highest legal authority in the realm, Thomas Wriothesley, and Sir Richard Rich, a former Speaker of the House of Commons, who would himself become Lord Chancellor in 1547. And though, according to her own account and that of gaolers within the Tower, she was tortured only once, her own

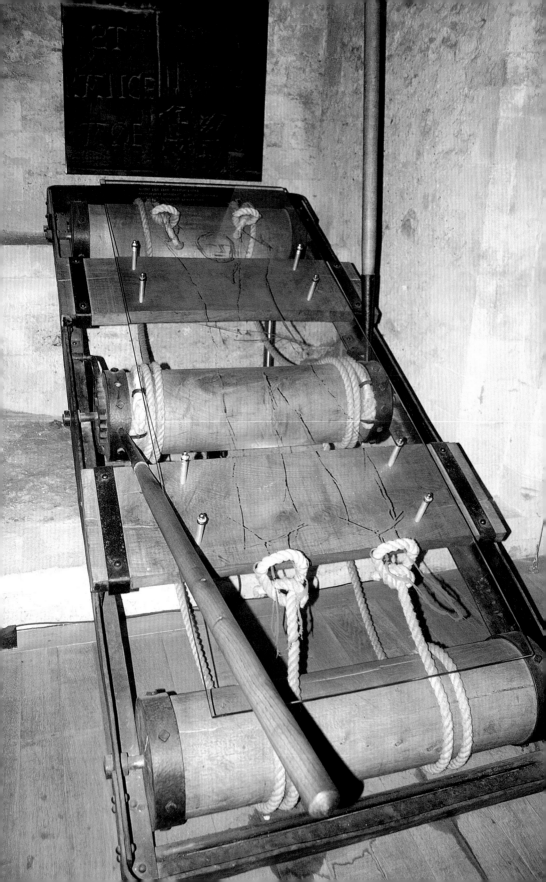

description of what ensued makes truly harrowing reading. Taken from her cell at about 10 a.m. to the lower room of the White Tower, she was first shown the rack in the customary manner and asked to divulge the names of other heretics, which she duly declined to do. In consequence, she was then asked to remove all clothing other than her shift before being fastened to the machine by her wrists and ankles, whereupon, after refusing once again to provide the required information, the wheel of the rack was turned, lifting her so that she was held taut about 12cm above its bed and slowly stretched. At this point, Askew's account, written from prison, suggests that she fainted from pain, and was subsequently lowered and revived – a procedure twice repeated before the Lieutenant of the Tower, Sir Anthony Kingston, refusing to witness the spectacle, left the scene and sought a meeting with the king to explain his position and seek pardon.

In the meantime, however, Wriothesley and Rich continued their work, turning the handles with such vigour that Askew's shoulders and hips were pulled from their sockets and her elbows and knees became dislocated. By this time, the victim's cries could be heard in the garden next to the White Tower where the Lieutenant's wife and daughter were walking. And although Askew gave no names before her ordeal was finally ended by order of the Lieutenant, even this would not spare her a martyr's death at Smithfield on 16 July 1546. So weakened was she by her previous ordeal that she had to be carried on a chair to the stake, where she became, at merely 25 years of age, the only Englishwoman on record to be both tortured and subsequently burned.

It was the reign of Elizabeth I that witnessed the high point of the rack's popularity as an instrument of state policy. It had first been employed in the Tower as long ago as 1447 by John Holland, 2nd Duke of Exeter, but by the 1590s, according to one Catholic source at least, its use had become 'so odious and so much spoken of by the people' that the government's principal torturer, Richard Topcliffe, had thought it preferable to install one in the privacy of his own house. He did so, moreover, with the full consent of the Privy Council, Sir Robert Cecil and, it seems, the queen herself. Writing to her on 26 June 1592, Topcliffe informed his sovereign, in surprisingly familiar fashion, that the Jesuit Robert Southwell was secure in 'my strong chamber in Westminster churchyard' and that preparation had already been made for 'hurting of himself by putting upon his arms a pair of hand gyves'. 'So humbly submitting myself to your majesty's direction in this, or in any service with any hazard,' the letter concludes, 'I cease, until I hear your pleasure.'

Ultimately, on 21 February 1595, Southwell would be hung, drawn, and quartered at Tyburn, where, as the executioner prepared to cut him down

David Bjorgen

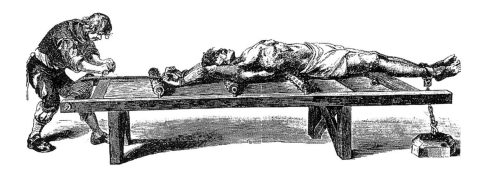

Wikimedia Commons

alive, prior to castration and disembowelment, Lord Mountjoy and some other onlookers tugged at his legs to hasten his death. Topcliffe, on the other hand, who had once served as Member of Parliament of Beverley, would eventually die of old age at his Derbyshire estate in 1604, albeit after an earlier brief spell in the Marshalsea Prison for extortion. Twenty-four years later the rack itself would finally be consigned to history, as judges, called to consider the case against John Felton, assassin of the Duke of Buckingham, unanimously declared its use to be contrary to the laws of England.

Execution cauldron

On 18 February 1531, according to the 'Acte for Poysoning' which ensued later that year, a certain Richard Roose, cook to the household of John Fisher, Bishop of Rochester, 'did cast poison into a vessel of yeast' at the bishop's Lambeth residence, 'by means of which two persons who happened to eat of the pottage made with such yeast died'. For some time Fisher's principled stand against the king's divorce had placed him in growing danger, and it would eventually cost the bishop his life on the scaffold. But on this occasion, at least, his saintly lifestyle seems to have saved him, for he never ate more than the barest minimum and consequently survived the ordeal with nothing more, according to some sources, than excruciating stomach cramps. Two paupers, Bennett Curwen and Alice Tryppytt, however, were not so fortunate, as they had been treated to the leftovers at the bishop's gate and paid the ultimate price for their hunger.

Nor would Roose's subsequent claim that he had merely added purgatives to the food 'as a jest' save him. On the contrary, he was subsequently attainted of high treason under the new poisoning statute rushed through Parliament at Henry VIII's personal behest, and subsequently boiled to death at Smithfield. Notwithstanding Fisher's ongoing opposition to his divorce, the king had acted out of genuine disapproval of the deed and a long-standing personal fear of the poisoner's craft. There would therefore be no hint of clemency or grain of moderation in Roose's treatment. For the cook was not to be immersed in one fell swoop, but, according to the *Chronicle of the Grey Friars of London*, 'lockyd in a chayne and pullyd up and downe with a gybbyt at dyvers tymes tyll he was dede'. The same treatment would also be applied some months later to a maidservant at King's Lynn accused of poisoning her mistress, and to a certain Margaret Davy who was boiled to death at Smithfield on 17 March 1542 for poisoning 'three houses that she dwelt in'.

Ultimately, the act sanctioning such cruelty was repealed in 1547 under the influence of Edward VI's more enlightened Lord Protector, the Duke of Somerset. But death by boiling was neither new nor finished in Europe as a whole. It had been, on the one hand, a common execution method for swindlers and counterfeiters during the Middle Ages, and had also been employed in the Holy Roman Empire for graver types of murder. In 1392, for instance, a man was boiled alive in Nuremberg for having raped and murdered his own mother, while in Scotland, William de Soules, a nobleman involved in a conspiracy against Robert the Bruce and reputed to be a sorcerer, was boiled alive at Ninestane Rig in 1321. North of the border, indeed, the criteria for boiling appear to have been laxer still on occasion, for in 1420 the laird of Glenbervie had been apprehended by a noble clique and 'thrown into the kettle' for no other reason than that his strictness was resented, whereafter the guilty nobles are said to have taken a spoonful each of the steaming brew.

Cauldrons like the one pictured here would in fact continue to be used as execution vessels in Northern Europe well after Tudor governments had abandoned the practice. Indeed, the copper example featured, which now embellishes the north façade of the *Waag* or 'weighing house' at Deventer in Holland, where goods were weighed for tax assessment and coins were checked for metal content, was employed against counterfeiters throughout the sixteenth century, since tampering with the coinage by substituting base metals for precious ones was deemed high treason in its own right. Even as late as 1687 a man from Nuremberg was boiled to death for assisting a group of coin forgers who had escaped justice.

On this last occasion the chosen medium was oil, though tar, tallow or molten lead were also favoured from time to time. In all cases, however, death was both agonising and surprisingly slow. Prolonged scalding would result in anything up to fourth-degree burns of the skin, as a result of which the epidermis and dermis were destroyed, leading to the complete breakdown of subcutaneous fat. Yet only when the heat had exposed muscle, leading to breaches in major arteries and veins, would death finally ensue. In Richard Roose's case, therefore, a contemporary chronicler had little difficulty capturing the horror involved. 'He roared mighty loud,' the account records, 'and divers women who were big with child did feel sick at the sight of what they saw, and were carried away half dead'. Indeed, even those less squeamish, it seems, would have preferred 'to see the headsman at his work'.

90

The Halifax gibbet

'From Hell, Hull and Halifax, Good Lord deliver us.' So ran the old Yorkshire saying, made famous later by John Taylor's *Beggar's Litany*, written in 1622. For if Hull's vagrancy laws were exceptionally harsh, even by the standards of the day, then Halifax's treatment of petty thieves gained a notoriety that reverberates even to the present. As part of the manor of Wakefield, where ancient custom and law gave the lord of the manor the authority to impose summary justice upon any felon found guilty of stealing more than 13½*d*, the West Yorkshire town became a byword for cruel and summary justice, embodied, appropriately enough, in one of its most notable landmarks. Probably installed some time during the sixteenth century as a more efficient alternative to the headsman's axe, the Halifax gibbet was an early guillotine employed for any petty thief unlucky enough to have pilfered more than the stipulated sum. Its stone base was rediscovered and preserved in about 1840, and a full-size non-working replica erected upon it in August 1974, incorporating a blade made from a casting of the original, which is displayed in the Bankfield Museum in Boothtown.

The device, which today stands close to St Mary's Catholic church in Gibbet Street, consisted of an axe head fitted to the base of a heavy wooden block that slid in grooves between two 4.5m-tall uprights, mounted on the stone base standing about 1.2m high. A rope attached to the block then ran over a pulley, allowing it to be raised, after which it was secured by attaching it to a pin in the base, and ultimately released either by withdrawing the pin or by cutting the rope once the prisoner was in place. Prior to execution a convicted felon was usually detained in custody for three market days, on each of which he was publicly displayed in the stocks, accompanied by the goods that had been stolen. Only after sentence had been carried out, however, would a county coroner visit the town and convene a jury of twelve men to give a sworn account of

Tim Green

the circumstances of the conviction and execution. The preceding trial at which sentence had been delivered therefore involved no presiding judge, defence council or oaths, and the convicting jury of sixteen who were summoned by the local bailiff were often the same individuals subsequently summoned by the county coroner to consider the propriety of their own actions.

Almost 100 people were executed in this fashion between the first recorded execution in 1286 and the last in 1650, though official records were not maintained until parish registers were first instituted in England in 1538. Between then and 1650, fifty-six men and women are known for sure to have been decapitated, by which time public opinion was increasingly opposed to such severity for common thieves. To Puritans, in particular, it was merely one more 'ancient ritual' to be jettisoned along with all the old feasts and celebrations of the medieval world and the Church of Rome, with the result that the Halifax Gibbet Law was finally rescinded by Oliver Cromwell in 1650.

Today the names of fifty-two people known to have been beheaded by the device are listed on a nearby plaque. But it is the contemporary account of Raphael Holinshed, written in 1586, that captures most vividly the scenes witnessed by Tudor men and women who once gathered at the spot to see justice done. 'In the nether end of the sliding block,' wrote Holinshed:

> Is an axe keyed or fastened with an iron into the wood, which being drawn up to the top of the frame is there fastened by a wooden pin ... unto the middest of which pin also there is a long rope fastened that cometh down among the people, so that when the offender hath made his confession, and hath laid his neck over the nethermost block, every man there present doth either take hold of the rope (or putteth forth his arm so near to the same as he can get, in token that he is willing to see true justice executed) and pulling out the pin in this manner, the head block wherein the axe is fastened doth fall down with such violence, that if the neck of the transgressor were so big as that of a bull, it should be cut in sunder at a stroke, and roll from the body by an huge distance.

Novelties and New Horizons

91

Printing press

Some twelve years before the Tudor age began, William Caxton described his reasons for producing the first book to be printed mechanically by an Englishman. 'And for as much as in the writing of the same my pen is worn, my hand weary and not steadfast, my eyes dimmed with overmuch looking on the white paper', he wrote:

And also because I have promised to diverse gentlemen and to my friends to address to them as hastily as I might the said book, there-fore I have practised and earned at my great charge and dispense to ordain this said book in print after the manner and form as you may here see.

The book, he added, had not been 'written with pen and ink as other books been' but by the new method 'to the end that every man may have them at once'. Born in Kent between 1415 and 1424, around thirty years before Johannes Gutenberg built the first printing press in Mainz, Caxton had become the governor of the English Merchant Adventurers in Bruges and learned how to print in Cologne around 1469 with commercial possi-bilities uppermost in mind. By Michaelmas 1476 his name had appeared on the account roll of John Estency, Sacrist of Westminster Abbey, as paying a year's rent in advance for the premises – probably a shop – in which he set up his press. And by the time of his death in 1491, he had published more than a hundred books including Chaucer's *Canterbury Tales*, Malory's *Morte D'Arthur, the Golden Legend* and a series of historical works and romances, which he himself translated.

Yet if Caxton blazed the trail, it was his successors in Tudor England, many of whom were foreigners largely ignored in today's history books, who transformed the printing press into a genuine mass medium. Working from premises in Westminster, Southwark, St Paul's

Churchyard, Fleet Street and elsewhere, men like Peter Treveris from Trier in Germany, the Dutchman Steven Mierdeman and Julian Notary, a native of Vannes on the south coast of Brittany, helped Englishmen like Richard Pynson, William Rastell and Robert Wyer both generate and satisfy the needs of a burgeoning reading public. In 1530 it was a Frenchman, Thomas Berthelet, who was appointed King's Printer by royal charter. A resident in the London parish of St Dunstan in London's famous printing quarter where Fleet Street lay, Berthelet would assume responsibility for the printing of royal proclamations and statutes, and by 1549 had been awarded his own coat of arms for his sterling efforts on the government's behalf.

More than any other, however, it was Wynkyn de Worde, a native of Alsace, who improved the quality of Caxton's work as a typographer and moved English printing away from its late medieval beginnings toward a recognisably modern model. Where Caxton had depended more heavily on noble patrons to sustain his enterprise, de Worde shifted his emphasis to the creation of relatively inexpensive books for a commercial audience and the beginnings of a mass market, and while Caxton had used paper imported from the Low Countries, de Worde exploited the cheaper product of John Tate, the first English papermaker. As a result, de Worde was able to publish more than 400 books in over 800 editions, including children's books, works on good housekeeping and animal husbandry, and a range of romantic novels and poetic works, including those of John Skelton. Moreover, while only twenty of Caxton's editions contained woodcuts, around 500 of de Worde's were illustrated.

By the time of de Worde's death in late 1534 or early 1535, the Gutenberg printing press had revolutionised both access to and demand for the written word. Indeed, the two-volume Bible first published in Germany in 1455 at a cost of 600 florins had ultimately given birth to a continent-wide explosion in literature, which yielded not only abstruse works of theological controversy or high literature but also an increasingly broad-based and practically orientated output. Where Johannes Gutenberg had produced books costing the equivalent of approximately three years' wages for an average clerk, Tudor printers were reducing prices at every turn. And where Caxton by and large serviced the few, de Worde was altogether more aware of the wider potential of the printing press. Appropriately enough, therefore, it is de Worde rather than his better-known English counterpart who is commemorated today on a plaque outside Stationers' Hall in London as the 'Father of Fleet Street'.

92

Spectacles

By the time of Gutenberg's invention of the printing press, spectacles were already used by artisans as well as monks and scholars. But when the availability of books increased, the demand for them rose so dramatically that by the end of the fifteenth century spectacle pedlars were already a familiar sight on English streets. Bow spectacles, like the ones pictured, were particularly popular and even found their way on to one of the statues adorning the Lady Chapel at Westminster Abbey, which was built by Henry VII between 1502 and 1509. Possessing a bow-shaped continuous bridge that was sometimes flexible depending upon the material employed, their appearance was remarkably modern, unlike the earliest type of spectacle, first mentioned in an Italian manuscript of 1289, where the bridge took the form of an inverted 'v', riveted at the centre to allow for adjustment. This latter type may well have persisted in use until about 1600, and there is even a pair attached to a display helmet of German origin presented to Henry VIII by Maximilian I. In both types of spectacle, however, the bridge was as much an area to be gripped as to rest upon the nose, and spectacles continued to be held in place with the hand either for extended periods of reading or close inspection until designs with arms began to appear in the late eighteenth century.

Certainly, failing eyesight was no respecter of rank and the inconvenience involved is brought home pointedly by a letter of Henry VII written to his mother, the Countess of Richmond, in 1501, by which time the ageing king's vision was, it seems, well beyond the assistance of spectacles or any other aid. 'For verily madame', Henry confessed:

> My sight is nothing so perfect as it has been ... wherefore I trust that you will not be displeased though I write not so often with mine own hand, for on my faith I have been three dayes or I could make an end to this letter.

Henry VIII, too, appears to have suffered from impaired sight, as an inventory of his possessions makes clear. More than twenty pairs of spectacle cases are itemised, including one 'of lether like a booke harnessed with syluer', another of 'Morisco worke', and one 'golde engraven with the Armes of England'. There is reference, too, to a 'brode glasse to loke vppon a boke' and a number of 'stones' which were to be placed directly upon the page for magnification of individual words.

Yet while kings might collect them avidly, Tudor spectacles nevertheless remain comparatively rare, and the occasional discovery of humbler specimens like the ones featured here are always significant. In this case, the discovery occurred in Guisborough in 1880 when the old almshouses and grammar school on the site of the former priory were being torn down to make way for a new school. John Cook, the clerk of the works at the time, offered his labourers free beer if they found anything interesting under the foundation stone, and they did not disappoint him, for not only did they find the spectacles with one lens intact, but after careful work, even went on to uncover the second lens – only for it to be lost years later. Nevertheless, the glasses remain in a remarkable state of preservation, especially when it is remembered that the frames are made from leather. And although their date of manufacture can only be surmised, they are almost identical to a haul of dozens of leather-framed spectacles dating to the late sixteenth century which were found by archaeologists investigating an old shipwreck off the coast of Croatia. Today they reside within the archive of Prior Pursglove College, Guisborough.

Prior Pursglove College, Guisborough

93

Pocket watch

In 1511, the German humanist Johann Cochlaeus wrote of a young man who 'fashions works which even the most learned mathematicians admire'. The works concerned were 'many-wheeled clocks' made out of 'small bits of iron', which, added Cochlaeus, 'run and chime the hours without weights for forty hours, whether carried at the breast or in a handbag'. And the man responsible was the locksmith and horologist, Peter Henlein, who produced the earliest surviving 'clock-watch'. Contained in a copper housing, measuring 4.5cm in diameter, it is spherical in form and hinged to allow access to the face, which displays only an hour hand. The total weight is 92g and the object also bears the date of its manufacture, beside an Old Latin inscription noting that while time flies, 'I will perceive it correctly'. Boasting a running cycle of forty hours, accompanied by chimes, it is still working today – a testament both to its creator's skill and the developing technology that would eventually transform early modern society into its twenty-first century, intensively time-driven equivalent.

Doubtless, it would be hard to imagine modern industrial societies without the existence of personal timepieces and while Henlein's watches were not the first of their kind – or particularly efficient, for that matter, sometimes losing more than an hour in a single day – they were nevertheless part of a broader trend that would fundamentally alter perceptions of the passage of time. For whereas life had flowed at a more flexible and indeed leisurely pace earlier, the widespread adoption of watches in subsequent centuries created an altogether busier and more hectic lifestyle. Key to all was the invention of the mainspring, which had already been employed in spring-driven clocks of the early 1400s, and the invention of the balance spring, which facilitated the manufacturer of smaller timepieces than the table-top variety that were being manufactured in Germany in significant

numbers in the early Tudor period. For the balance spring, moreover, Henlein must take particular credit, since without its operation the force of the mainspring and the impact of movement – so critical in the efficiency of watches – created serious problems of accuracy. The new balance spring was completely even in thickness to ensure uniform power and was designed as a fine spiral to manage any vibrations.

Yet beyond the fact that Henlein was born in Nuremberg around the very time that Henry VII was establishing the Tudor dynasty in England, very little is known about his early life. Apprenticed initially as a locksmith, he was involved, it seems, in an ugly brawl on 7 September 1504 in which his friend and fellow locksmith George Glaser was killed, after which he sought safety in the local Franciscan monastery. It was during this time that he refined the skills of his trade, for upon his return to the outside world, he swiftly established a far-reaching reputation. By 1509 he had already become a master in Nuremberg's locksmith guild and was soon making both scientific instruments and pendant timepieces which brought him into regular contact with high-ranking noblemen demanding ever smaller and more beautiful designs.

Accuracy, however, became an increasing priority as the sixteenth century progressed, and in the process Swiss timepieces became increasingly sought after. One of the more important stabilising mechanisms, for example, was the fusee, which underwent refinement at the hands, first, of Jacob Zech in 1525 and then his fellow Swiss, Arnaud Gruet, who later perfected it. Between 1550 and 1600, moreover, screws, brass wheels, and crystals began to be used, and during the same period it became increasingly common for English courtiers to wear watches purchased from the Continent. Edward VI appears to have been the first Tudor monarch to possess one, and Elizabeth I is said to have worn a 'ring' watch that alerted her to the arrival of a pre-set hour by scratching her finger with a metal projection.

English clockmakers, by contrast, remain virtually unheard of until the appearance of Thomas Tompion, who was born in 1639, the son of a Bedfordshire blacksmith. Indeed, the Worshipful Company of Clockmakers would not receive its royal charter until 1631, and while Hampton Court had been graced with its famous astronomical clock at some time between 1540 and 1542, its designers, Nicholas Kratzer and Nicholas Oursian, were both foreign. Certainly, there was no Tudor equivalent of Swiss craftsmanship or indeed of Peter Henlein, who would die in August 1542, lauded by his compatriot, the writer Johann Neudorfer, as 'very nearly the first of those who invented how to put small clocks into little boxes'.

www.peterhenlein.de

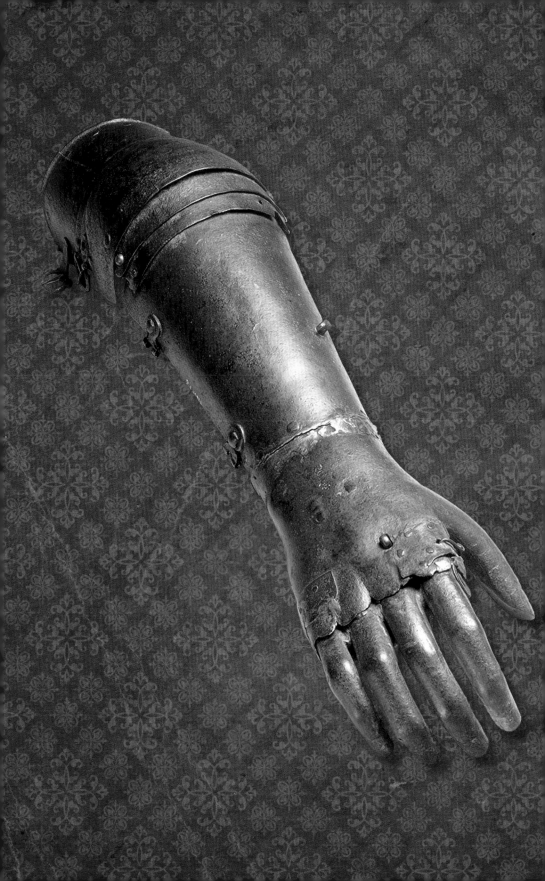

94

Prosthetic arm

This artificial iron arm, which now resides in London's Science Museum, was purchased in 1928 by the American–British pharmaceutical engineer, Henry Wellcome, who founded one of the world's largest medical charities, the Wellcome Trust, and was himself a keen collector of medical artefacts. At the time, the object was thought to have belonged to Götz von Berlichingen (1480–1562), the German mercenary knight and adventurer who was seriously injured at the age of 24 during the siege of Landshut in 1504 when a cannon ball blew shrapnel from his sword and side armour through his arm and hand. Thereafter he was fitted with at least three prosthetic limbs during the course of his life, which allowed him against all odds to pursue a distinguished military career immortalised by Goethe in a play of 1773 named after him. According to contemporary reports the spring-operated fingers of his replacement hand enabled him to remain a fearsome figure on the battlefield, leading a group of rebels against the Holy Roman Empire in 1525, fighting a campaign against the Ottoman Empire of Suleiman the Magnificent under Emperor Charles V in 1542, and serving under Francis I during the imperial invasion of France in 1544.

However, while two of Berlichingen's prostheses are kept today at Jagsthausen Castle and a third is located at Castle Grüningen in Riedlingen, the example at the Science Museum can no longer be connected with him, since it is now known that the knight's left arm rather than the right was actually the one lost at Landshut. We know, too, that the Science Museum's exhibit dates from the period between 1560 and 1600, making it likely to have been manufactured after von Berlichingen's death. Nevertheless, it remains a particularly interesting specimen, not least because a number of other examples have now been recognised as later copies. Equipped with hinged fingers, which were designed to lock for gripping a variety of implements, it is pictured here fully extended, but was designed to be manipulated at the elbow in a range of positions

John Cummings

according to use. In more sophisticated examples of the period, both the thumb and the paired fingers are capable of being independently locked in several positions by means of an elaborate system of ratchets and spring-operated pawls that can be instantly released by pressure on a push-button protruding from the back of the hand. Usually attached to the stump of the arm by leather straps, artificial limbs of this kind were considered miracles of technology at the time and were consequently as expensive as they were rare.

Perhaps the most sophisticated examples, however, were produced not in Germany but in France, where Ambroise Paré was able to augment the technical skill of the armourer with his own detailed knowledge of surgery and human anatomy. As a battlefield surgeon, he had been disturbed by the reaction of some of the people whom he had saved, observing that some soldiers subsequently took their own lives rather than live with the consequences of amputation. Nor was Paré satisfied with the cruder types of prostheses that had been fashioned since ancient Egyptian times. Instead he sought designs that emulated nature and emphasised functionality, fashioning in the process mechanical knees that were controlled by string and could be locked when standing and bent at will, as well as flexible spring-operated feet: designs, in fact, which attracted the suspicion of the Church, since they appeared to mimic God's own handiwork.

It was, however, Paré's mechanical hand that captures most aptly the Frenchman's ingenuity and expertise. Operated by multiple catches and springs, it simulated the joints of a biological hand, as the following list of design features, provided by Paré himself, makes clear:

1. Sprockets attached to each finger, part of the fingers themselves, added and assembled from the back of the hand.
2. Metal shaft going through the centre of the sprockets, upon which they turn.
3. Trigger to hold each finger.
4. Stoppers for the triggers, with a pin in the centre, to receive the triggers.
5. Main trigger to open the four smaller triggers, which hold the fingers.
6. Button at the end of the main trigger; push to open the hand.
7. Spring under the main trigger, which makes it go back, and keeps the hand closed.
8. Springs for each finger, which make the fingers go back and open when closed.

A masterpiece of artistry and innovation, it appears to have outshone even its most impressive contemporary rivals and was soon attracting the notice of both craftsmen and surgeons throughout Europe after it was first produced in prototype around 1551 and had been worn into battle by a French army captain. The Frenchman had not only survived the fray but had also ridden at the head of his cavalry troop, gripping and releasing the reins of his horse, we are told, with perfect ease.

A plaine plot of
This is Don A I A X-houſe, of the new faſhion, all in ſunder, that a workeman may ſee what he hath to do.

Here are the parts ſet downe with a rate of the pryſes, that a builder may gueſſe what he hath to pay.
A, the ceſterne ſtone or bricke, priſe. o 6 8.
B.D.E the pype that comes from the ceſterne, with a ſtopple to the waſher. o.5.6.
C.a waſt pype, o.1.0.
F.G, the ſtem of the great ſtopple, with a key to it. o.1.6.
H, the forme of the vpper brim of the veſſell or ſtoole pot.
M.the ſtoole pot of ſtone, priſe. o.8.0
N, the great braſſe ſluce, to which is three inches currant, to ſend it downe a gallop into the Iax. o.10.0
And leaſt you ſhould miſlike with this phraſe I had it in a verſe of a graue author, that was wont to walke vp and downe the Court, with a foreſt bill, I haue forgot how it begun (like a beaſt as he was) but it ended in ryme.

Archimedes

The rare Enginer.

O that I were at Oxenford, to eate ſome Banberie cakes.
I, the ſeate with a peke deuant for elbow roome, the whole charge 30. ſhillings eight pence, yet a maiſon of my maiſters was offered thirtie pounds for the like.
Memorandum the ſcale is about halfe an inche to a foote.

A priuie in perfection.
Here is the ſame all put together, that the worke-man may ſee if it be well.

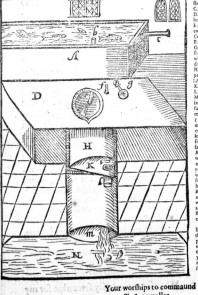

A.the Ceſterne.
B. the litle waſher.
C.the waſt pipe.
D.the ſeate boord.
E.the pipe that comes from the Ceſterne.
F. the Screw.
G. the Scallop ſhell to couer it when it is ſhut downe.
H.the ſtoole pot.
I.the ſtopple.
K.the current.
L.the ſluce.
M.N the vault into which it falles, alwayes remember that ( )at noone and at night, emptie it, and leaue it halfe a foote deepe in fayre water. And this being well done, and orderly kept, your worſt pri-uie may be as ſweet as your beſt chamber. But to conclude all this in a few wordes, it is but a ſtanding cloſe ſtoole eaſilie emptyed. And by the like reaſon (o-ther formes and proportions obſerued) all o-ther places of your houſe may be kept ſweet.

Your worſhips to commaund
T. C. traueller.

95

Flushing toilet

In his book of 1596, entitled *A New Discourse of a Stale Subject, called the Metamorphosis of Ajax,* Sir John Harrington proudly announced a new device that 'would make unsavoury Places sweet, noisome Places wholesome and filthy Places cleanly'. 'Ajax', appropriately enough, was a pun on the word 'jakes', the Elizabethan term for toilet, since Harrington had invented 'for publike benefite' nothing less than the first fully functioning and self-contained flushing lavatory. Costing £1 10s 8d, the gadget represented a major breakthrough in sanitary science, though it appears that only two examples were ever constructed at the time: one at Harrington's own Kelston Manor in Bath, the other for Elizabeth I's personal use at Richmond Palace.

Today only a single replica model bears lasting testament to Harrington's ingenuity. Installed in 1981 at the Gladstone Pottery Museum in Stoke, it is an authentic reconstruction based on detail from the designer's book, which posed a number of problems in its own right, since the text was much more a literary exercise in wordplay and satire than a technical manual for modern-day engineers. Opening with a letter from the character 'Philaretes', who appears to have represented Harrington's cousin, the author is urged to make his invention known to the world, so that he 'may not only please many great persons, but do her Majestie good service' and become 'a great benefactor to the City of London, and all other populous townes'. But though he replies at length to this message under the name 'Misacmos', 'hater of filth', it is only in the book's later sections that Harrington provides us with a description of the device itself. Consisting of a brick, stone or lead receptacle, termed a 'stoole pot', which could be placed over an existing privy shaft, the toilet was serviced by a 'great brasse sluce' leading to an underground cesspool. The stool pot, we are told, had 'sides all smooth' and was dressed with pitch, resin and wax to 'keep it from taynting with the urine', while the sluice was sealed with a 'stopple', or plug, probably of leather. Meanwhile, an iron stem 'as bigge as a curten rod' was attached to the stopple so that it could be operated from above the wooden seat which it penetrated. To accommodate the user, the seating plank had a circular hole with a chamfered rim and a V-shaped notch at the front 'for elbow roome'.

The cistern, in its turn, 'containing a barrell or upward' of water, was to be placed either behind the seat or at some convenient spot elsewhere in the room or above it, and attached to the stool pot by means of a lead pipe, 2.5cm in diameter, and a fitted 'cocke', or tap, which was intended to 'yeeld water with some pretie strength, when you would let it in'. By means of a 'force' costing 20s and further piping at 18d per yard, Harrington also suggested that water could be pumped from the lowest to the highest part of any house. And as if this was not impressive enough, his design also included a number of further features, such as an overflow pipe for the cistern, and a T-shaped key screwed on to the end of the stopple stem to allow the user to empty the closet. The key, in its turn, was removable in order to prohibit unauthorised use of the closet by uninvited parties, and nor, predictably, did Harrington neglect the crucial question of fumes. Once the closet had been installed, he advised, the stool pot, privy shaft and their vicinity were to be 'passing close plastered with good lyme and hayre that no ayre come up from the vault'. Likewise, it was recommended that the closet be emptied 'at noone and at night', though if water was in short supply 'once a day is inough, for a need, though twentie persons should use it'.

No item, then, was neglected in the toilet's design, and Harrington's high status as Queen Elizabeth's godson seemed to ensure the invention's success. Yet at the time of his death at the age of 51, it appeared that the inventor's water closet would die with him. It had not, in fact, caught on and serious improvement in the standard of English lavatories would have to wait until the eighteenth century and the advent of the S-bend. Even the queen, it seems, had been reluctant ultimately to use the gadget, since the noise of the flush betrayed the uncomfortable fact that she, too, like the humblest of her subjects, was answerable to nature's calls. So when the water closet was first patented in London in 1775, it was Alexander Cummings rather than Harrington's descendants who would reap the material rewards. Small consolation, then, that the device would ultimately be dubbed the 'John' after its originator's own Christian name.

96

Matchlock revolver

Though the first recorded use of a firearm dates to 1364 and handguns had become known across Europe by the end of the following decade, an important limiting factor in the development of such weapons was the time involved in reloading. Before the appearance of the matchlock, guns were fired by holding a burning wick to a touch hole in the barrel, igniting the powder inside, as the shooter employed one hand for firing, and a prop to steady the gun. However, the first device or lock for purely mechanical firing was the matchlock, whereby powder contained in a flash pan was ignited by a wick, or match, held in a movable firing clamp known as a serpentine. This design removed the need to lower a lit match manually into the weapon's flash pan and made it possible to have both hands free to keep a firm grip on the weapon at the moment of firing. More importantly still, it allowed the shooter to keep both eyes on the target. Thereafter, from 1509 onwards, the wheel lock allowed ignition sparks to be generated mechanically without the need for any burning wick at all, making guns both easier to use and more reliable.

Yet matchlocks, at half the cost, not only remained in use but underwent significant development, evolving eventually into multi-chambered revolvers like the example shown. Made around 1580 and of shoulder-gun length, this state-of-the-art weapon, which can be seen today at the Germanisches Nationalmuseum, Nuremberg, the city of its original manufacture, fired eight shots in all before reloading became necessary. It appears to have been effective at a distance of 80m, which was especially impressive when it is remembered that the Duke of Alba was recommending to his own 'harquebusiers' around this time an effective range 'of a little more than two pike lengths', i.e. approximately 11 metres. Not only more deadly than many contemporary weapons, the matchlock revolver was also more reliable and safer, too – no small consideration

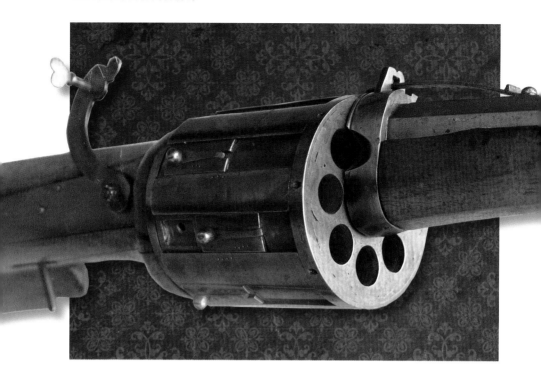

when the danger involved in firing many contemporary weapons is taken into account. Hitherto, misfires could be expected in every six to eight shots and after thirty the barrel normally became too hot to hold in any case. Significantly, only a decade or so earlier a Spanish observer had noted how troops priming their guns were inclined to turn their faces away 'just like those who are waiting for the blood-letter to open a vein'. 'And even when they fire,' he added, 'they close their eyes and go pale, and shake like an old house.'

In the sixteenth century as now, therefore, war had proved an important incentive to innovation and technological advance. In 1498 the rifling principle had been discovered, and as early as the 1540s a multi-shot wheel lock pistol had been presented to Emperor Charles V. In this particular weapon two locks were combined in a single mechanism, giving each barrel separate ignition, but later guns, called pepper-box pistols, used a revolving cylinder containing multiple barrel passages. Single-barrel weapons were, however, both cheaper and lighter and early revolvers were developed for this very reason. This Nuremberg example, with its rifled barrel of 115cm length and 18.3mm calibre was, by the standards of the day, a most impressive item; as manageable as it was effective, and representing a significant advance in both engineering and ballistic science.

Bullenwachter

This is not to say, of course, that it was by any means the final word in terms of design. Lacking an automatic mechanism, it was set by means of sliding catches on the chamber and restricted, like other matchlock weapons, by the ongoing need to keep alight a match soaked in potassium nitrate – a particular problem in wet weather when match cord became damp. Furthermore, the amount of smoke produced by black-powder weapons of this kind was considerable, making it hard to see the enemy after anything more than a single shot, unless there was enough wind to disperse the smoke quickly. Even more problematic was the process of reloading after the chamber had been fully discharged in battlefield conditions. If eight shots were inadequate to the task of stopping an advancing enemy, the sharpshooter still had little choice but to resort to using his weapon as an expensive club.

Yet guns of this kind were still in use until at least the 1720s and as Tudor troops in France, the Netherlands and elsewhere found themselves embroiled in the endemic warfare that characterised the age, the technology of killing would continue to evolve apace. 'I was dreaming of an age that was really golden and isles that were really happy,' mused the humanist Erasmus, reflecting forlornly upon the renewal of Europe-wide war in 1511. And the same refrain was no less apt a century later as the Continent drifted this time towards the prolonged agony of the Thirty Years War.

97

Microscope

More, perhaps, than any other area of sixteenth-century science, the history of optics has been dogged by debate and uncertainty. As besieged Antwerp was about to fall to the Spaniards in 1588, so Hans Jansen fled with his family to Middelburg to ply his trade as a pedlar-cum-optician, establishing before long a successful shop and travelling to nearby fairs to sell his wares. Around that time, too, Jansen appears to have been blessed with a son, Zacharias, who is often credited with the invention of the microscope. But the younger Jansen's claim to fame has been hotly contested, since the date of the first microscope seems to date back to his early childhood – in which case the father himself may be the rightful claimant – or even earlier, since rival evidence supporting an unnamed Italian inventor also has its proponents. Certainly, Zacharias himself, though a convicted counterfeiter in later life, never claimed responsibility for the invention, advancing instead his father's right to recognition. And to compound matters, the German bombardment of Middelburg on 17 May 1940 destroyed extensive archives detailing the Jansens' activities, resulting in a wilderness of speculation that continues to this day.

The nature of the Jansen microscope is, however, altogether less doubtful, for, although no physical specimens are known to exist today, written descriptions have supplied more than enough information for the construction of reliable replicas like the one, made by John Mayall in the 1890s and presently residing at the National Museum of Health and Medicine in Washington DC. Dating to 1590 and consisting of three hand-manipulated draw tubes, its basic design is undeniably rudimentary, though the lenses inserted into the two flanking tubes display uncommon sophistication. The eyepiece lens, for example, was bi-convex and the objective lens plano-convex – a very advanced arrangement by the standards of the day, which allowed the item to achieve threefold magnifications when fully closed and magnifications of up to ten times when entirely extended. Certainly, the advent of this 'compound' type of microscope marked a crucial advance from the type of the single lens magnification that had been available hitherto, and though its reception in England seems to have been limited initially, by the end of the next century further work by Robert Hooke among others would allow the detailed study of organisms such as fossils, diatoms and even the first cells.

Nor would it be entirely fair to underplay the role of all Tudor Englishmen in this particular area of scientific advance. Leonard Digges, for example, a well-known mathematician and surveyor, is not only credited with the invention of the theodolite, but is also associated these days with what may well have been one of the earliest reflecting telescopes, built at some point between 1540 and 1559. According to notes written by his son, Thomas, to accompany the posthumous publication of his *Pantometria* in 1570, Digges had made use of a 'proportional glass' to view distant objects. 'My father by his continual painfull practices,' wrote the younger Digges:

> Was able and sundrie Times hath by proportionall glasses duly situate in convenient angles, not onely discovered things farre off, read letters, numbered peeces of money with the very coyne and superscription thereof, cast by some of his freends of purpose uppon Downes in open fields, but also at seven miles declared what had been doon at that instant in private places.

And notwithstanding the manifest hint of exaggeration in the son's account, the intriguing possibility of an English rival to Hans Lippershey, who is normally credited with the invention of the telescope, and even to Zacharias Jansen, who has his advocates for this achievement too, retains its attraction. Significantly, perhaps, the diagrammatic representations of the planets produced in Thomas Digges' *A Perfit description of the Caelestiall Orbes* (1576) might well suggest that a telescope had been employed at least thirty-three years before Galileo's first observations. And there is even the intriguing possibility that Digges' description of his father's telescope may actually have been barred from publication, in view of the invention's crucial military applications as war with Spain approached. In the meantime, however, the elder Digges had died not only unsung but penniless, as a result of his participation in Sir Thomas Wyatt's rebellion of 1554 against Mary Tudor. Initially condemned to death, his sentence was finally commuted on forfeiture of his entire estate.

98

Sebastian Cabot's 'planisphere'

This world map, or 'planisphere', created by Sebastian Cabot and published in Antwerp in 1544, was found by Dr Jon Martius in the home of a Bavarian curate in 1843. Obtained by the French government the following year, the map was then deposited in the Bibliothèque Nationale in Paris, where it remains today. Although the map displays neither maker, title nor date, when a second edition circulated in London in 1549, Cabot's name appeared unchallenged as its creator, and its significance in the history of Tudor exploration has only increased with the years. Comprising four leaves of parchment and measuring 120cm by 213cm, it bears inscriptions, not written by Cabot himself, that are lettered on paper and pasted to both sides of the map. These inscriptions make reference, among other things, to the geographical writings of ancient authors and a variety of fantastical creatures and curious customs including 'men whose ears are so big that they cover their entire bodies' and the women of Bengal who 'joyfully', we are told, fling themselves onto the funeral pyres of their deceased husbands.

But the most intriguing feature of this map lies elsewhere, for its creator, the son of the Venetian explorer Giovanni (John) Cabot, was born in Bristol in 1474 and had sailed with his father from the port of his birth in the *Matthew* on 20 May 1497 in search of a new sea passage to China. Making landfall in June in southern Labrador, Newfoundland, or Cape Breton Island, the Cabots took possession of the new territory in the name of Henry VII, believing that they had reached the north-east coast of Asia, before returning to Bristol on 6 August of the same year. By the time that Cabot's map was produced in 1544, however, the English-born

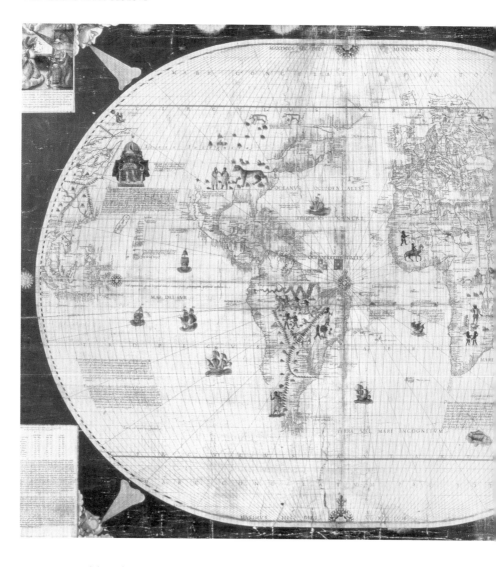

Bridgeman Images

seaman and his father were being credited, in the accompanying Latin text, with the discovery of North America. Columbus's famous voyage of 1492 had, after all, penetrated no farther than the Caribbean islands and it was not until 1498 that Columbus reached the American mainland, a full year after Cabot and his father. Furthermore, Sebastian Cabot's map is quite explicit that father and son not only made landfall on the 'big island' of America on 'Saint John holiday' but that they did so in 1494 – three years earlier than their more famous voyage under the patronage of the King of England. 'People there wander wearing animal furs', the map records, before going on to relate how the inhabitants 'use bow and arrow to fight'. We find, too, that the land itself was inhabited by a

large number of 'white bears and very big deers, big as horses, and many other animals', and that the surrounding waters contained 'infinite' fish – 'plaices, salmons, very long soles, one yard long' and, above all, cod.

Even more intriguing, however, is the possibility that Englishmen may well have set foot on American shores earlier still. The evidence for this is a ledger entry in 1496 from the Bardi banking house in Italy, detailing a loan of 50 nobles, apparently made out to John Cabot – referred to as 'Giovanni Chabotte of Venice' – and a yellowed parchment map, also belonging to Cabot's Italian backers, for a journey to the 'new land'. Since this reference was preceded in Italian by the definite article, *il*, rather than the indefinite *un*, some scholars have therefore suggested that the existence of the Americas was already a known fact, thanks to reports of earlier explorers who may well indeed have been English. Certainly, Bristol mariners were already claiming credit for the discovery of the 'Isle of Brasil', and a letter of 1498 written to Columbus by an English merchant named John Day confirms as much. In it, Day asserted how it was 'considered certain' that the North American mainland, which Cabot had visited the previous year, had been 'found and discovered in the past' by seamen from the port of Bristol, and further papers unearthed more than half a century ago by the scholar Alwyn Ruddock appeared to suggest that these pioneering Englishmen may well have traversed the Atlantic as long ago as 1470.

It is a truly tantalising suggestion, particularly when it is remembered that a Bristol merchant and customs officer by the name of Richard Ameryk may well have been a financier of the early transatlantic voyages who linked his name to the new continent forever. Yet Ruddock ordered all seventy-eight bags of her detailed notes and research destroyed at her death in 2005, and now we are left once more with a riddle wrapped inside an enigma. If only for the expertise involved in its production, of course, Cabot's map of 1544 remains a document of immense geographical and historical interest in its own right – a testament to the expanding horizons of European civilisation at a time when the continent itself was racked by inward-looking discord and division. But if the map really is part of a broader tale of English exploration and discovery, its historical significance is incalculable.

99

William Lee's knitting frame

Almost two centuries before the Industrial Revolution is generally considered to have begun, a humble Elizabethan curate was developing at Calverton near Nottingham a new machine that represented the first major stage in the mechanisation of the knitting industry. Born around 1563, William Lee had graduated from St John's College, Cambridge, at the age of 19 and went on only seven years later to develop his first knitting machine, a gadget capable of producing fine, patternless, 12-gauge stockings at a rate of 600 stitches per minute. Operating at more than six times the rate of a hand knitter, it would remain largely unrivalled until the 1780s when demand for cotton items finally began to predominate. And in the meantime, machines like the one preserved today at the Framework Knitters' Museum in Ruddington in Nottingham had established that city, along with Leicester, as the hub of a thriving industrial base, rivalling the dominance even of London's own Company of Framework Knitters, which had been granted a royal charter in 1663.

Lee's frame brought together a number of components to create a machine capable of closely replicating the movements of a hand knitter at considerably enhanced efficiency. Firstly, a wooden frame provided a seat for the framework knitter and pedals to control the knitting bed, which were bolted on to the frame and could be removed for maintenance. The knitting process itself, meanwhile, started with the framework knitter laying a thread across a horizontal row of hooked needles, after which 'jack sinkers', attached to a metal block known as a 'slurrock', were placed between the needles and allowed to fall one at a time on to the yarn to form loops. Two pedals then pulled the slurrock from side to side. Once the sinkers had dropped they were used to bring the partially formed loops forward and under the hooks of the needles, after which a metal presser bar was brought down by a further pedal to close the hooks and trap the new course of loops. To complete the task, the sinkers were then used to bring the old course of loops over the closed hooks, after which a locker bar finally pushed the jacks back under the springs to fix them in place ready for a new thread to be laid.

According to one tradition, Lee's invention is said to have originated in frustrated courtship: the curate is said to have fallen deeply in love with a young lady of his village who devoted much more attention to knitting stockings than to him. Determined to cure her of her time-consuming obsession, Lee allegedly laboured for all of three years to design a more efficient mechanical device, abandoning his curacy and seeking royal patronage. Yet, the queen, notwithstanding her well-known partiality for knitted stockings, proved hesitant, and fearing the invention's impact upon the large number of her subjects dependent upon hand knitting for their livelihoods, denied him a patent. 'Thou aimest high, Master Lee,' the inventor was told. 'Consider thou what this invention could do to my poor subjects. It would assuredly bring to them ruin by depriving them of employment, thus making them beggars'. In consequence Lee was be left scavenging for recognition and the commercial success that would elude him until the day he died.

He entered into a partnership with a certain George Brooks on 6 June 1600, but this too would end in failure when Brooks was arrested on a charge of treason and executed. Thereafter, Lee sought better fortune in France, taking nine workmen and frames with him, in 1605, which led for a while to better support from Henry IV of France, who granted him a patent and allowed him to begin manufacture in Rouen. Indeed, shortly before Henry's assassination in 1610 Lee would sign a contract with Pierre de Caux to provide further knitting machines for the manufacture of silk as well as woollen stockings. But the political climate changed abruptly upon the king's death and his claims were ignored.

Ultimately, then, Lee would die in distress in 1614, leaving his brother to return to England and dispose of most of the remaining frames in London. Lee's apprentice, however, a miller named Ashton, continued to work on the design, producing a number of improvements, such as the introduction of leaden sinkers, that kept the invention alive. And though the industry would take another century to develop, Lee's name, at least, would not be forgotten in the longer term, for he and the young maiden who supposedly inspired him remain proudly emblazoned to this day upon The Worshipful Company of Framework Knitters' coat of arms.

100
Gresham's grasshopper

Any regular visitor to the City of London is unlikely to ignore for long the golden insect suspended so strikingly above the entrance to 68 Lombard Street. Representing enterprise and activity, the grasshopper was the personal emblem of Sir Thomas Gresham, one of the most quietly gifted men of Elizabethan England. As the founder of the Royal Exchange and the father of English banking, he epitomised the thrusting spirit of enterprise – and appetite for personal wealth – that characterised so many of his contemporaries. Nor is it any surprise that the year 1563 should feature so prominently at the top of the sign on either side of Gresham's initials, since this was the year in which he offered to build the Royal Exchange at his own expense in an attempt to rival Antwerp as Europe's financial hub. Appropriately enough, Gresham had founded his own bank at the very same address during the previous decade, and though the area had been synonymous with finance since Edward I had expelled the Jews from England in 1290 and replaced their goldsmiths with Lombards from Italy, it was he who left his own indelible mark, not only upon the area but upon the entire financial well-being that underpinned so many of Tudor England's broader successes.

For Gresham was no ordinary private banker. When in 1551 the mismanagement of Sir William Daunsell, Edward VI's financial agent in the Low Countries, had brought the king's government to the brink of financial disaster, it was the 33-year-old Gresham whom the authorities called upon for advice, allowing him to raise the value of the pound sterling on the Antwerp bourse and thereby eradicate almost all the king's debts, amounting to some £40,000, over the next few years. In consequence, the government was soon seeking Gresham's advice in all their financial difficulties, and rewarding him, though he had no stated salary, with various grants of lands from the king, totalling around £400 a year.

Neither was his temporary eclipse at the start of Queen Mary's reign long-lived, for the incompetence of William Dauntsey in undoing his work on the rate of interest only served to make Gresham more indispensable than ever. When Charles V imposed a ban on the export of bullion from the Netherlands, Gresham proved equally adept at smuggling to safeguard his country's wealth, attempting first to transport English funds in bales of pepper, before resorting to soldiers' armour as an alternative. And though the queen's debts totalled some £226,910 at her death, he was soon raising cheap loans on her younger sister's behalf, while insisting that Elizabeth borrow as little abroad as possible and take all possible steps to restore the purity of the coinage after her father's debasement of it two decades earlier. In an effort to curtail exchange fluctuations, which increased the amount paid by the English government on foreign loans, Gresham also operated with characteristic guile on the foreign exchange markets, even suggesting the creation of an exchange-equalisation account, not dissimilar in principle to the system in operation today.

Yet it was Gresham's establishment of the Royal Exchange that probably encapsulated both the man and, indeed, his era most aptly. At a time when the growing volume of financial trading was still often conducted in the City's muddy streets, it was Gresham's earlier experience as a royal agent for both Edward VI and Mary Tudor on the Antwerp bourse that encouraged him to invest his own funds in the creation of a similar purpose-built building in England's capital. As a result, on land provided by the City Corporation between Cornhill and Threadneedle Street, the grand new structure duly emerged between 1566 and 1570, with a Flemish-style and Italianate trading floor and an imposing bell tower on one side of the main entrance, crowned by a huge grasshopper. On two upper floors, Gresham saw fit to gain more than adequate recompense for his original outlay by opening what amounted to England's very first shopping mall, consisting of a hundred or so kiosks, all of which were rented out at a substantial profit.

In effect, then, Gresham's Royal Exchange, like his career in general, embodied that same mix of patriotism, enterprise and self-interest that lay, arguably, at the heart of so much of the Tudor achievement. Elizabeth I was quick to license legal landing quays for goods on the banks of the Thames, ensuring the Crown got its share of the wealth, while underpinning London's emerging status as a major trading centre. And in the meantime Gresham consolidated his status as both financial innovator and one of England's wealthiest commercial magnates – a man who would bequeath an annual income of around £2,400 to his widow upon his death in 1579. By 1565 he had reduced the royal foreign debt to a mere

£20,000, and in the process his skill, acumen and studied disinterest in religion and politics had given him a cloak of immunity throughout the upheavals of the previous three reigns. Ultimately, he proved the perfect servant for an ambitious and thrifty monarch like Elizabeth and a fitting symbol for a vigorous, self-confident age which had placed England on the threshold of future greatness.

Index

abortion, 69, 205
Act for the Maintenance of Archery (1514), 211
Act of Succession (1534), 221
Act of Supremacy (1534), 221, 237
Alba, Duke of, 327
alnager, 79
Ameryk, Richard, 335
Angel, Islington, 261
Anjou, René, Duke of, 19
Anjou, Robert of, 102
Antwerp, 94, 230, 331, 333, 339, 341
apprentices, 52, 83–5, 121, 190, 209
Arthur, Prince, eldest son of Henry VII, 13, 15, 18, 52, 147
Artificers, Statute of (1563), 88
artillery, 287–9
Arundell family, 237
Aske, Robert, 241–2
Askew, Anne, 301–3
astrology, 200, 258
Aylmer Bishop John, 41
Aztecs, 37, 105

Backhouse, James, 128
Bankfield Museum, 309
Barbaro, Daniel, 77
Barclay, Alexander, 195
Bartmann jugs, 272
Baule, William, 167
Beaufort, Lady Margaret, 17, 52, 191, 226
Beaurieux, Dr Gabriel, 296
Beccles, 170

Bedingfield, Sir Henry, 248
belladonna, 266
Belloc, Hillaire, 41
Bergavenny, Lord, 184
Berkeley, Sir Richard, 299
Berlichingen, Götz von, 321
Bermondsey, 88
Bernardino da, Siena, 191
Bertelli, Pietro, 134
Berthelet, Thomas, 314
Bethencourt, Jacques de, 203
Bibliothèque Nationale, 333
Bigod, Sir Francis, 242
billiards, 190
Birmingham, 88
Biron, Duke of, 183
Blagrave, Joseph, 272
Blomefield, Frances, 28
Bocardo prison, 245
Bodin, Jean, 269
Boleyn, Anne, 22–3, 65, 111, 296
Boleyn, Thomas, Earl of Wiltshire, 22
Bonetti, Rocco, 283
Bonner, Edmund, 245
Book of Common Prayer, 57–8, 65
Boorde, Andrew, 109, 117, 145, 161, 187
Bora, Katharina von, 57, 59
border ware, 145, 163
Bostocke, Jane, 69–70
Bosworth Field, Battle of, 11–2
Boulogne, siege of, 289
bowling, 190
Bradmore, John, 211–2

Brandon, Charles, Duke of
  Suffolk, 185, 193
breastfeeding, 205
Bristol, 77, 79, 88, 124, 172, 333,
  335
Broke, John, 62
Brooks, George, 338
Brownewend, John, 128
Bruyn, Abraham de, 138
Brydges, Sir John, 31
Brydges, Sir Thomas, 29
Bulleyn, William, 209
Butler, Charles, 165
Buxton, 217
Byrche, George, 128
Byrd, William, 181

Cabot, John, 333–5
Cabot, Sebastian, 333–5
Calais, 34
Calvin, John, 222
Candell, Frances, 97–8
Cardan of Milan, 212
Carew, Edward, 289
Carey, Robert, 173
Carlisle Castle, 195
Carré, Jean, 89
Castiglione, Baldassare, 55, 139
Castiglione, Sabba de, 69
Catherine of Aragon, 21, 33, 52,
  65, 147, 221
Caux, Pierre de, 338
Caversham, 225, 229
Caxton, William, 19, 186, 313–4
Cecil, Sir Robert, 249, 303
Cecil, William, 258, 301
Charles V, Emperor, 18, 22, 105,
  321, 328, 341
Charles VIII, 201
Chelmsford, 125, 215, 267
Cheseman, Creature, 49

Chester, 13, 71, 88, 125
Chetham's Library, 230
China, 107, 201, 333
chopine, 123
Christ's College, Cambridge, 191
Cicognara, Antonio, 191
Cloth Act (1552), 88
Clowes, William, 212, 262
Clyff Park, 187
cochineal, 141–2
Cochlaeus, Johann, 317
cockentrice, 115
Colchester, 79
Coleorton, 81–2
College of Physicians, 73, 146,
  199, 209
Colte, John, 134
Constable, Sir Robert, 242–3
Cook, John, 316
Copenhagen, University of, 75
cordwainers, 125
Cornwall, 82
Cortés, Hernán, 37, 103, 105
Coryate, Thomas, 103
Coventry, 88, 106, 111, 117
Cranach, Lucas, 57
Cromwell, Oliver, 171, 237, 310
Cromwell, Thomas, 171, 187, 221,
  229, 232, 237–9, 241–2, 295–6
Crowley, Aleister, 258
Cruelty to Animals Act (1835), 182
Ctesias, 266
Culpeper, Nicholas, 203
Cumberland, 243
Cummings, Alexander, 326
Cunny, Joan, 269
Curwen, Bennett, 305
cutlery, 102–3, 285

D'Arcy family, 113
Dale, Richard, 151

Darcy, Edward, 193
Darcy, Lord, 242
Darvel Catherne, 235
Daunsell, Sir William, 339
Dauntsey, William, 341
Daventry, 137–8
Davis, John, 196
Davy, Margaret, 305
Dawson, Thomas, 105
Day, John, 335
Deal Castle, 288
Dedham (Massachusetts)
    Historical Society, 93
Defoe, Daniel, 205
Delicado, Francisco, 203
Deventer, 307
Devon, 77, 82, 172, 290
Digges, Leonard, 332
Digges, Thomas, 332
Drake, Sir Francis, 41, 290
'duck's bill' shoe, 123
Dudley Castle, 205–6
Dudley, Guildford, 31
Dudley, John, Earl of Warwick and
    later Duke of Northumberland,
    23, 25, 65
Dudley, Robert, Earl of Leicester,
    127–8, 259
Dürer, Albrecht, 61, 233
Dyer, Edward, 259
dysentery, 41, 61, 207, 292

East India Company, 94
East Indies, 107
Edward III, 163, 169
Edward IV, 13, 101, 180
Edward VI, 23, 31, 45, 55, 57, 65,
    91, 180, 196, 218, 222, 235, 262,
    307, 319, 339, 341
Effingham, Lord Howard of, 292
Egmond, Maximilian van, 287, 289

Elizabeth I, 25, 34, 39, 53, 98,
    116–7, 122–3, 128, 133–5, 139,
    151, 171, 173, 179, 193, 195, 242,
    247, 262, 266, 269, 272, 290
Elizabeth of York, 13, 163, 193
Elyot, Sir Thomas, 55, 69, 196
Epping, 72, 172, 271
equine armour, 277–9
Erasmus, 215, 231, 329
Essex, Robert Devereux, Earl of, 295
Exeter, 88, 269, 303
extreme unction, 222

Fallopio, Gabriele, 206
Faucil, Valery, 191
Fécamp, 225
Feckenham, John, 29
Feeld, Henry, 62
Felton, John, 304
Fen Hole, 12
Field, John, 184
Finsbury Fields, 211
Finsbury Square, 121
Fisher, Bishop John, 221, 305
Fitzroy, Henry, Duke of
    Richmond, 65
Flodden, Battle of, 65, 275–6
Florence, 52, 196, 207
'Florentine kick', 196
Forest, John, 235
Fracastoro, Girolamo, 201
Framework Knitters' Museum,
    Ruddington, 337
Framlingham, 65, 275–6
Francis, Elizabeth, 267, 269
Franco, Pierre, 215
Frizer, Ingram, 286
'fulhams', 189

Galen, 218
Gardiner, Bishop Stephen, 245

Garrick, David, 178
Gateshead, 85
Gerard, Fr John, 247, 299
Germanisches Nationalmuseum, 327
Girona, 37
Giustiniani, Vincenzo, 199
Glaser, George, 319
Glastonbury, 237–9
Gloriana, Cult of, 41
Gloucester, 88
glove-making, 88
Glyn Henry, 72–3
Great Debasement, 23
Great North Road, 173
Great Yarmouth, 95
Greenwich, 179, 271
Gresham, Sir Thomas, 339–42
Grey, Henry, Duke of Suffolk, 31
Grey, Lady Jane, 29–31, 55, 65, 245
Groom of the Stool, 161
Gruet, Arnaud, 319
Gryndall, William, 110
Guisborough, 316
Gutenberg, Johannes, 313–5

Hailes Abbey, 229
Hakluyt, Richard, 196, 206
Hall, Edward, 276, 295
Hall, John, 177
Hampton Court, 319
Hardwick Hall, 152
Hariot, Thomas, 209
Harrington, Sir John, 325–6
Harris, Anne, 158
Harris, Richard, 111
Harrison, William, 89, 101, 159, 169
'Harry Hunks', 183
Harvington Hall, 247
Hatfield Peverell, 267
Hatton, Sir Christopher, 117, 259

Hawksmoor, Sir Nicholas, 179
'hazard', 190
Hearst, William Randolph, 154
Henlein, Peter, 317–9
Henry V, 17, 211–2
Henry VI, 11, 229
Henry VII, 13, 15, 17, 61, 77, 139, 159, 163, 189–91, 193, 225, 262, 275, 317, 319, 333
Henry VIII, 13, 15, 18, 21–2, 25, 33, 55, 62–5, 91, 93, 102, 111, 115–7, 122, 139, 161, 163, 173, 180–1, 185–7, 190, 196, 211, 218, 221, 225–7, 232–3, 237, 242, 261–2, 269, 275, 279, 287–9, 296, 300, 305, 315–6
Herbert, Lord, 289
'Hinky punk', 172
Hippocratic Oath, 214
Hoby, Lady Margaret, 167
Hockley, 227, 229
Holinshed, Ralph, 310
Holme, Randle, 137–8
Hooke, Robert, 332
Horman, William, 159
Hornsey Wood, 122
horses, 76, 279
housework, 156–8
Huggate, 51
humours, 200
Hurstpierpoint, 265
Hutten, Ulrich von, 201

influenza, 146
Ingatestone Hall, 145
Ipswich, 95, 226

James I, 55, 173, 193, 279
James IV, 65, 275
Jansen, Hans, 331
Jansen, Zacharias, 331–2

Johanna of Austria, 193
Johnson, John, 106
Jonson, Ben, 47

Kelly, Edward, 257–8
Kett, Robert, 26–8
Kett, William, 28
Keynsham, 172
Kingston, Sir Anthony, 303
Kirkby Lonsdale, 128
Kitchener, William, 128
Knollys, Sir Francis, 195
kohl, 141
Kratzer, Nicholas, 319

L'Ange, Jean, 205
Lacada Point, 37
Laguille, Henri, 296
Landsknechte, 27
Laneham, Robert, 183–4
Langland, William, 72
Langton, Dr Christopher, 73
Latimer, Bishop Hugh, 25, 211,
    235, 245–6
Lavenham, 79
Leather Act (1563), 88
Leatherhead, 119
Lee, William, 337–8
Leinberger, Hans, 61
Leiva, Don Alonzo Martinez de, 37
Leland, John, 19, 172
Leominster, 71–3
leprosy, 217–8
Lessius, Leonardus, 205
Linacre, Thomas, 199
Lippomano, Jérôme, 130
literacy, 53, 55
Little Moreton Hall, 151–2
Louth, 241
Lucas, Seymour, 121
Lucy, Sir Thomas, 178

Lull, Ramon, 186
Lund, 206
Luther, Martin, 57, 59, 116, 222, 232

Machiavelli, Niccolò, 180
Maddocke, Walter, 73
Maisse, André Hurault-Sieur de,
    39–40
malaria, 146, 209
Marlowe, Christopher, 97, 286
Martius, Dr John, 333
Mary Queen of Scots, 164
Mary Rose, 125, 164, 203, 289
Mary Tudor, 29, 31, 33–4, 65, 123,
    135, 171, 193, 245, 257, 332, 341
Mascall, Leonard, 158
Matthew Bible, 15
Maximilian I, Emperor, 315
May Day riots, 52
Mayall, John, 331
mead, 165–6
Meade, Alice, 269
Medici, Catherine de, 134
Mercers' Company, 233, 235
mercury, 131, 141–2, 189, 203
merrills, 190
Metcalf, Michael, 95
Miagh, Thomas, 300
miasma, 146
midwifery, 45–6
Mierdeman, Steven, 314
Mile End, 217–8
Millot, Michel, 205
mining, 81–2
Monmouth, Sir Humphrey, 231
Monson, John, 253
Montague, Alice, 122
More, Sir Thomas, 77, 186, 221,
    233
Moreton, William, 151
Mortlake, 259

Mountjoy, Lord, 303
Mousehold Heath, 26
Mulcaster, Richard, 196
Murano, 89, 91
Museo Correr di Veneziani, 123

National Archives, 22, 61
National Museum of Health and
    Medicine, Washington DC, 331
Netherbury, 119
Neudorfer, Johann, 319
Newcastle, 77, 82–3, 85
Nonsuch Palace, 93
Norfolk, Thomas Howard, 2nd
    Duke of, 275–6
Norfolk, Thomas Howard, 3rd
    Duke of, 65, 242
Northampton, 88
Northampton, Earl of, 27
Norton Folgate, 97–8
Norton, Thomas, 299
Norwich, 26–8, 70, 77, 79, 88, 95,
    128, 185
Norwich Museum, 138
Notary, Julian, 314
Nottingham, 88, 125, 337
Nuremberg, 307, 319, 327

Oursian, Nicholas, 319
Owen, Agnes, 184
Owen, Nicholas, 247

Packwood House, 167
Padua, University of, 199
Paré, Ambroise, 322
Paris Gardens, 182–4
Parke, Matilda, 269
Parker, Matthew, 28
Parr, Katherine, 30, 45
Partridge, John, 106
Paston, John, 191

Paston, Margaret, 191
Pembroke, earls of, 39
Pepys, Samuel, 138, 215
Perrenoto, Don Tomas, 37
Persia, 107
pessaries, 135, 205
Petre, Sir William, 145
Pfalz-Neuburg, Dorothea von, 133
Philip II, 31, 35
Phillips, Henry, 232
Phillips, John, 267
Pinkie Cleugh, Battle of, 279
Plat, Hugh, 164
poisoning, 266, 305
Pole, Cardinal Reginald, 245
Pole, Edmund de la, 18
Pole, Lady Margaret, 242, 295–7
pomanders, 146
Ponet, Bishop John, 75
Poor Act (1575), 98
Porter, John, 128
Prentice, Joan, 269
'primero', 193
Prior Pursglove College, 316
property tax, 145
puerperal fever, 30, 45
Puritans, 184, 253, 310
Pynson, Richard, 314

Quebec House, 167

Rabelais, François, 131
Raleigh, Sir Walter, 183, 209
Rastell, William, 314
Ravenna, Cardinal of, 22
Remy, Nicholas, 269
'rhythm method', 205
Rich, Richard, 301
Richard III, 11–2
Richeson, Frances, 83, 85
Richmond, Countess of, 315

Ridley, Nicholas, 245–6
Rogers, John, 245
Rombaud, Jean, 297
Roose, Richard, 305, 307
Rosicrucian movement, 257
Royal Exchange, 339, 341
Ruddock, Alwyn, 335
Rudolf II, Emperor, 237, 258
Rummynge, Eleanor, 119
Russell, John, 159
Russia Company, 94
Ryston Hall, 28

Samuel, William, 110
sanitary pads, 135
Saviolo, Vincento, 283
Sawston Hall, 247
Scaino, Antonio, 196
Schuch, Anton, 281–2
scold's bridle, 71
scrofula, 261
Seymour, Edward, Duke of
    Somerset and Lord Protector,
    23, 25, 307
Seymour, Jane, 23, 45–6
Sforza, Cardinal Ascanio, 193
Shakespeare, Hamnet, 47
Shakespeare, William, 47, 62, 91,
    119, 141, 177–8, 193, 254, 263
Shaxspere, Jane, 62
Shireburn, Sir Richard, 171
Shrewsbury, Battle of, 211
Sidney, Sir Henry, 63, 259
Sidney, Sir Philip, 39
Silver, George, 282–3
Skeffington, Sir Leonard, 300
Skelton, John, 119, 314
sleeping habits, 149
Smith, William, 178
Smithfield, 245, 303, 305
Smythe, Sir John, 282

Sommerling, S.T., 296
Southwark, 91, 93, 155, 183, 303
Southwell, Robert, 303
Spenser, Edmund, 149, 206, 254
Spitalfields, 261
Spurs, Battle of, 277
St Albans, 118
St Alfege's Church, 179, 181
St Asaph, 226
St Bartholomew's fair, 50
St Bridget, 226
St George, 225
St Helena, 227
St Michael's, church of,
    Framlingham, 275
St Paul's Cathedral, 70, 313
St Thomas, shrine of, 225–6
Stafford, Thomas, Duke of
    Buckingham, 18, 115, 169
Statute of Bridges (1531), 172
Stinchcombe, 231
Stirling Castle, 195
Stooe, John, 128
Stow, John, 65, 133
Stratford-upon-Avon, 62, 167
Stuart, Lady Arbella, 152
Stubbes, Philip, 119, 125, 137–8
suffumigation, 203
sugar, 41, 105–6, 165
Sutton Cheney, 12
Swannington, 28, 82
sweating sickness, 23, 61, 164
syphilis, 131, 201–3, 206, 218

Tagliacozzi, Gaspare, 212
Tallis, Thomas, 179–81
tallow, 81, 167, 307
Tanner, Matthias, 300
Tatterford, 95
Tawstock, 172
Taylor, John, 308

tertian fever, *see* malaria
Thérouanne, 277, 287, 289
Thetford Priory, 276
Thornbury Castle, 167, 170
Tickenhall Manor, 147
Titchfield Abbey, 167
tobacco, 119, 149, 209
Tolhuys, Jan, 287
Tompion, Thomas, 319
'Topcliffe rack', 249
Topcliffe, Richard, 299, 303–4
Towton, Battle of, 11, 212
Treveris, Peter, 314
Tryppytt, Alice, 305
Tudor, Owen, paternal grandfather of Henry VII, 11
tumbrel, 72
Tunstall Chapel, 182
Tunstall, Bishop Cuthbert, 182
Turner, William, 50
tussie mussies, 146
Tyndale, William, 230–2
Tytmarche, John, 153

unicorns, 89, 266
Upney, Joan, 269
Upton Warren, 62

vagabonds, 97–8
Venice, 89, 91, 123, 141, 207, 335
Vergil, Polydore, 58
vermillion, 141
Verzelini, Jacopo, 89–92
Voltaire, 201, 269

Wakefield, 309
Walsingham, 225–6,
Walsingham, Sir Francis, 63, 258

Wardour Castle, 237
Warwick 'the Kingmaker', 11
Waterhouse, Agnes, 267
Wellcome, Henry, 321
Wellcome Trust, 213, 321
Westminster Abbey, 133, 190, 229, 313, 315
Weston, Fr William, 248–9
Wheler, Robert Bell, 352
White, Sir John, 93
Whiting, Abbott Richard, 237–9
Whythorne, Thomas, 155
Wills, Statute of (1540), 70
Wilton House, 39
Winchester, 18–9, 33
Wisdom, Robert, 62
Witchcraft Act (1563), 269
Wolsey, Cardinal Thomas, 23, 161, 232, 239, 288
Woodall, John, 212
Worde, Wynkyn de, 314
Worshipful Company of Clockmakers, 319
Worshipful Company of Framework Knitters, 338
Worshipful Company of Pewterers, 101
Wriothesley, Thomas, 25, 301, 303
Wyatt, Sir Thomas, 31, 332
Wyer, Robert, 314
Wylede, Thomas, 70
Wymondham, 26, 28

York, 77, 85, 88, 125, 243

Zech, Jacob, 319
Zutphen, Battle of, 39

If you enjoyed this book, you may also be interested in…

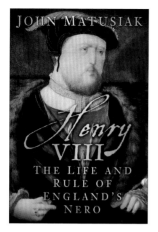

Henry VIII: The Life and Rule of England's Nero
John Matusiak

This compelling account of Henry VIII is by no means yet another history of the 'old monster'. This ground-breaking book demonstrates that his priorities were always primarily martial rather than marital, and accepts neither the necessity of his all-consuming quest for a male heir nor the severance of ties with Rome. As the story unfolds, Henry's predicaments prove largely of his own making. Five hundred years after he ascended the throne, the reputation of England's best-known king is being rehabilitated and subtly sanitised. Yet John Matusiak paints a colourful and absorbingly intimate portrait of a man wholly unfit for power.

978 0 7509 6089 2

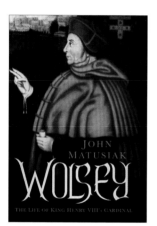

Wolsey: The Life of King Henry VIII's Cardinal
John Matusiak

Cardinal Wolsey is a controversial figure: a butcher's son, a man of letters and the Church, a divisive political expert, a man of principle – yet, to some, an arrogant upstart. As Lord Chancellor to VIII he achieved much both at home and abroad, but his failure to achieve the king's divorce from Catherine of Aragon saw him brought to his knees. John Matusiak explores the pragmatic cardinal's life and career to uncover a man of contradictions and extremes. This is the gripping story of how talent, noble intentions and an eye for opportunity can contrive with the vagaries of power politics to raise an individual to unheard of heights before finally consuming him.

978 0 7509 6535 4

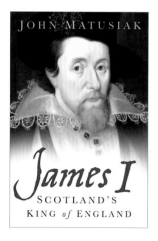

James I: Scotland's King of England
John Matusiak

Few kings have been more savagely caricatured or grossly misunderstood than England's first Stuart. Yet, as this biography demonstrates, the tendency to downplay his defects and minimise the long-term consequences of his reign has gone too far. In spite of genuine idealism and flashes of considerable resourcefulness, James I remains a perplexing figure. A flawed, if well-meaning, foreigner in a rapidly changing and divided kingdom, his passionate commitment to time-honoured principles of government would, ironically, prove his undoing, as England edged unconsciously towards a crossroads and the shadow of the Thirty Years War descended upon Europe.

978 0 7509 5562 1

The destination for history
www.thehistorypress.co.uk